"The Reformation was about countering what was wrong in Catholicism, but its central principles, the five *solas*, are not only negations. Reformational Protestantism is also about being *for* something. The *solas* are therefore principles for shaping a robust theology. It is this constructive task that Vanhoozer has undertaken in this book, and he has done so with rigor, vigor, and an infectious enthusiasm."

—**David F. Wells**, Gordon-Conwell Theological Seminary

"A fresh appraisal of the core principles of historic Protestant Christianity. Written with conviction, nuance, and wisdom, this is Vanhoozer at his best—a treasure."

—**Timothy George**, Beeson Divinity School, Samford University; general editor, Reformation Commentary on Scripture

"More than a rousing three cheers for the Reformation—though it is that—Vanhoozer's book is a sparkling proposal for Protestant unity based on the five *solas* and also based on a differentiation between central gospel truths that are absolutely required and areas where disagreement should not divide Protestants denominationally. Catholic theologians like myself, seeking paths for deeper ecumenical dialogue, need to listen to Vanhoozer's rigorous, gracious, and erudite defense of the truth of Protestant Christianity."

—**Matthew Levering**, Mundelein Seminary

"Are rumors of Protestantism's demise greatly exaggerated? May it actually be the case that the authority, unity, and mission of the whole church could be served precisely by reengaging with the Reformation *solas* rather than running from them? While wrestling frankly with the Reformation's unintended consequences, Vanhoozer makes a penetrating argument that must be taken seriously."

—**Michael Horton**, Westminster Seminary California

"The authority of Scripture in the life of the church is a perennial theme of debate. In this book, Vanhoozer links the subject to the five *solas* of the Reformation era, explaining the part that each one of them plays in our interpretation and application of the Bible today. Half a millennium later, he shows how there is still life in these classical formulations and why they should be recovered by the church today. *Biblical Authority after Babel* will

T0339235

be a stimulating discussion starter and will help to shape the evolution of Protestant hermeneutics in the years ahead."

—**Gerald Bray**, Beeson Divinity School, Samford University

"At a time when the terms 'evangelical' and 'catholic' both face bewildering internal and external pressures, Vanhoozer helps to shine Scripture's light on an authentically Protestant path forward. Amid newfound interest in the Reformation *solas*, this book's distinctive contribution lies in discerning their hermeneutical import. This approach challenged me to think afresh about the gospel, Scripture, and the church at several points."

—**Daniel J. Treier**, Wheaton College Graduate School

"Protestants in general, and evangelicals in particular, are often challenged to manifest a robust grasp of the catholicity of the church. The difficulty of such a task can be compounded by (mis)understandings of *sola scriptura*, as well as of the authority of—and authority in—the church. In *Biblical Authority after Babel*, Vanhoozer summons evangelical Protestants to squarely face these and related issues in their particular stream of Christianity, and he proposes a way forward by both faithfully and creatively drawing upon the five *solas* of the Reformation. This is an astute and constructively thought-provoking book."

—**W. David Buschart**, Denver Seminary

"Protestantism has been charged with many schisms and with spawning modern secularism and its varied ills. While some have sought solace in other folds, Vanhoozer responds not by looking elsewhere for another defense but by doubling down through retrieval of basic principles of Protestant theology. Further, he shows that those reformational *solas* were themselves retrievals of earlier biblical faith and practice. Readers of Vanhoozer have learned to expect to be charitably guided and imaginatively provoked, and this book delivers similar wisdom and provocation."

—**Michael Allen**, Reformed Theological Seminary, Orlando

BIBLICAL AUTHORITY
AFTER BABEL

Retrieving the *Solas*
in the Spirit of Mere Protestant Christianity

KEVIN J. VANHOOZER

BrazosPress
a division of Baker Publishing Group
www.BrazosPress.com

© 2016 by Kevin J. Vanhoozer

Published by Brazos Press
a division of Baker Publishing Group
P.O. Box 6287, Grand Rapids, MI 49516-6287
www.brazospress.com

Paperback edition published 2018
ISBN 978-1-58743-423-5

Printed in the United States of America

All rights reserved. No part of this publication may be reproduced, stored in a retrieval system, or transmitted in any form or by any means—for example, electronic, photocopy, recording—without the prior written permission of the publisher. The only exception is brief quotations in printed reviews.

The Library of Congress has cataloged the hardcover edition as follows:
Names: Vanhoozer, Kevin J., author.
Title: Biblical authority after Babel : retrieving the solas in the spirit of mere Protestant
    Christianity / Kevin J. Vanhoozer.
Description: Grand Rapids : Brazos Press, 2016. | Includes bibliographical references and index.
Identifiers: LCCN 2016017619 | ISBN 9781587433931 (cloth)
Subjects: LCSH: Calvinism. | Reformed Church—Doctrines.
Classification: LCC BX9422.5 .V365 2016 | DDC 230/.42—dc23
LC record available at https://lccn.loc.gov/2016017619

Unless otherwise noted, Scripture quotations are from The Holy Bible, English Standard Version® (ESV®), copyright © 2001 by Crossway, a publishing ministry of Good News Publishers. Used by permission. All rights reserved. ESV Text Edition: 2011

Scripture quotations labeled ASV are from the American Standard Version of the Bible.

Scripture quotations labeled KJV are from the King James Version of the Bible.

Scripture quotations labeled NIV are from the Holy Bible, New International Version®. NIV®. Copyright © 1973, 1978, 1984, 2011 by Biblica, Inc.™ Used by permission of Zondervan. All rights reserved worldwide. www.zondervan.com

Scripture quotations labeled NRSV are from the New Revised Standard Version of the Bible, copyright © 1989, by the Division of Christian Education of the National Council of the Churches of Christ in the United States of America. Used by permission. All rights reserved.

In keeping with biblical principles of creation stewardship, Baker Publishing Group advocates the responsible use of our natural resources. As a member of the Green Press Initiative, our company uses recycled paper when possible. The text paper of this book is composed in part of post-consumer waste.

18 19 20 21 22 23 24   7 6 5 4 3 2 1

To the faculty and principals of Moore College,
past and present

Contents

Preface

Experience is not the primary norm for Christian theology, but events often serve as catalysts or occasions for theologizing. I was awakened from my pre-dogmatic slumbers one summer by a curious incident while ministering in southern France. I was there for a summer in partial fulfillment of my seminary internship requirement. The local pastor with whom I was working accompanied me to the *marché*, the weekly open-air market that is a staple of every town in Provence. We set up a bookstall with standard Christian literature: Bibles, Gospels of John, and assorted evangelistic tracts. Most people ignored us: it was hard to compete with freshly picked apricots, *herbes de Provence*, and ripened wheels of Camembert. Time passed, until eventually a man approached. "Bonjour, monsieur!"

The man thumbed through some of our pamphlets, checked the sign over our booth identifying us as an *Église Libre* (Free Church), and then said something unexpected: "Alors, vous êtes anarchiste?" ("So, you're an anarchist?"). Several things went through my mind: first, did I hear him correctly; second, he wouldn't be saying that if he knew my parents; third, if only my college friends could see me now! Seeing my surprise, he proceeded to set out what I would later discover was a customary Roman Catholic objection to Protestantism: "The Roman Catholic Church has a head [Gk. *archē*], a figure of authority who directs the body and says what the Bible means. You Protestants lack such a figure: you are headless [Gk. *an* + *archē* = "without a head/ruler"]—hence, anarchists."[1]

1. The *a(n)*- prefix is the alpha privative, which expresses negation or absence.

The man in the *marché* was the first to alert me to the perceived parallel between the Protestant Reformation and the babble that followed Babel (Gen. 11:9): both were events that apparently resulted in more rather than less confusion. The implication of his remark was that the Reformation resulted in a confusion not of languages but of interpretations, authorities, and interpretive communities. I don't remember how I responded that day, though I do recall being eager to complete my seminary training so that I could pursue this and other questions, such as: What does it mean to be biblical? Who can say, with authority, what the Bible means? How can the Bible have authority *after interpretive Babel*? How should Bible-believing Christians navigate the conflict of church interpretations?

My doctoral studies provided a second catalyst for this book. I will never forget the way Henry Chadwick, the Regius Professor of Divinity, peered at me over the rim of his glasses as I concluded my dissertation proposal hearing at the end of my first year at Cambridge University. I had gone to England to pursue further my life question: What does it mean for Christian disciples and theologians to be biblical? Professor Chadwick sighed, then rendered his judgment with classic British understatement: "Mr. Vanhoozer, I'm afraid that topic has been studied before." Indeed.

The problem of competing claimants to the mantle "biblically authorized" is older than Protestantism itself. Yet, for the reasons we will examine in this study, the Protestant Reformation exacerbated the problem, fanning scattered embers into a raging fire that engulfed the whole of European Christianity. The ashes are still smoldering. As arborists know, the impact of a fire on a forest depends on the forest's condition, and opinions differ on whether this conflagration was purely destructive or produced more ecological good than harm. *Sola scriptura* continues to generate much heat, but few would go so far as to describe the Reformation's effect on the church as a controlled burn.[2] On the contrary: the conflict of interpretations that has divided the church resembles a wildfire that is still only 10 percent contained.

It is widely assumed that the Reformers' careless play with biblical matches is responsible for the hermeneutical havoc that has been unleashed upon the modern world. Despite the abundance of supporting empirical evidence, the present work sets out to refute the *necessity* of this development. The accidental

---

2. The Forest Service of the United States Department of Agriculture warns: "Understanding fire is a science. The ability to know when an ecosystem is ready for controlled burning is science" (http://www.fs.usda.gov/detail/dbnf/home/?cid=stelprdb5281464 [accessed August 29, 2015]).

truths of European history ought never become the proof of necessary truths of Protestant theology. Yes, Protestants have disagreed and split churches over divergent biblical interpretations; there is no disputing the course of church history since the Reformation. Yet things could and should have proceeded otherwise, and sometimes did. The burden of the present work is therefore to reclaim elements for a normative Protestantism from the ruins of present-day Protestantism by revisiting historical Protestantism (the Reformation *solas*). I argue that the *solas* provide not an alternative to orthodox tradition but rather a deeper insight into the one true gospel that undergirds that tradition.

I originally presented the contents of the present book in Sydney, Australia, as the Annual Moore College Lectures 2015 under the title "Mere Protestant Christianity: Why Singing *Sola* Renews and Reforms Biblical Interpretation, Theology, and the Church." Though I have taken the liberty of editing and supplementing my lectures with extra material, not least in the footnotes, and changing the title, I have otherwise sought to preserve their original oral flavor. The expectation of the Moore College lectures was that they would "deal with some aspect of the Reformed and Evangelical faith either by way of biblical exposition or systematic theology."[3] I was pleasantly surprised to discover that previous lecturers included scholars such as F. F. Bruce, J. I. Packer, and my former dean, Kenneth Kantzer, who delivered the 1984 series on a theme similar to my own: "Reformation Theology at the End of the Twentieth Century." I do not know what approach he took, but I would like to think he would have approved of what I set out in these pages.

I am pleased to acknowledge receiving helpful points and bibliographic suggestions from my Trinity colleagues David Dockery, David Luy, Scott Manetsch, and Doug Sweeney. I am indebted to my doctoral students—Isuwa Atsen, Kessia Reyne Bennett, Jeff Calhoun, Daniel Fleming, Austin Freeman, Geoff Fulkerson, Jonathan King, Matt La Pine, Paul Maxwell, Derek Rishmawy, Todd Saur, Brian Tung, and Paul Uyen—for their willingness to meet and discuss the manuscript chapter by chapter, and to Chris Donato for his insightful editorial comments. Finally, I owe a special thanks to Jim Kinney, editorial director of Baker Academic and Brazos Press, for both his advocacy of my work and his shrewd suggestions for improving it, including the revised title, and to Tim West, my editor at Brazos, for improving the wording of the manuscript more times than I care to acknowledge.

3. https://www.moore.edu.au/annual-moore-college-lectures (accessed September 6, 2015).

I am most grateful to the Rev. Dr. Mark Thompson, principal of Moore College, for the invitation to deliver the lectures, and to his family for their gracious hospitality (which included a memorable Sydney harbor ferry trip) during my stay. I wish, finally, to thank the several faculty members and their families who invited me to dinner, and the students who submitted handwritten questions after each lecture. In ways that I had not anticipated, the writings of several Moore College folk—in particular Graeme Goldsworthy, Peter O'Brien, David Broughton Knox, Peter Jensen, John William Woodhouse, and Mark Thompson—had a disproportionate influence on my preparation for the lectures. It is therefore only appropriate that I have dedicated this published version to the principals and faculty members of Moore College, past and present.

Introduction

Should the Church Repent
or Retrieve the Reformation?
Secularism, Skepticism, and Schism—Oh My!

"By Their Fruits Ye Shall Know Them": Assessing a Revolution

"By their fruits ye shall know them" (Matt. 7:16 ASV). This is one of the key points in Jesus's Sermon on the Mount, and in context he is speaking of false prophets *in the church* who come in sheep's clothing "but inwardly are ravenous wolves" (Matt. 7:15), leading disciples astray. The Reformation was a movement, not a person, a movement that gave birth to Protestantism "as a distinct form of Western Christianity,"[1] but the principle still stands: "Every healthy tree bears good fruit, but the diseased tree bears bad fruit" (Matt. 7:17).

Five hundred years is more than enough time to assess the harvest, yet the jury is still out.[2] On the one hand, Protestants have indeed been fruitful and multiplied: the 2010 edition of the *Atlas of Global Christianity* estimates that there are more than four million congregations worldwide and thirty-eight

---

1. Mark A. Noll, *Protestantism: A Very Short Introduction* (Oxford: Oxford University Press, 2011), 1.
2. For an interesting survey of the ways that earlier anniversaries of the Reformation have celebrated it, see Thomas Albert Howard and Mark A. Noll, "The Reformation at Five Hundred: An Outline of the Changing Ways We Remember the Reformation," *First Things* 247 (November 2014): 43–48.

thousand denominations.[3] One therefore wonders whether Protestants have been not only fruitful but excessively so: If Charles de Gaulle could complain about the difficulty of governing a country that has 246 varieties of cheese, how much more difficult is it to achieve consensus among thirty-eight thousand Protestant denominations?

We need to do more than crunch numbers, however, to assess properly the Reformation's fruit. Jesus was concerned with truth and good deeds as criteria of authentic discipleship. Similarly, we need to assess whether and to what extent the Reformation encouraged faithfulness to God's Word and godly obedience—conformity to Christ. Christlikeness is ultimately the only fruit that counts. As C. S. Lewis says, "The church exists for nothing else but to draw men into Christ, to make them little Christs."[4] If a fruitful church makes disciples (cf. Matt. 28:19–20), a fruitful movement makes disciple-making churches.

One need not be a historian to know that, on this scorecard, Protestantism gets mixed marks. The Reformation begat not simply disciples but Lutherans, Calvinists, Wesleyans, Zwinglians, Mennonites, and more. Some family lines have remained intact; others have suffered through various divorces. Critics of the Reformation (their name is Legion) accuse it of begetting a bevy of bastard children too, including capitalism, subjectivism, and naturalism (so much for practicing birth control). There are mainline and evangelical, conservative and liberal, Western and non-Western varieties of Protestants, and their disagreements on various points of faith and practice make it difficult to speak of *the* Protestant position on any doctrinal or social issue.

"Decentralization" is the Protestant watchword. In the beginning, decentralization took denominational form. At present, it is taking the form of *de*-denominating. Historians like Alister McGrath think it more accurate to speak of Protestantisms, in the plural.[5] Some commentators think that Protestantism has no future. The tank is empty. On one telling of the story, Protestantism is like the fig tree that Jesus cursed (Matt. 21:18–19). It was meant to bear fruit, but when a hungry Jesus came to it, it had leaves only—and we know what fig leaves are good for: covering up nakedness (cf. Gen. 3:7). Sheer numbers

3. Todd M. Johnson and Kenneth R. Ross, eds., *Atlas of Global Christianity* (Edinburgh: Edinburgh University Press, 2009).

4. C. S. Lewis, *Mere Christianity* (New York: Touchstone, 1996), 171.

5. Alister McGrath, *Christianity's Dangerous Idea: The Protestant Revolution—A History from the Sixteenth Century to the Twenty-First* (New York: HarperOne, 2007), 62–63.

cannot cover up Protestantism's failure to display consistently the fruit of the Spirit: denominational love, joy, peace, patience, kindness, and especially denominational faithfulness and self-control (cf. Gal. 5:22–23). Many of the thirty-eight thousand denominational grapes are indeed withering on the vine. Still, many Christians continue not only to identify with the Reformation but also to name their blog sites and their seminaries after its leading lights. Is Protestantism a cursed fig tree, or is it a tree "planted by streams of water that yields its fruit in its season" (Ps. 1:3)?

Narrating the Story of Protestantism

How can we tell the story of the Protestant Reformation? In this book I will make several claims, some of them counterintuitive, about the abiding significance of the Reformation for theology today. I am not a professional historian. I have unearthed no new facts about the Reformation, though I have sought to refresh our memory about certain things that we may have forgotten.[6] The basic narrative (Martin Luther's story) is well known: boy loves church; boy leaves church; boy finds new church friend. Wait a moment—is that the story? Is there such a thing as a "new" church? To repeat: I am not a historian, nor have I discovered new facts. However, I will dispute some interpretations of the facts, including popular ways of telling the story of the Reformation, in light of certain Reformation ideas and practices that tend to get passed over. Admittedly, these are deep waters: Isn't all storytelling ideologically driven? Won't my story simply reflect my location—my prejudices, my people, my power interests?

I acknowledge the dilemma. To make any claim is to risk having people suspect that it ultimately serves one's own self-aggrandizing interests. In this case, however, I will be arguing not for the superiority of my own Reformed tribe but for "mere Protestant Christianity." This refers neither to a lost "golden age" nor to a particular cultural instantiation of Protestantism, but rather to a set of seminal insights—encapsulated by the five *solas*—that represent a standing challenge, and encouragement, to the church. To borrow from G. K. Chesterton: mere Protestant Christianity (theological unity in ecclesial diversity) has not been tried and found wanting; it has been found arduous

6. To mention two examples to be developed in later chapters: the Reformers' concern for the unity of the visible church (a catholicity rooted in the gospel rather than Rome); the sixteenth-century Genevan *congrégation* as an ecclesial institution and paradigm for biblical interpretation.

and left unfinished.[7] Internecine tumult over non-Nicene theology—in other words, first-order discord over second-order doctrine—has been the bane of Protestant theology. But before I give my account, it may be helpful to examine other ways of telling the story.

To what biblical story may we liken the Reformation? Martin Luther cast himself as an Old Testament prophet leading Israel back to Jerusalem after the Babylonian captivity, or alternately as a New Testament apostle (Martin Luther Paul) who had to confront the Galatian heresy all over again after its migration to Rome. Although Luther did not compare himself to one of Israel's kings, his rediscovery of Romans—the gospel according to Paul—and subsequent reform of the church parallel King Josiah's reform of the temple and rediscovery of the law (2 Kings 22:8–23:3; cf. 2 Chron. 34:8–33), namely, the book of Deuteronomy, "the Gospel according to Moses."[8] When Josiah heard the law, he tore his clothes; when Luther heard the gospel, his heart was set free. Of course, that is not the end of the story, which is why others are disposed to view the Reformation in terms of an earlier chapter in the book of Kings: the story of the divided kingdom (1 Kings 12).[9]

Other, less charitable storytellers cast Luther as the serpent in the church garden, tempting the bride of Christ to eat the forbidden fruit, namely, the power-knowledge of interpreting the Bible for oneself and thus to be "like God," having textual knowledge of words and meaning. McGrath does not come right out and identify Luther with Lucifer, but he does call Protestantism—in particular, the notion that individuals can read the Bible for themselves—"Christianity's dangerous idea."[10]

Protestantism's Progress? (Ernst Troeltsch)

Friedrich Schleiermacher praised the Reformers for introducing academic freedom into theology, namely, the critical (i.e., scholarly) principle that is the

---

7. The original reads, "The Christian ideal has not been tried and found wanting. It has been found difficult; and left untried" (G. K. Chesterton, *What's Wrong with the World* [New York: Dodd, Mead, 1912], 48).

8. Daniel I. Block, *The Gospel according to Moses: Theological and Ethical Reflections on the Book of Deuteronomy* (Eugene, OR: Cascade, 2012).

9. Ephraim Radner, *The End of the Church: A Pneumatology of Christian Division in the West* (Grand Rapids: Eerdmans, 1998). Radner argues that a divided church is a church without the Holy Spirit, and thus a church that is unable rightly to read Scripture.

10. Note the title of his book. Specifically, the dangerous new idea "was that all Christians have the right to interpret the Bible for themselves" (McGrath, *Christianity's Dangerous Idea*, 2).

only antidote to (Roman Catholic) dogmatism.[11] The biblical scholar Wilhelm de Wette generalized the idea: "The spirit of Protestantism . . . leads necessarily to political freedom."[12] Indeed, the philosopher G. W. F. Hegel viewed the Reformation as an essential step in the history of *Geist* toward freedom: "This is the essence of the Reformation: Man is in his very nature destined to be free."[13] Paul Tillich similarly depicted the "Protestant principle" as dialectical: a prophetic "no" to any earthly authoritarianism, and a creative "yes" to the ground of being (love) that empowers new shapes of human freedom.[14]

These optimistic narratives of Protestantism's progress are perhaps best represented (and critiqued) by Ernst Troeltsch's 1906 work *Protestantism and Progress: The Significance of Protestantism for the Rise of the Modern World*.[15] Instead of hailing Luther as the pioneer of modern freedom, Troeltsch was more circumspect: "early" Protestantism (Luther's) was a "second blooming" of medievalism, which led only indirectly to the "new" Protestantism that coexisted happily with secular science and the secular state.[16] For Troeltsch, Protestantism's progress is a matter of basing beliefs not on external authority but on inner personal conviction: "Protestantism became the religion of the search for God in one's own feeling, experience, thought, and will."[17] The Reformation may have begun as a revival of medievalism, but it indirectly paved the way toward the individualism of the modern world—that is, a civilization freed from (church) authority.

"Constructive Protestantism" (H. Richard Niebuhr)

Richard Niebuhr's 1937 work *The Kingdom of God in America* examines how Protestant pilgrims newly arrived in America, the land of opportunity,

11. Address to the theology faculty of the University of Berlin, on the occasion of the 300th anniversary of the Reformation (November 3, 1817), cited in Howard and Noll, "Reformation at Five Hundred."

12. Cited in Howard and Noll, "Reformation at Five Hundred," 45.

13. G. W. F. Hegel, *The Philosophy of History*, trans. J. Sibree (Mineola, NY: Dover, 1956), 417. See also Merold Westphal, "Hegel and the Reformation," in *Hegel, Freedom, and Modernity* (Albany: State University of New York Press, 1992), 149–64.

14. Paul Tillich, *The Protestant Era* (Chicago: University of Chicago Press, 1948).

15. Philadelphia: Fortress, 1986. Originally published in German as *Die Bedeutung des Protestantismus für die Entstehung der modernen Welt* (Munich: R. Oldenbourg, 1906).

16. "It was not until modern Protestantism had lost sight of the idea of a universal Church-civilization that it could characterise as genuine Protestant principles, the duty of historico-philological criticism, the organisation of Churches formed by voluntary association, independent of the State, and the doctrine of revelation by inner personal conviction and illumination" (Troeltsch, *Protestantism and Progress*, 37).

17. Ibid., 98.

used their freedom no longer to protest (the negative part of the Reformation) but rather to practice a positive citizenship of the gospel: "Whatever else then America came to be, it was also an experiment in constructive Protestantism."[18] Niebuhr devotes a chapter to "The Problem of Constructive Protestantism," where he sets out the basic challenge. Protestants confessed the direct rule of God, apart from any institutional mediation, but it was not clear how God's Word was to order society: "The new freedom was not self-organizing but threatened anarchy in every sphere of life."[19]

Although Niebuhr does not mention it, what happened among the Puritans in the Massachusetts Bay Colony makes for an excellent case study in the problem of constructive Protestantism. The Puritans distrusted any interpretive authority but the Holy Spirit speaking in Scripture; as Lisa Gordis notes, "Puritan interpretive practices privileged techniques that theoretically allowed the Bible to interpret itself."[20] The preachers at Massachusetts Bay claimed simply to "open" the text, with the Spirit's illumination, and assumed that a community that read "in the Spirit" would achieve interpretive consensus. Given this assumption, dissent over what God is saying in Scripture could not help but be troubling, not only practically but also theoretically.[21] The "troubles" came to a head in 1636, in what is now known as the Antinomian or "Free Grace" Controversy. It is a sobering illustration of how Puritan hermeneutics generated, managed, and ultimately failed to contain interpretive diversity.

The story has everything one could want in a Hollywood blockbuster: courtroom drama, intrigue, religious figures coming to grief in public, and perhaps the first feminist in America. I refer to the trial of Anne Hutchinson, also known as the "American Jezebel."[22] Hutchinson was at the center of a theological controversy that took the Massachusetts Bay Colony to the brink of collapse and spurred a significant exodus of the disaffected. The particular issue—did God's grace transform sinners?—is less important for present purposes than is the phenomenon of a Christian community that aspired to interpretive unity falling into greater and greater interpretive disarray. The

18. H. Richard Niebuhr, *The Kingdom of God in America* (1937; repr., Middletown, CT: Wesleyan University Press, 1988), 43.

19. Ibid., 30.

20. Lisa M. Gordis, *Opening Scripture: Bible Reading and Interpretive Authority in Puritan New England* (Chicago: University of Chicago Press, 2003), 3.

21. Ibid., 9.

22. An expression used in the title of chap. 10 in Michael Winship's *Making Heretics: Militant Protestantism and Free Grace in Massachusetts, 1636–1641* (Princeton: Princeton University Press, 2002).

explicit issue concerned the relationship of grace, transformation, and the work of the Holy Spirit, but the underlying question was this: Whose reading of the Bible counts, and, in particular, how are church members to proceed in the face of interpretive disputes?[23]

Like the Bereans (Acts 17:11), Hutchinson searched the Scriptures, hosting meetings in her house to discuss, and dissect, the sermons being preached by John Cotton in the First Church of Boston, the most important in the colony. She worried that the preachers in the Massachusetts Bay Colony so emphasized moral obedience as evidence of salvation as to be guilty of teaching a covenant of works. In contrast, she believed that only an inner intuition associated with the sealing of the Spirit could provide assurance of one's election. In any case, the meetings at the Hutchinson home drew up to sixty people and rivaled the influence of the church's official ministers. What further complicated matters was the previously mentioned conviction that people who interpret Scripture in the Spirit ought to agree: "They [did not] have room in their theories of exegesis to account for legitimate differences of opinion about scripture-derived doctrine."[24]

What to do with an intelligent woman who called into question the views of the established clergy in Boston, thus threatening to undermine the Puritan New England "holy experiment"? Answer: put her on trial for slandering ministers (and disturbing the peace of the commonwealth)! Governor John Winthrop presided over the trial in 1637. The climax of the trial came on the second day when Anne testified as to "the ground of what I know to be true," which apparently proved to be an immediate revelation of the Holy Spirit.[25] The verdict: banishment to Rhode Island—and the Baptists.

What Anne Hutchinson had opened in the Massachusetts Bay Company was the Pandora's box of Protestantism: "Left alone with her Bible . . . and with the Holy Spirit, Hutchinson interpreted the text in a way that put her at odds with her community."[26] Unlike Luther, she was a layperson, but like

23. "Leaders of the Bay Colony expected consensus: indeed, expectations of interpretive consensus enabled by the Holy Spirit were high enough that church polity rested on assumptions of unanimity" (Gordis, *Opening Scripture*, 149).

24. Ibid., 151.

25. "The Examination of Mrs. Anne Hutchinson at the Court at Newtown," in *The Antinomian Controversy, 1636–1638: A Documentary History*, ed. David D. Hall, 2nd ed. (Durham, NC: Duke University Press, 1990), 337.

26. Gordis, *Opening Scripture*, 172. For example, at her trial Hutchinson appealed to Dan. 6:16–24, claiming that God had shown her that he would deliver her as he had delivered Daniel from the lion's den ("Examination," in Hall, *Antinomian Controversy*, 337–38).

Luther, she argued that her reading of the biblical text, illumined by the Spirit, was superior to that of the resident clergy, in her case the Boston pastors. This was an interpretive dispute that threatened civil unrest, even violence. John Winthrop worried that the different sides of the debate might come to use the Bible not as a source of isolated proof texts with which to refute one another but rather as a weapon with which to break the head of one's opponent.[27] The controversy eventually resulted in the second generation of New England's ministers "ground[ing] their authority in learning and expertise, emphasizing the need for academic training along with the assistance of the Holy Spirit."[28]

"Christianity's Dangerous Idea"? (Alister McGrath)

Anne Hutchinson's case perfectly illustrates why McGrath can speak of "Christianity's dangerous idea." He is playing off the title of Daniel Dennett's book *Darwin's Dangerous Idea: Evolution and the Meanings of Life*.[29] Darwin's dangerous idea was the supposition that we can account for the design that we discover in nature through the impersonal process of natural selection without positing a designer. McGrath, who has a PhD in molecular biology as well as one in historical theology, takes more than Dennett's title, for he goes on to compare Protestantism to a microorganism, a virus capable of rapid mutation, proficient at adapting, and thus surviving, under a wide range of diverse conditions.

McGrath identifies the priesthood of all believers as the key Protestant gene, or rather meme: an idea, value, or practice that spreads from person to person, culture to culture, nation to nation through not genetic but cultural replication, in the case of the Reformation thanks largely to the printing press.[30] To tell the story of Protestantism as the transmission of memes from one generation to the next may seem a nonstarter, but McGrath sticks with the metaphor, arguing that Protestantism's ability to mutate accounts both

27. See Hall, *Antinomian Controversy*, 293–94.

28. Gordis, *Opening Scripture*, 10. See further Michael Winship, *The Times and Trials of Anne Hutchinson: Puritans Divided* (Lawrence: University Press of Kansas, 2005). See also Marcus Walsh, "Profession and Authority: The Interpretation of the Bible in the Seventeenth and Eighteenth Centuries," *Literature and Theology* 9 (1995): 383–98.

29. Daniel C. Dennett, *Darwin's Dangerous Idea: Evolution and the Meanings of Life* (New York: Simon & Schuster, 1995).

30. Like genes, memes are packets of information that can be passed on to subsequent generations. Unlike genes, the information that memes encode is done via culture rather than biology. The term "meme" was coined by Richard Dawkins in *The Selfish Gene* (Oxford: Oxford University Press, 1976), chap. 11.

for the unpredictability of new developments (such as Pentecostalism) and its capacity to adapt to new situations.

In invoking this evolutionary model, McGrath takes a stand on the question of the essence of Protestantism: "There was no single, unambiguous Protestant template, gene, or paradigm."[31] He rejects the idea that there is a moment in time that defines Protestantism once and for all. On the contrary, the essence of Protestantism is dynamic, consisting in "its constant self-examination in the light of the Bible and in its willingness to correct itself."[32]

To be Protestant is to strive to be biblical, yet no single way of being biblical can be used as a standard to judge the others. This, to McGrath's mind, is what makes Protestantism dangerous, for what else should one call an uncontrolled division of cells that mutate and spread throughout a body but cancer? This is indeed how its critics regard the Reformation notion of the priesthood of all believers, a meme so dangerous it almost deconstructed Massachusetts! Luther got a taste of his own medicine too. The Peasants' War in 1525 showed him a possible consequence of his position: radical religious individualism. McGrath writes, "Too late, Luther tried to rein in the movement by emphasizing the importance of authorized religious leaders, such as himself, and institutions in the interpretation of the Bible. But who, his critics asked, had 'authorized' these so-called authorities?"[33] Precisely.

We come, then, to the question that this book seeks to address: Should the church repent or retrieve this dangerous Protestant idea? Can the Protestant principle *sola scriptura* ever produce consensus, or is the result always chaos? Does Protestantism contain a fail-safe device that can be used to forestall or regulate the proliferation of divergent readings of the Bible that, left unchecked, are a cancer that ravages the body of Christ? Did the Reformation set loose interpretive anarchy upon the world, and, if so, should Christians everywhere file a class-action suit?

Repenting the (Unintended) Iniquities of Our Reformation Fathers

There is no merit in giving pat answers to complex questions. It is an uncomfortable fact that even those who are united in their affirmation of the supreme authority of Scripture often disagree over what the Bible says. The

31. McGrath, *Christianity's Dangerous Idea*, 463.
32. Ibid., 465.
33. Ibid., 3.

question is what to make of, and how to resolve, such interpretive disagreements. The subtitle that I chose for this chapter (playing off "Lions and tigers and bears—oh my!" in *The Wizard of Oz*) expresses the scope of the challenge. The cancerous Protestant meme combines the lion of skepticism (crouching at the door of modernity), the tiger of secularism, and the bear of schism. These are the alleged consequences, albeit unintentional, of the Reformation. Others have, of course, accused the Reformers of involuntary church slaughter and defamation of papal character. The particular charges for which I will seek their acquittal, however, are hermeneutical recklessness and criminal negligence of tradition. We begin by hearing testimony from three witnesses for the prosecution.

The Reformation Begat Secularization (Brad Gregory)

Surely the most important recent critique of the Reformation is Brad Gregory's *The Unintended Reformation: How a Religious Revolution Secularized Society*,[34] a magisterial deconstruction of the magisterial Reformation. Gregory claims that we can understand our present "hyperpluralized" situation only by returning to the past, the scene of the crime. The "crime" in question is secularization, and Gregory lays the blame at the doorstep of Protestantism: the Wittenberg door to which Luther affixed his challenge to church authority. In doing so, Luther set in motion a series of events that has led to what Gregory believes is an unsustainable and unhealthy modern situation. The unintended consequence of the Reformation's refusal of the church's final say-so was the loss of "any shared framework for the integration of knowledge"[35]—a loss whose effects continue to loom large.

Gregory readily admits that the Reformers did not set out to secularize the world. That is precisely why he speaks of the "unintended" Reformation. The Reformers worked an inadvertent Copernican revolution as concerns knowledge of God: instead of seeing Scripture as a planet that revolves around the system of theology, the Reformers made Scripture the sun that illumines the whole theological system. Instead of making Scripture conform to tradition, Scripture would speak for itself. In Luther's words: "This is not a Christian teaching, when I bring an opinion to Scripture and compel Scripture to follow it, but rather, on the contrary, when I first have got straight what Scripture

---

34. Cambridge, MA: Belknap Press of Harvard University Press, 2012.
35. Gregory, *Unintended Reformation*, 327.

teaches and then compel my opinion to accord with it."[36] The problem, as Gregory points out, is that from the 1520s onward, "those who rejected Rome disagreed about what God's word said."[37]

Protestant churches in cities like Geneva, and later nation-states like Holland, appeared to enjoy consensus on doctrinal matters, but Gregory claims that these agreements often were politically motivated and backed by political authority, like the German princes who supported Luther. By way of contrast, in the hands of the Radical Reformers, *sola scriptura* "produced not even rough agreement, but an open-ended welter of competing and incompatible interpretations."[38] Protestant pluralism—and eventually postmodernism— "derived directly from the Reformation's foundational truth claim,"[39] namely, the dangerous idea that individuals read the truth out of the Bible for themselves, apart from church authority: *sola scriptura*.

Why call this interpretive situation "secularization"? Because, Gregory argues, the Reformers rejected the whole hierarchical worldview of late medieval Christianity and replaced it with a flattened-out picture of *sola scriptura* whereby each person claimed independent authority to interpret the supreme religious authority. This eventually led to religious wars over disagreements as to precisely what Scripture said and, eventually, to the Enlightenment's elevation of *sola ratio* (reason alone) to the position of unbiased referee. Moreover, when reason became the privileged route to universal truth, faith was demoted to the realm of private (subjective) opinion.[40]

Gregory wants his readers to appreciate the full extent of the Reformation's failure. Not only did Protestants fail to agree about what the Bible said, they also failed to agree about the criteria to be used for deciding what was essential to believe and what was not, leading to the further problem of who gets to determine what true Christianity is, and how. Against their best intentions, "the church became the churches."[41] Gregory then fast-forwards to the present: "The Reformation is the most important distant historical source for contemporary Western hyperpluralism with respect to truth claims about

36. Cited in ibid., 88.
37. Ibid., 89.
38. Ibid., 94.
39. Ibid.
40. "Christian doctrinal pluralism set the Western world on an unintended trajectory in which knowledge was secularized as faith was subjectivized" (ibid., 327). See also Carlos M. N. Eire, *War against the Idols: The Reformation of Worship from Erasmus to Calvin* (Cambridge: Cambridge University Press, 1986).
41. Gregory, *Unintended Reformation*, 369.

meaning, morality, values, priorities, and purpose."[42] Gregory thus goes further than Max Weber: apparently, Protestants invented not only capitalism but consumerism too.[43] The net result of the Reformation was a proliferation of conflicting truth claims, each of which marketed itself as biblical and competed for the hearts and minds of Protestant church shoppers.

The Reformation Begat Skepticism (Richard Popkin)

The intellectual historian Richard Popkin opens his magisterial *History of Scepticism* with a chapter on "The Intellectual Crisis of the Reformation."[44] Of course, skepticism has an ancient pedigree; it would be unjust to accuse the Reformers of inventing it. This is not Popkin's claim. Rather, he argues that the Reformers let the skeptical views of antiquity into Europe through the back door of their dispute with Rome over the proper standard of religious knowledge.[45] Luther cracked open this back door in his 1519 Leipzig debate with Johann Eck by declaring *sola scriptura* to be the basis of Christian belief: Luther "took the critical step of denying the rule of faith of the Church and presented a radically different criterion of religious knowledge."[46]

For Luther, citing church tradition—the fathers—is not a sufficient argument: "For that which is asserted without the authority of Scripture . . . may be held as an opinion, but there is no obligation to believe it,"[47] much less count it as theological knowledge.[48] According to Popkin, Luther's claim precipitated an intellectual crisis that shook "the very foundation of Western civilization."[49] Luther had changed the rules of the legitimation game, namely, the criteria by which one determines something as true or false, and

42. Ibid. "Modernity is failing partly because reason alone in modern philosophy has proven no more capable than scripture alone of discerning or devising consensually persuasive answers to the Life Questions" (377).

43. In chap. 5 I discuss Max Weber's hypothesis set out in his classic work, *The Protestant Ethic and the "Spirit" of Capitalism*.

44. Richard H. Popkin, *The History of Scepticism: From Savonarola to Bayle*, rev. and expanded ed. (Oxford: Oxford University Press, 2003).

45. Ibid., 1.

46. Ibid., 4.

47. Cited in ibid., 4.

48. The Reformers did appeal to the church fathers as secondary authorities (because faithful expositors of Scripture), first, to justify their break from medieval scholasticism, but also, second, to authenticate their respective confessional traditions vis-à-vis one another. See further Esther Chung-Kim, *Inventing Authority: The Use of the Church Fathers in Reformation Debates over the Eucharist* (Waco: Baylor University Press, 2011).

49. Popkin, *History of Scepticism*, 4.

his alternative criterion—"that which conscience is compelled to believe on reading Scripture is true"[50]—was dangerously subjective. Popkin identifies the underlying crisis—in fact, an epistemological dilemma—as a dispute about the fundamental criterion to which people can nonarbitrarily appeal when trying to decide between two or more possibilities. How could one refute Luther's claims if the ultimate appeal was Luther's conscience? This was precisely what Luther's Roman Catholic opponents were afraid of: a chaotic situation where the ultimate criterion is subjective, where everyone exercises the right to appeal to his or her own conscience rather than to the established objective authority of the institutional church. Erasmus went so far as to appeal to skepticism as a reason to remain Roman Catholic: in view of the difficulty in establishing the true meaning of the biblical text, he reasoned, is it not better to adhere to the age-old wisdom of the church? As Popkin observes, "The Reformers were continually occupied with trying to justify their own type of subjective, individual criterion and at the same time were using this criterion as an objective measure by means of which they condemned as heresies their opponent's appeals to conscience."[51]

The Reformation Begat Schism (Hans Boersma and Peter Leithart)

One adjective seems custom-made to describe the unintended consequence of the Reformation. It is a word that I never come across except in the descriptions or criticisms of Protestantism: "fissiparous"—"inclined to cause or undergo division into separate parts of groups," from the Latin *fissus*, past participle of *findere* (to split; cf. "fissure"). Here, for example, is how Brad Gregory uses it: "The fissiparous particularity of Protestant truth claims, theology, and experiential knowledge was an insuperable problem."[52] Think of it as the centrifugal force or, more provocatively, the Big Bang behind interpretive pluralism.

It is largely because of its fissiparousness that Hans Boersma regards the Reformation "not as something to be celebrated but as something to be lamented."[53] In particular, he laments the tearing of what he terms the "sacramental tapestry"—the premodern worldview where visible realities point

---

50. Ibid., 5.
51. Ibid., 7.
52. Gregory, *Unintended Reformation*, 355.
53. Hans Boersma, *Heavenly Participation: The Weaving of a Sacramental Tapestry* (Grand Rapids: Eerdmans, 2011), 85. See also Boersma, Nouvelle Théologie *and Sacramental Ontology: A Return to Mystery* (Oxford: Oxford University Press, 2009).

to the invisible heavenly realities in which they sacramentally participate. Boersma sees the Reformers' insistence on reading for the literal (i.e., "natural") sense rather than the allegorical (i.e., supernatural, spiritual) sense to be symptomatic of the modern turn away from mystery to history and the grammatical-historical method for reading Scripture: "The rise of modernity corresponded with the decline of an approach that regarded the created order as sacramental in character."[54] This fissure between the natural sign (*signum*) and supernatural thing (*res*), between this-worldly history and its participation in heavenly reality, constitutes an *ontological* schism that encourages, as it were, an epistemological fissiparousness.[55]

According to Boersma, the Reformers rent not only the sacramental tapestry that held together heaven and earth but also the previously seamless garment of the body of Christ: the church "was pulled apart by arguments over faith and works, Scripture and tradition, baptism and Eucharist."[56] In sum, Boersma views the Reformers as dividers rather than uniters in both an ecclesial and an ontological sense: "The reason the Reformation was a tragedy is that it split the unity of the church while it failed to address the problematic decline of the Platonist-Christian synthesis."[57]

In a widely discussed article in *First Things* on "The Future of Protestantism," Peter Leithart decries the Protestant tendency to "just say *no*," that is, to identity itself oppositionally, in contrast to the "other" of Roman Catholicism.[58] He thinks that they (Protestants) protest too much. As T. S. Eliot put it, "The life of Protestantism depends on the survival of that against which it protests."[59] However, history does not stand still, and the Roman Catholic

54. Boersma, *Heavenly Participation*, 17.
55. Boersma locates the beginning of the tear in the sacramental tapestry in late medieval developments (e.g., nominalism) that began to separate the natural from the supernatural (ibid., 84).
56. Ibid., 84.
57. Ibid., 87.
58. Peter J. Leithart, "The Future of Protestantism: The Churches Must Die to Be Raised Anew," *First Things* 245 (August/September 2014): 23–27.
59. T. S. Eliot, *Notes towards the Definition of Culture* (London: Faber & Faber, 1949), 75. Compare Friedrich Schleiermacher's famous formulation of the contrast:

> Insofar as the Reformation was not simply a purification and reaction from abuses which had crept in, but was the origination of a distinctive form of the Christian communion, the antithesis between Protestantism and Catholicism may provisionally be conceived thus: the former makes the individual's relation to the Church dependent on his relation to Christ, while the latter contrariwise makes the individual's relation to Christ dependent on his relation to the Church. (*The Christian Faith*, ed. H. R. Mackintosh and J. S. Stewart [Edinburgh: T&T Clark, 1999], 103)

See also Paul Tillich, *A History of Christian Thought* (New York: Touchstone, 1967), 228.

Church today looks quite different from what the Reformers had to confront. Leithart takes exception to Protestants who act as if the Reformation were the summit of church history: "But if God is alive, why would we think that the Church reached its final form in 1517 or 1640? . . . We cannot. Division *cannot* be the final state of Christ's Church."[60] Insofar as definitional opposition to Roman Catholicism is constitutive of Protestant identity, says Leithart, "Jesus bids Protestantism to come and die."[61] Protestantism seems all too willing to accept the call, if present trends in declining membership of the mainline churches are any indication.

As a sociological and historical phenomenon, Protestants are, of course, susceptible to the same kind of blind spots or myopic thinking that characterizes every other human group. However, contra Leithart, the fundamental gesture of Protestantism is not negative but affirmative. The Reformers did not view themselves as schismatics, nor were they. To protest is to testify *for* something, namely, the integrity of the gospel, and, as we will see, this includes the church's catholicity. It also includes prophetic protest (the negative gesture) whenever and wherever the truth of the gospel is at risk. Unity alone (*sola unitas*) is not enough unless the unity in question is a *unitas* of *veritas* (truth).

What Luther objected to was not the church's catholicity per se but the narrowness of its Roman qualifier—that is, to constricting catholicity to the city limits (so to speak) of Rome. In John McNeill's words: "It was, then, the narrowness of Rome's alleged catholicity that antagonized Luther."[62] C. S. Lewis concurs: "The Roman Church where it differs from this universal tradition and specifically from apostolic Christianity I reject. . . . In a word, the whole set-up of modern Romanism seems to me to be as much a provincial or local *variation* from the ancient tradition as any particular Protestant sect is."[63] Continuing in this vein, the present work argues that the only true Protestant—a biblical, Christ-centered Protestant, whose conscience is indeed captive to the gospel—is a *catholic* Protestant.[64] For true Protestants, schism

---

60. Leithart, "Future of Protestantism," 24.
61. Ibid., 26.
62. John T. McNeill, *Unitive Protestantism: The Ecumenical Spirit and Its Persistent Expression* (Richmond: John Knox, 1964), 68.
63. Letter to Lyman Stebbins, May 8, 1945, in C. S. Lewis, *The Collected Letters of C. S. Lewis*, vol. 2, *Books, Broadcasts, and the War, 1931–1949*, ed. Walter Hooper (New York: HarperSanFrancisco, 2004), 646–47.
64. Compare Leithart's "Reformational Catholicism," where the accent is on Catholicism and what Protestants share with Roman Catholics. By way of contrast, my formula makes

is, as Matthew Henry put it, "an uncharitable distance, division, or alien-
ation of affections among those who are called Christians, and agree in the
fundamentals of religion, occasioned by their different apprehensions about
little things."[65] Be that as it may, the distinction between "fundamentals"
and "little things" brings us back to what many consider the Achilles heel of
Protestantism: the lack of centralized interpretive authority.[66] For who decides
what belongs to the fundamentals and what to the little things?

Fine-Tuning the Problem; Deepening the Dilemma

To this point, I have said little that is edifying. In order to build, one must first
clear the ground. We need to dig deeper before we can lay a positive foundation
for construction. There are indeed positive insights from the Reformation to
cherish: both the *material principle* (justification by grace alone through faith
alone) and the *formal principle* (the supreme authority of Scripture alone).
However, the present work focuses on what we could call the *material problem* of the Reformation (the conflict of biblical interpretation in the church
and the lack of visible church unity) and the *formal problem* that generated
it (the lack of a consensual criterion for discerning whose interpretation of
Scripture is right). The problems are linked, and they derive from three inter-
related crises, all allegedly by-products of *sola scriptura*.

An Interpretive Crisis: Which Biblical Meaning?

Saint Peter may not have had Protestants in mind when he wrote, but surely
it is a good idea for every child of the Reformation always to be prepared
to make a defense to anyone who asks for a reason for the hope that is in us
(cf. 1 Pet. 3:15)—namely, that we will one day all agree about what the Bible
means. For the proliferation of opinions and disagreements over just about
every single passage in the Bible is staggering. As the experiment of Puritan
theology in North America revealed, the de facto diversity and individualism

---

"catholic" the adjectival qualifier and "Protestant" the noun that it modifies. In other words,
"Protestant" stands for the core content of what is confessed (i.e., the five *solas*, themselves
indications of the gospel), while "catholic" describes the scope of its confessors.

65. Matthew Henry, *A Brief Enquiry into the True Nature of Schism: Or a Persuasive to
Christian Love and Charity* (London, 1690).

66. So Devin Rose, *The Protestant's Dilemma: How the Reformation's Shocking Consequences Point to the Truth of Catholicism* (San Diego: Catholic Answers Press, 2014), 213.

of Protestant truth claims about what Scripture says "could not be reconciled with the epistemological demands of science for universality and objectivity."[67]

Call it the "Protestant perplex," so named after Frederick Crews's wonderful little book, *The Pooh Perplex*, a brilliant parody of the multifarious means by which literary critics have their way with texts. The subtitle says it all: "In Which It Is Discovered That the True Meaning of the Pooh Stories Is Not as Simple as Is Usually Believed, but for Proper Elucidation Requires the Combined Efforts of Several Academicians of Varying Critical Persuasions."[68] Whereas the *Pooh Perplex* pokes fun at various critical theories (Crews provides Freudian and Marxist readings of the Pooh stories, for example), the Protestant perplex describes the odd state of affairs where readers using no particular literary theory nevertheless produce a bewildering variety of readings.

Christian Smith's *The Bible Made Impossible* does for Protestantism what Crews does for Pooh: it exposes the multifarious meanings that have been made by various readers.[69] Smith is clear that the problem is not the Bible but *biblicism*—a theory about the authority of the Bible that posits its clarity, self-sufficiency, self-evident meaning, and universal applicability.[70] Smith, a sociologist, tries to demonstrate how the practice of biblicism belies the theory. Specifically, what falsifies biblicism is the *pervasive interpretive pluralism* that results: "It becomes beside the point to assert a text to be solely authoritative . . . when, lo and behold, it gives rise to a host of many divergent teachings on important matters."[71] Biblicists must be in denial, Smith thinks, if they cannot see what everyone else sees: "*On important matters the Bible apparently is not clear, consistent, and univocal enough to enable the best-intentioned, most highly skilled, believing readers to come to agreement as to what it teaches.*"[72]

Devin Rose, an apologist for Roman Catholicism, makes a similar point with a simple syllogism: if *sola scriptura* is true, then Protestants should be

---

67. Gregory, *Unintended Reformation*, 355.

68. Frederick C. Crews, *The Pooh Perplex* (London: Robin Clark, 1979).

69. Christian Smith, *The Bible Made Impossible: Why Biblicism Is Not a Truly Evangelical Reading of Scripture* (Grand Rapids: Brazos, 2011).

70. The situation is somewhat more complex, for Smith goes on to acknowledge that the Bible is multivocal: "It can and does speak to different listeners in different voices that appear to say different things"; "The words of scripture themselves can and usually do give rise to more than one possible, arguably legitimate interpretation" (ibid., 47, 53). In subsequent chapters I will argue that the way forward is not to abandon biblicism but to distinguish between a naïve and a critical biblicism, between a pervasive interpretive pluralism, on the one hand, and a unitive interpretive plurality, on the other (I will also refer to the latter as a plural interpretive unity).

71. Ibid., xi.

72. Ibid., 25 (emphasis original).

united in their interpretations of the Bible; Protestants are not united in their biblical interpretations; therefore, *sola scriptura* is not true. Strictly speaking the logic is impeccable (it is an example of *modus tollens*, or denying the consequent, a valid rule of inference), but everything rides on how one understands the premises: *sola scriptura* and Protestant unity. We will return to these notions in due course. Rose succinctly states the presenting problem of the Reformation's legacy: "No honest religious historian can deny that the result of *sola scriptura* has been doctrinal chaos."[73] Wittenberg, we have a problem.

A Legitimation Crisis: Whose Theological Authority?

The problem is not simply the sheer multiplicity of interpretations but the lack of a viable shared criterion or central authority to help sort through them. We're back to McGrath's dangerous idea of Christianity—the priesthood of all believers—namely, the right of each believer to interpret the Bible for himself or herself. This is the mutant gene in the Protestant DNA, the ultimately uncontrollable meme that spawned developments that the Reformers themselves could never have imagined.[74] As McGrath points out, "the nature of Protestantism makes it very difficult to use the term 'heresy' to refer to divergent schools of thought."[75] John Dryden's poem "Religio Laici" ("A Layperson's Religion" [1682]) exposes the Protestant nakedness at this point:

> The Book thus put in every vulgar hand,
> Which each presumed he best could understand,
> The common rule was made the common prey,
> And at the mercy of the rabble lay.[76]

Elsewhere Dryden asks,

> Have not all heretics the same pretence,
> To plead the Scriptures in their own defence?[77]

---

73. Rose, *Protestant's Dilemma*, 87.
74. McGrath, *Christianity's Dangerous Idea*, 2.
75. Ibid., 230.
76. John Dryden, "Religio Laici," lines 400–403, in *Selected Poems* (London: Penguin, 2001), 184.
77. John Dryden, "The Hind and the Panther," part 2, lines 154–55 (ibid., 243).

The underlying issue is how to determine who has the authority to define the Christian faith and interpret its defining document.[78] According to Bruce McCormack, "The greatest theological problem confronting Reformed theology today—and I suspect that this is true not only for the American church but for other western churches as well—is the problem of ecclesial authority."[79] Here is how Devin Rose paraphrases Luther's principle of the priesthood of all believers: "If Protestantism is true, we all decide for ourselves what God's revelation means."[80] And, "If Protestantism is true, all we have is fallible opinions about infallible books."[81] Here, in a nutshell, is the Protestant dilemma: *sola scriptura*, coupled with the priesthood of all believers, seems to make each individual the final authority, and yet various Protestant individuals, each guided and illumined by the Holy Spirit, disagree with one another. That's the bad news.[82]

The good news—to be developed over the course of the next five chapters—is that God alone saves, and that he saves us even from this. As we will see, a misleading picture of the priesthood of all believers holds its critics captive. Make no mistake: the danger is real. Schism happens. I remember once asking my students in a doctoral seminar on theological hermeneutics, "What do you do when people in your church agree that the Bible is authoritative but disagree over its implications for doctrine and practice?" I had meant it as a rhetorical question, intended (like the present introduction) to create a sense of urgency about what I was planning constructively to propose. However, no sooner had I posed the question than a student from the Philippines raised his hand and said, "That's easy. We start a new church." It was (descriptively) and was not (normatively) the right answer. It was not the right answer because there is only one church. In any case, it provided an excellent teaching moment.

This misleading picture of the priesthood of all believers as granting every individual the right to start a church fits hand in glove with what we may call *interpretive egoism*. Interpretive egoism is first cousin to the modern value

78. McGrath, *Christianity's Dangerous Idea*, 3.
79. Bruce McCormack, "The End of Reformed Theology?," in *Reformed Theology: Identity and Ecumenicity*, ed. Wallace M. Alston Jr. and Michael Welker (Grand Rapids: Eerdmans, 2003), 54.
80. Rose, *Protestant's Dilemma*, 89.
81. Ibid., 95.
82. It is worth noting that John Dryden, himself an Anglican at the time, believed that Scripture's truths are clear and distinct to all grace-enabled readers: Scripture "speaks itself, / and what it does contain, / In all things needful to be known, is plain" ("Religio Laici," lines 368–69 [p. 183]).

of individual autonomy that its critics want to blame on the Reformation. *Extreme interpretive egoism* is the view that privileges my interpretations simply because they are mine.[83] The question is whether Martin Luther and others who read the Bible under the rubric *sola scriptura* are interpretive egoists. I do not think that Luther, though (obviously!) an individual, was an interpretive egoist, and in chapter 4 I will refute the myth that the priesthood of all believers serves as a charter for mass interpretive egoism.

A Community Crisis: What Ecclesial Unity?

Most Christians probably do not worry about being interpretive egoists because they are members of a believing community, where there is both safety and sanctity in numbers. Church unity is here a function of unity of confession. Such complacency ignores the possibility of *communal interpretive egoism*—the attitude that regards the fact that other communities interpret the Bible differently as having no particular bearing on the interpretation by one's own community.[84] Why should we care whether our local church is singing with a denominational or ecumenical choir? Because, says John Howard Yoder, "Where Christians are not united, the gospel is not true in that place."[85] Yoder is no doubt thinking of Jesus's high-priestly prayer, when he asks the Father in heaven to sanctify Jesus's followers in the truth (John 17:17, 19) "that they may become perfectly one, so that the world may know that you sent me and loved them even as you loved me" (John 17:23).[86] What is ultimately at stake in repenting or retrieving the Reformation is the witness of the church, including its visible unity, and hence the integrity of the gospel.

We do not prosper the gospel when we pit unity against truth. Furthermore, *unity* is an elusive concept. As to what the unity of the church ought to be, there are several models, which raises the question of whether there can be such a thing as mere Protestant *polity* (see chap. 4). There is, first, the model

83. I am borrowing, and modifying, these categories from Linda Trinkhaus Zagzebski's study *Epistemic Authority: A Theory of Trust, Authority, and Autonomy in Belief* (Oxford: Oxford University Press, 2012). The modifications stem from my different starting point, namely, an attempt in the chapters that follow to give a dogmatic description of the pattern of interpretive authority.

84. Here too I am adapting what Zagzebski says about communal epistemic egoism (ibid., 223).

85. John Howard Yoder, *The Royal Priesthood: Essays Ecclesiological and Ecumenical*, ed. Michael G. Cartwright (Scottdale, PA: Herald, 1994), 291.

86. I will argue in the conclusion that being "perfectly one" is compatible with a plural unity or "Pentecostal" plurality in which different churches make common confession in their own idioms.

of Christendom—the Holy Roman Empire—though the church has already been there, done that, and found it both coercive and divisive (absolute ecclesial power corrupts absolutely). A kinder, gentler version might be the Holy British Empire, a commonwealth of holy nations. Ecumenists might prefer a third model: the United Holy Nations (though which denominations get to sit on the Security Council would make for interesting debate). Then there is the American experiment, Puritan New England, and eventually the Wild West, with locally elected sheriffs in every town. Lastly, there is my favorite model: the Democratic Republic of Biblical Letters, about which more in due course.[87]

In step with historical Christian orthodoxy, I take the Bible's authority as a given. The problem is not biblical authority but how to negotiate the conflict of interpretations of that authoritative source. The present book addresses the crisis concerning the authority not of the Bible but of its interpretation: Whose interpretation counts, and what makes one person's (or church's) interpretation more authoritative than another's?[88] "If there's a post-Reformation epistemological crisis in the West," says Peter Leithart, "we [are] all in it, not just Protestants. None of the strategies for building consensus—neither Protestant nor Catholic—have been successful in uniting the *whole* church."[89]

In writing this book, I did what any right-thinking research professor of systematic theology would do: I searched amazon.com for books pertaining to "interpretive authority." There were 2,652 results. At the top of the list was a title I knew well: Stanley Fish's *Is There a Text in This Class? The Authority of Interpretive Communities*.[90] Just under it was Mark Thompson's *A Sure Ground on Which to Stand: The Relation of Authority and Interpretive Method in Luther's Approach to Scripture*.[91] I knew then that I was on the right track.

For Stanley Fish, a secular literary critic, textual meaning is a function of the interpretive assumptions that happen to be in force in a particular

87. See Kevin J. Vanhoozer, "Interpreting Scripture between the Rock of Biblical Studies and the Hard Place of Systematic Theology: The State of the Evangelical (dis)Union," in *Renewing the Evangelical Mission*, ed. Richard Lints (Grand Rapids: Eerdmans, 2013), 201–25, esp. 217.

88. Compare Rupert Davies's statement of the problem of authority in religion: "Is there any accessible source of religious truth which is wholly authoritative? and, if so, what is it?" (*The Problem of Authority in the Continental Reformers: A Study in Luther, Zwingli, and Calvin* [London: Epworth, 1946], 9).

89. Peter J. Leithart, "Epistemological Crisis," *First Things*, August 9, 2013, http://www.first things.com/blogs/leithart/2013/08/epistemological-crisis.

90. Cambridge, MA: Harvard University Press, 1980.

91. Eugene, OR: Wipf & Stock, 2007.

interpretive community. Neither text nor reader is the self-sufficient source of meaning; rather, the interpretive community encompasses both: "There is no single way of reading that is correct or natural, only 'ways of reading' that are extensions of community perspectives."[92] In dethroning objectivity and subjectivity in favor of intersubjectivity, Fish follows philosophers of science like Thomas Kuhn, who claims that even scientists examine the world through paradigms that their interpretive community, the scientific community, treats as authoritative. How ought rival scientific or, for that matter, rival Protestant communities negotiate their interpretive disagreements? Is there anything that can arbitrate the conflict of communal interpretive paradigms? For those who swim in Fish's school, there is no authoritative authorial voice in the text: it is community reading conventions all the way down.

Always Retrieving? "Ressourcing" the Debate about Interpretive Authority

Attentive readers may at this point think that my situation is hopeless. Surely the evidence is irrefutable: the Reformers agreed *that* Scripture is supremely authoritative yet routinely disagreed as to *what* it says. The case against *sola scriptura* seems insurmountable. Even Harry Houdini could not escape these chains.

Earlier I spoke of the Reformation as a "revolution," which is the way many of its critics view it: a "radical and violent overthrow of an existing system,"[93] namely, Roman Catholicism. Philip Schaff disagrees. In his view, the Reformation was neither a revolution nor a restoration but "a deeper plunge into the meaning of the gospel."[94] There is continuity with the past (this is what Schaff calls the Reformation's "retrospective" aspect) and also forward progress (its "prospective" aspect).

Schaff does not use the word, but I will: the Reformation was a *retrieval*, first and foremost of the biblical gospel, particularly the Pauline articulation,

---

92. Fish, *Is There a Text?*, 16. McGrath says something similar: "It is important to note that biblical interpretation is partly a socially constructed enterprise that rests on inherited assumptions concerning what is 'natural' or 'obvious' within a community" (*Christianity's Dangerous Idea*, 468).

93. Philip Schaff, *The Principle of Protestantism*, trans. John W. Nevin, ed. Bard Thompson and George H. Bricker, Lancaster Series on the Mercersburg Theology 1 (1845; repr., Eugene, OR: Wipf & Stock, 2004), 57.

94. Philip Schaff, *Creeds of Christendom, with a History and Critical Notes*, vol. 1, *The History of Creeds* (New York: Harper, 1877), 204.

but also, secondarily, of the church fathers.[95] The Reformers were engaged in theology as retrieval long before it became trendy. Retrieval theology is the name for a "*mode or style of theological discernment* that looks back in order to move forward."[96] In their book *Theology as Retrieval*, David Buschart and Kent Eilers argue that Christian theology has always been about receiving and transmitting the deposit of faith. For example, the apostle Paul sees himself as "passing on" (*paradidōmi*) what he had "received" (*paralambanō*) from the Lord (1 Cor. 11:23). Retrieval is a mode of "handing down"— traditioning—"the faith that was once for all delivered to the saints" (Jude 3). At the same time, retrieval does more than repeat: it reforms. And it reforms not according to the standard of a past formula but according to the living and active Word of Scripture: "Christian allegiance is not to a single tradition but to the gospel, not to the task of reform for reform's sake but to Christ."[97] Sometimes viewing the past from our present situation makes the past (and the present) come alive in new ways. That is what I hope to do with this book.

We typically associate retrieval with Vatican II's and Henri de Lubac's *ressourcement* of patristic theology.[98] *Ressourcement* describes a return to authoritative sources for the sake of revitalizing the present. Unsurprisingly (given the principle "scholar see, scholar do"), there is now a call for evangelicals to retrieve the patristic and medieval heritage, based in part on the realization that the Reformers too relied in important ways on the church fathers. To my knowledge, however, no one has called for a properly Protestant *ressourcement*—that is, a retrieval of distinctly Reformation insights—to address the problem of interpretive pluralism. Such is my purpose here. As the Reformers

95. See further Anthony N. S. Lane, *John Calvin: Student of the Church Fathers* (Edinburgh: T&T Clark, 1999); Chung-Kim, *Inventing Authority*.

96. W. David Buschart and Kent D. Eilers, *Theology as Retrieval: Receiving the Past, Renewing the Church* (Downers Grove, IL: IVP Academic, 2015), 12.

97. William Stacy Johnson, "Theology and the Church's Mission: Catholic, Orthodox, Evangelical, and Reformed," in Alston and Welker, *Reformed Theology*, 67.

98. Michael Allen and Scott Swain survey ten other retrieving trends, including Thomas Oden's "paleo-orthodoxy," Robert Webber's "ancient-future" Christianity, and Radical Orthodoxy's Christian Platonism. They also commend their own model, reformed catholicity, in their *Reformed Catholicity: The Promise of Retrieval for Theology and Biblical Interpretation* (Grand Rapids: Baker Academic, 2015), 4–15. See also John Webster, "Theologies of Retrieval," in *The Oxford Handbook of Systematic Theology*, ed. John Webster, Kathryn Tanner, and Iain Torrance (Oxford: Oxford University Press, 2007), 583–99; and Webster, "*Ressourcement* Theology and Protestantism," in *Ressourcement: A Movement for Renewal in Twentieth-Century Theology*, ed. Gabriel Flynn and Paul D. Murray (Oxford: Oxford University Press, 2014), 482–95.

retrieved the gospel to meet the challenges of their time, so I want to retrieve certain aspects of the Reformation to meet present challenges. The purpose is not to provide a full-fledged hermeneutical theory but to address the criticism that Protestant biblical interpretation is essentially uncontrollable—anarchic.

Some may think the idea of retrieving the Reformers old hat. There are whole denominations already devoted to that, committed to preserving not only the legacy but also the doctrines and confessional statements of the Reformation. Yes, there are. But we ought not to confuse retrieval with either retrenchment or repristination: retrieval is not a simple return to the past (it can't be done).[99] Nor is it primarily a matter of rehabilitating the reputation of the Reformers, though correcting certain caricatures would be a welcome secondary outcome.[100] No, the main purpose of retrieval is the revitalization of biblical interpretation, theology, and the church today. *To retrieve is to look back creatively in order to move forward faithfully.*[101] In particular, what needs to be retrieved is the Reformers' vision for catholic unity under canonical authority, and also their strategy for making this vision visible through table talk: conciliar deliberation around not simply a conference table but a Communion table.

Andrew Walls, a historian of mission, views translation into vernacular languages as the principal means by which the gospel is transmitted. Walls's special interest is the rise of Christianity in the non-Western world, and though he does not mention Luther, I see no reason why we should not consider Luther as part of the gospel's missionary advance. Luther translated and contextualized the gospel—which is to say, *retrieved* it—into the vernacular language and cultural situation of his day.[102] Theology is always missiologi-

99. For a criticism of retrenchment and repristination as models of retrieval, see Buschart and Eilers, *Theology as Retrieval*, 270–72.

100. Robert McAfee Brown helpfully distinguishes between looking *at* the Reformers (i.e., in admiration) and looking *through* them, "using them as a helpful means of looking at something else more clearly, namely that which the Reformers themselves looked at—the redemptive work of God in Jesus Christ" (*The Spirit of Protestantism* [Oxford: Oxford University Press, 1965], 20).

101. Elsewhere I describe this looking back and moving forward in terms of theatrical improvisation. See Kevin J. Vanhoozer, *The Drama of Doctrine: A Canonical-Linguistic Approach to Christian Theology* (Louisville: Westminster John Knox, 2005), 335–44. See also Vanhoozer, "Improvising Theology according to the Scriptures: An Evangelical Account of the Development of Doctrine," in *Building on the Foundations of Evangelical Theology: Essays in Honor of John S. Feinberg*, ed. Gregg R. Allison and Stephen J. Wellum (Wheaton: Crossway, 2015), 15–50.

102. For a study of the ways in which sixteenth-century struggles over biblical translation were related to the issue of authority, see Allan K. Jenkins and Patrick Preston, *Biblical Scholarship and the Church: A Sixteenth-Century Crisis of Authority* (Aldershot, UK: Ashgate, 2007).

cal to the extent that the search for understanding requires us to speak that understanding into new contexts. The Reformation thus appears in this light as a missiological retrieval of the gospel as set forth in the original languages of the Bible.

Walls's understanding of mission and transmission helps us to see better how retrieval looks back creatively in order to move forward faithfully. Vernacular translation—the attempt to contextualize the gospel in a particular language—results in a net conceptual gain for the whole church. We see this at Nicaea, when the West and East had to come together to articulate the Son's relationship to the Father. I think that we also see it in the Reformation. Consider the way Walls describes the process of transmitting the faith: "As Paul and his fellow missionaries explain and translate the significance of the Christ in a world that is Gentile and Hellenistic, that significance is seen to be greater than anyone had realized before. It is as though Christ himself actually grows through the work of mission."[103]

To retrieve the Reformation, then, is not to repeat but to *translate* it into our new cultural contexts, thus enlarging our understanding of its achievement.[104] *The present work contends that retrieving the five Reformation* solas *helps to address the contemporary problem of pervasive interpretive pluralism, and that retrieving the priesthood of all believers (ecclesiology) helps to address the problem of the authority of interpretive communities.* The retrieval of the *solas* constitutes the *material principle* of mere Protestant Christianity insofar as they summarize the economy of the gospel, while retrieving the priesthood of all believers (disciples under the domain of Jesus Christ's commissioned witnesses) constitutes its *formal principle*, especially as concerns the particular problem that is the focus of the present work: whose biblical interpretation counts, and why. Together, these two principles will enable us to retrieve a third, what I will call the *final principle* of the Reformation, namely, catholicity: a differentiated or "plural" interpretive community, a rich communion that is both creature of the Word of God and fellowship of the Spirit.

103. Andrew F. Walls, *The Missionary Movement in Christian History: Studies in the Transmission of Faith* (Maryknoll, NY: Orbis; Edinburgh: T&T Clark, 1996), xvii.

104. Elsewhere I have distinguished between two kinds of sameness: *idem* (permanence in time; numeric identity) and *ipse* (continuity in time; narrative identity). Theology as retrieval in the sense that I intend here partakes more of *ipse* than of *idem* identity, though because the faith is "one" there are aspects of each. However, while what God has done remains the same, our understanding of it grows. See Vanhoozer, *Drama of Doctrine*, 127–31.

Retrieving the Solas: *The Ontology of Interpretive Authority*

I have written this book not to bury or even repent of the *solas* but rather to sing their praise. I realize that my claim is at first blush counterintuitive: How can *sola scriptura* save us from pervasive interpretive pluralism? Isn't *sola scriptura* the epitome of a mind-set that leads in anticatholic directions? Many people today, including some Protestants, consider *sola scriptura* to be toxic to the project of church unity. In this respect, it is like the Greek word for "drug," *pharmakon*, which according to context can mean either "poison" or "remedy," as Jacques Derrida famously pointed out in his essay "Plato's Pharmacy."[105] What first appears to be the poison of Protestantism (a cause of solitariness) proves upon further inspection, and retrieval, to be the cure (a cause of salutariness).

What exactly are the *solas*, the "alones"? We are familiar with the list: grace alone, faith alone, Scripture alone, Christ alone, for the glory of God alone. Some people call them "doctrines" insofar as they express key theological convictions about the essentials of the Christian faith, as when we conjoin *sola gratia* and *sola fide* to express the doctrine of justification by faith. Others view the *solas* as rallying cries summarizing the Reformers' chief disagreement with the Roman Catholicism of their day: Scripture alone over tradition; grace alone over merit; faith alone over works. Still others view the *solas* as positive "principles."[106] The Wesleyan theologian Albert Outler approaches the matter differently: "All the great Reformation watchwords—*sola Scriptura, sola fide, sola gratia*—have one essential meaning: *solus Christus* . . . Jesus Christ is the Christian dogma."[107]

Outler raises an interesting point: Can we group the five *solas* into a single big idea? While books today commonly treat the five *solas* together, it was not until the twentieth century that they were mentioned collectively,[108] and

---

105. Jacques Derrida, "Plato's Pharmacy," in *Dissemination*, trans. Barbara Johnson (London: Athlone, 1981), 61–172.

106. See Terry L. Johnson, *The Case for Traditional Protestantism: The Solas of the Reformation* (Edinburgh: Banner of Truth Trust, 2004).

107. Albert Outler, *The Christian Tradition and the Unity We Seek* (Oxford: Oxford University Press, 1957), 128–29.

108. To be precise, *sola fide, sola gratia*, and *sola scriptura* can be found in the sixteenth-century Reformers' writings, but *solus Christus* and *soli Deo gloria* appeared somewhat later—the latter on a regular basis in the compositions of J. S. Bach. However, the absence of the actual phrase does not imply the lack of the concept, and I would argue that all five *solas* reflect core Reformation theological convictions. See Theodore Engelder, "The Three Principles of the Reformation: Sola Scriptura, Sola Gratia, Sola Fides," in *Four Hundred Years: Commemorative Essays on the Reformation*, ed. W. H. T. Dua (St. Louis: Concordia, 1916), 97–109.

discussions about what links them together remain rare.[109] Graeme Golds-worthy's *Gospel-Centered Hermeneutics* is one of the few books that do.[110] Also noteworthy is Herman Bavinck's 1917 reference (on the occasion of the Reformation's four hundredth anniversary) to three *solas* as expressing the essential Reformation confession: *"Scriptura sola, gratia sola, fides sola . . .* This was not a new principle, only the old Gospel."[111]

Goldsworthy views the *solas* as basic hermeneutical presuppositions for reading Scripture.[112] He asks how there can be five "alones" and answers that "they are distinct emphases on the one essential truth of the gospel."[113] And, because salvation is connected to the work of Father, Son, and Spirit, he suggests that the "alones" have their organic unity in the Triune God: "The gospel of our salvation through faith alone, in Christ alone, by grace alone, revealed in the Bible alone, is what it is only because God is the kind of God he is."[114] From this insight Goldsworthy goes on to link the *solas* to the basic ontological, epistemological, and hermeneutical presuppositions that under-gird Christian faith.

Thus encouraged by Bavinck's precedent and Goldsworthy's example, I make so bold as to suggest that the *solas*, taken together, represent what we might call the *first theology* of mere Protestant Christianity.[115] *The solas are not isolated doctrines; they are theological insights into the ontology,*

109. Bruce Atkinson, "The Seven Solas: Toward Reconciling Evangelical and Anglo-Catholic Perspectives," *Virtue Online*, December 31, 2009, http://www.virtueonline.org/seven-solas -toward-reconciling-evangelical-and-anglo-catholic-perspectives.

110. Graeme Goldsworthy, *Gospel-Centered Hermeneutics: Foundations and Principles of Evangelical Biblical Interpretation* (Downers Grove, IL: IVP Academic, 2006).

111. Herman Bavinck, "De Hervorming en ons nationale leven," in *Ter herdenking der Her-vorming, 1517–1917: Twee redevoeringen, uitgesproken in de openbare zitting van den senaat der Vrije Universiteit op 31 October 1917*, ed. H. Bavinck and H. H. Kuyper (Kampen: Kok, 1917), 7. Translation in Henk van den Belt, "The Problematic Character of *Sola Scriptura*," in *Sola Scriptura: Biblical and Theological Perspectives on Scripture, Authority, and Hermeneutics*, ed. Eric Peels, Arnold Huijgen, and Hans Burger (Leiden: Brill, forthcoming).

112. Goldsworthy, *Gospel-Centered Hermeneutics*, 39. Goldsworthy adopts John Frame's definition of a presupposition as "a belief that takes precedence over another and therefore serves as a criterion for another" (*The Doctrine of the Knowledge of God* [Phillipsburg, NJ: P&R, 1987], 45).

113. Goldsworthy, *Gospel-Centered Hermeneutics*, 46. Strictly speaking, he focuses on only four of the *solas* but acknowledges that some, like me, add a fifth: *soli Deo gloria.*

114. Ibid., 50.

115. Though it lies beyond the scope of the present chapter, I believe that there is a parallel of sorts between the way I propose to use the five *solas* here and what I call "strong Trinitarian-ism"—that is, an approach to theology that treats the Trinity not simply as one doctrine among others but as the lens through which all other doctrines are viewed. See Kevin J. Vanhoozer, "Three (or More) Ways of Triangulating Theology: On the Very Idea of a Trinitarian System,"

epistemology, and teleology of the gospel. The *solas* are not a substitute for creedal orthodoxy but its servants. The *solas* do not develop the doctrine of the Trinity but presuppose it. Indeed, their special function is to preserve the integrity of the triune economies of revelation and redemption. As such, they are guides to theological judgment that both generate and govern mere Protestant theology. *They also provide resources with which to respond to the charge that the Reformation unintentionally loosed interpretive anarchy upon the world*. In subsequent chapters I argue that the *solas* provide a pattern for reading Scripture theologically that enables Protestant unanimity on theological essentials, and thus the possibility of genuine fellowship in spite of secondary and tertiary doctrinal differences.

My aim is to retrieve the Reformation *solas* in order to refute the all-too-common charge that *sola scriptura* generates pervasive interpretive pluralism. I want to take what many believe to be the Achilles heel of Reformation Protestantism and show that it is not a mortal weakness when connected to the rest of the body—that is, the other four *solas*.[116] Though occasioned by the need to correct medieval excesses that misconstrued the church's role in the plan of salvation, the *solas* are essentially positive, rather than negative, insights into the presuppositions, implications, and entailments of the gospel. Accordingly, the *solas* are the permanent Copernican revolution at the heart of the Reformation, a synopsis of the story that "turned the world upside down" (Acts 17:6), namely, the proclamation of the exclusive lordship of Christ, the crucified king.[117]

Retrieving the Royal Priesthood of All Believers: The Economy of Interpretive Authority

Retrieving the *solas* yields the material principle of mere Protestant Christianity: the triune economy of the gospel. "Economy" is the theological term for the work of Father, Son, and Spirit. It comes from two Greek terms, *oikos* (house) and *nomos* (law), and conveys the sense of "household management."

---

in *Revisioning, Renewing, and Rediscovering the Triune Center: Essays in Honor of Stanley J. Grenz*, ed. Derek Tidball, Brian Harris, and Jason Sexton (Eugene, OR: Cascade, 2015), 31–58.

116. See also Arnold Huijgen, "Alone Together: *Sola Scriptura* and the Other *Solas* of the Reformation," in *Sola Scriptura: Biblical and Theological Perspectives on Scripture, Authority, and Hermeneutics*, ed. Eric Peels, Arnold Huijgen, and Hans Burger (Leiden: Brill, forthcoming).

117. See further Jeremy R. Treat, *The Crucified King: Atonement and Kingdom in Biblical and Systematic Theology* (Grand Rapids: Zondervan, 2014).

To speak of the economy of the gospel is thus to highlight the ways in which the three divine persons manage to bring about the good news that Christ's death and resurrection make possible the reconciliation and restoration of the world. The *solas* summarize what the Father is doing in Christ through the Spirit to form a holy nation, and this summary—a rule of faith, hope, and love—functions as a hermeneutical tool with which to arbitrate the conflict of interpretations. However, in order to respond to the crisis of Protestant interpretation, we also need to recover a hitherto-underappreciated element in the pattern of Protestant interpretive authority: the principle of the priesthood of all believers. I call this the formal principle of mere Protestant Christianity for two reasons: first, the formation of a royal priesthood is part of the gospel's very content (the good news about Jesus includes the corporate dimension of being in Christ); second, discussions about biblical interpretation are "earthed" in local congregations.

Far from being a pathology that accords authority to autonomous individuals, the royal priesthood of all believers—briefly, the notion that all church members are ministers of God's Word—is actually part of a pattern of authority, indeed, part of a triune economy of authority. *"Royal" signals authority; "priesthood" signals interpretive community; "all believers" signals that individuals are not autonomous agents but citizens of the gospel.*[118] I will therefore speak of the "royal priesthood of all believers" to signal my intent to retrieve not only the principle of authority (the Triune God speaking in the Scriptures) but also the pattern of authority, which is to say the pattern of interpretive authority, an economy that identifies Jesus Christ alone as king but accords pride of interpretive place to his royal priesthood.

To put it more provocatively: in retrieving the royal priesthood of all believers, I am pursuing what amounts to a virtual sixth sola: *sola ecclesia* (church alone).[119] Before you light the match, hear me out. Church alone *what*? The short answer: *the church alone is the place where Christ rules over his kingdom and gives certain gifts for the building of his living temple.*[120] If we are to retrieve the promise of the Reformation but not its pathology, we must retrieve not merely the idea but the practice of the royal priesthood of all

118. In the Old Testament, one of the functions of priests was to teach and interpret the Torah, Israel's law (Deut. 33:10; cf. Lev. 10:10; Ezek. 22:26).

119. I am aware that in the context of Roman Catholic theology, *sola ecclesia* refers to the church's final authority to interpret Scripture. I am here putting the phrase to a different, distinctly Protestant use.

120. See further Michael J. Glodo, *"Sola ecclesia*: The Lost Reformation Doctrine?," *Reformation and Revival* 9, no. 4 (2000): 91–97.

believers, their place in the economy of triune communication. "Economy" is the operative term. There is a pattern, a divinely ordered way of being a people of the book, and this pattern helps explain whose biblical interpretation counts, why it counts, and in what way it counts.

Retrieving Catholicity: The Teleology of Interpretive Authority

The third theme to retrieve from the Reformation may be the most surprising of all: catholicity. Is this not what the Reformation was against? If you think that, you are not alone. Philip Schaff shocked his audience when, in an 1844 inaugural address on "The Principle of Protestantism" to the German Reformed Theological Seminary at Mercersburg (Pennsylvania), he declared the Reformation to be the "greatest act" of the catholic church.[121] Schaff judged the Church of Rome to be subcatholic in refusing to acknowledge the Reformation as its legitimate child.[122] This is not to say that he gave Protestant churches a free pass. He identified the great defect of modern Protestantism as its sectarianism: "the want of an adequate conception of the nature of the church and of its relation to the individual Christian."[123] From his mid-nineteenth-century perspective, Schaff believed the greatest threat to the Protestant principle to be not Rome but an exaggerated subjectivism that fails to acknowledge the objectivity of the church. The way forward, he claimed, was Protestant Catholicism,[124] no doubt a conceptual ancestor of what I am calling mere Protestant Christianity.

Catholicity is the final principle of the Reformation insofar as it regulates the process of biblical interpretation and the end toward which it tends, not the monological institutional unity of Rome but a dialogical or "plural" unity. Catholicity is an "Ephesian moment"—Andrew Walls's term for that quintessentially evangelical moment when churches take a step toward an even greater realization of the unity of the body of Christ.[125] "Ephesian moment" is Walls's way of referring to those times in church history when we catch a glimpse of the summing up of all things in Christ. Walls is thinking, in particular,

121. Schaff, *Principle of Protestantism*, 224.

122. Robert McAfee Brown agrees: "For [the Reformers] the issue of the Reformation was precisely the issue of catholicity. They contended . . . that medieval Christendom had surrendered the notion of catholicity to a limited and distorted understanding" (*Spirit of Protestantism*, 19).

123. Schaff, *Principle of Protestantism*, 227.

124. Ibid., 230.

125. Buschart and Eilers list reconciliation as an outcome of retrieval (*Theology as Retrieval*, 273–74).

of Ephesians 2:14–16, which speaks of Christ creating in himself one new humanity in place of the two (i.e., Jew and gentile): "Christ takes flesh as he is received by faith in various segments of social reality at different periods, as well as in different places. And these different manifestations belong together; they are part of the same story."[126] To the extent that different Protestant traditions are also different cultures that share their respective insights into the gospel, they too can experience Ephesian moments, moments when their diversity can be seen to be part of a larger unity. These Ephesian moments are often fleeting because of two dangers that Walls identifies as pride (the instinctive desire to protect our own version of Christian faith) and indifference (the postmodern decision that no one can know for sure, so why bother ruling some versions out). Catholicity is not chaos, however. It is the standing challenge for the church to display its unity in Christ despite its differences.[127]

Mere Protestant Christianity is catholic Christianity inflected by the Reformation. The name is an obvious allusion to C. S. Lewis's "Mere Christianity," which Lewis in turn took from the seventeenth-century Puritan pastor Richard Baxter.[128] Baxter lived in the early heyday of Protestant denominationalism, but instead of the traditional labels (e.g., Anglican, Presbyterian, Congregationalist), he preferred to call himself a "meer" or "catholick" Christian.[129] As Baxter and Lewis use it, "mere" means not what is "barely" or "minimally" the case (as in lowest common denominator) but rather what is "centrally" or "essentially" the case. In Lewis's words: "It is at her center, where her truest children dwell, that each communion is really closest to each other in spirit, if not in doctrine."[130]

Why Mere Protestant Christianity Matters

Does it matter if Protestants go the way of the dodo, eventually becoming extinct? Jacques Maritain once referred to the Reformation as "that immense

126. Andrew F. Walls, *The Cross-Cultural Process in Christian History: Studies in the Transmission and Appropriation of Faith* (Maryknoll, NY: Orbis; Edinburgh: T&T Clark, 2002), 74.

127. The recent joining of Reformed and Lutheran churches in France may represent an Ephesian moment. The two churches are now L'église Protestante unie de France (the United Protestant Church of France). As we will see in later chapters, however, catholicity need not entail institutional unification.

128. Timothy George, "A Thicker Kind of Mere," *First Things*, May 2015, http://www.first things.com/web-exclusives/2015/05/a-thicker-kind-of-mere.

129. Baxter uses both terms on the same page of his *Church History of the Government of Bishops and Their Councils* (London: John Kidgell, 1680), 6.

130. Lewis, *Mere Christianity*, 8–9.

disaster for humanity,"[131] and more recently Peter Leithart has called for the "end" of the kind of Protestantism that defines itself in opposition to Roman Catholicism.[132] "By their fruits ye shall know them." If we knew Protestantism only as a negative, critical gesture, then probably there would be no good reason to perpetuate it. Why waste water on a barren fig tree? It is my contention, however, that the Reformation was a key event, a precious Ephesian moment in the history and mission of the church, a moment in space and time that has yielded its fruit—a deeper theological insight into the gospel—in due season, a growth in understanding, and hence both a boon and a blessing to the *whole* church.

If mere Protestant Christianity indicates the way forward for the twenty-first-century church, it is not because it is a form of generic Christianity. This has sometimes been the tendency of the evangelical movement: to flatten out Protestant differences by locating identity in a common experience, spirituality, or ministry rather than a common confession (i.e., a definable set of doctrines).[133] The problem is that evangelicalism itself has become a fractious, fissiparous (there's that word again) movement that began as a renewal movement of confessional Protestantism but that now too often attempts to maintain itself by seeking renewal by means other than confessional theology. However, renewal without a direct object—the gospel as articulated by the Protestant confessions—is energy poorly spent. Moreover, for many evangelicals the visible church is a matter of secondary or incidental importance. This becomes especially problematic in the face of rival biblical interpretations and doctrinal differences. Bereft of an institutional means to deal with difference, evangelical cells simply continue to split: not "divide and conquer" but "divide and rancor." This is Protestantism's dangerous idea at work—the dissolution of interpretive authority—generating division and disunity.

Mere Protestant Christianity is an attempt to stop the bleeding: first, by retrieving the *solas* as guidelines and guardrails of biblical interpretation; and second, by retrieving the royal priesthood of all believers, which is to say, the place of the church in the pattern of theological authority—the place where *sola scriptura* gets lived out in embodied interpretive practices. Lewis

131. Jacques Maritain, *Three Reformers: Luther, Descartes, Rousseau* (London: Sheed & Ward, 1944), 13.

132. Leithart, "Future of Protestantism." See further his *The End of Protestantism: Pursuing Unity in a Fragmented Church* (Grand Rapids: Brazos, 2016).

133. John Stackhouse gives a winsome presentation of this position in "Generic Evangelicalism," in *Four Views on the Spectrum of Evangelicalism*, ed. Andrew David Naselli and Collin Hansen (Grand Rapids: Zondervan, 2011), 116–42.

associated mere Christianity with the hall of a house: we meet others in the hall, but we live in the rooms. My own proposal is that we think of the various denominations, interpretive communities, or confessional traditions ("communions") as houses, and Protestantism as the street—call it "Evangel Way." The Roman Catholic Church is the seven-story yellow house at the end of the street, at the intersection of Evangel Way and Tiber Road. At the other end of the street is a vacant lot where a few families live in mobile homes (independent Bible churches). With this image in mind, think of mere Protestant Christianity as a block party—and the neighborhood watch. Mere Protestant Christianity provides space and parameters for plural unity: on my Father's street there are many mansions.

To be a mere Protestant Christian, one must be not only a person of one book but also a person of one church. "Catholicity" belongs somewhere in the pattern of theological authority too: minimally, as the proper context for reading Scripture;[134] maximally, as a first earthly step in the triune mission "to unite all things in him, things in heaven and things on earth" (Eph. 1:10). The church's catholicity—the scope of what is "in Christ"—is a parable of the cosmic unity that will obtain in the kingdom of God. Scripture is never "alone" in one sense because it is never without the communal domain over which it rules: the people of God. *Mere Protestant Christianity uses the resources of the* solas *and the priesthood of all believers to express the unity-in-diversity that local churches have in Christ.* It calls churches to enact, on some level and in tangible ways, the oneness for which Jesus prayed, as evidence of the gospel—a project that requires a mere Protestant ecclesiology.

In the chapters that follow I present the *solas* as seeds for a perennial reformation of the church. *The kind of Protestantism that needs to live on is not the one that encourages individual autonomy or corporate pride but the one that encourages the church to hold fast to the gospel, and to one another.* The only good Protestant is a catholic Protestant—one who learns from, and bears fruit for, the *whole* church. In light of this exacting standard, I submit that the Reformers were good Protestants.[135] Hence the project of the present work: to retrieve mere Protestant Christianity, enabling the lion of biblical fidelity (*sola scriptura*) to lie down with the lamb of ecclesial fraternity (*sola ecclesia*).

---

134. To coin a Latin phrase: "Exegesis *extra ecclesiam nulla unitas*" (Exegesis outside the church [will ultimately yield] no unity).

135. As we will see, a "good" Protestant is one who displays the humility that characterizes those who attend to God's Word and the charity that characterizes those who walk in God's Spirit.

1

Grace Alone

*The Mere Protestant Ontology, Economy,
and Teleology of the Gospel*

The promises of God are altogether trustworthy; not so the promises of men, even those invited to deliver the 2015 Moore College Annual Lectures. The introduction made a number of promises. In particular, I claimed that retrieving the Reformation *solas* opens up a way to counter the fissiparousness that has dogged the Protestant commitment to *sola scriptura*. I here begin to make good on that bold claim by retrieving *sola gratia* (grace alone) to rebut the narrative in which the Protestant Reformation serves as the catalyst for secularization in biblical studies and more generally. On the contrary: this brief formula, *sola gratia*, stands for the all-embracing economy of revelation and redemption that precedes the work of interpretation and in which interpreters live, move, and have their being. As we will see, the grace of God concerns the way the Father, Son, and Spirit share their love, life, and light respectively with those who are not God: "God for us, Christ with us, the Spirit among us—that is the living drama . . . to which theology seeks to bear witness."[1]

---

1. Johnson, "Theology and the Church's Mission," 67.

Although all three persons are involved in everything that God does, we may assign to the Father the ontology of grace, the giving of the *love* that creates (originating grace); to the Son the economy of grace, the giving of the *life* that redeems (saving grace); and to the Spirit the teleology of grace, the giving of the *light* that sanctifies (illuminating grace).[2] These three correspond to the ontology, economy, and teleology of the gospel: "The Trinitarian shape of the gospel comes from the fact that God, by grace, gives himself to us by opening that eternal triune life to us."[3] Please note: "grace alone" should not be construed narrowly as a matter of soteriology only, but should be seen "as the very definition of who God is."[4] Grace is the way in which God extends himself to the world so that creatures can come to know and love him. The burden of this chapter is to reclaim *sola gratia* as the banner under which later chapters discuss what (for lack of a better term) I will call the "economy of interpretive authority."

Before I begin to fulfill my promises, however, it may be helpful to say something about my premises. First, I am not importing a foreign problem to Protestant theology, as if secularization, skepticism, and schism were invasive species. The sober truth is that the disturbing problem of doctrinal differences leading to church division has been on conspicuous display for some time now. Second, I disagree with critics who blame individual autonomy on the Reformers, even if the blood trail seems to lead back to Luther's "Here I stand." On the one hand, as concerns a unified Christendom, the handwriting was already on the wall or, rather, on the printing press, a powerful means for disseminating both opinion and knowledge. Given human nature and the lust for power, it was only a matter of time before the written word would be used to challenge centralized institutional authorities. On the other hand, division antedated the Reformation in the garden of Europe: in the fourteenth and fifteenth centuries the Roman Catholic Church suffered through a second great schism, when a rival papacy was

---

2. Although everything that God does is the work of all three persons, it is fitting to ascribe certain actions, or aspects of actions, to particular divine persons on the basis of what we observe in the outworking of God's plan (i.e., the economy). The technical term is divine "appropriation," which Calvin defines as follows: "To the Father is attributed the beginning of activity . . . to the Son . . . the ordered disposition of all things; but to the Spirit is assigned the power and efficacy of that activity" (*Institutes of the Christian Religion*, ed. John T. McNeill, trans. Ford Lewis Battles, Library of Christian Classics 20–21 [Philadelphia: Westminster, 1960], I.13.18).

3. Fred Sanders, *The Deep Things of God: How the Trinity Changes Everything* (Wheaton: Crossway, 2010), 25.

4. Johnson, "Theology and the Church's Mission," 69.

established in Avignon.[5] As to individual autonomy, well, it has been around since Adam's fall, which only a divine initiative can remedy ("There but for the grace of God go we").

"Grace" is indeed the operative term, and we begin with it in order to highlight the priority of God's presence, activity, and initiative in creation, redemption, and biblical interpretation alike. As mentioned previously, the Reformers themselves never formulated a complete list of the five *solas*, nor is there any indication that their successors ranked them in any particular authoritative sequence. There is no authorized *ordo sola-tis*, as it were. Still, there are good reasons to begin with grace, for arguably there is no better or broader framework for theological understanding than the grace of God expressed in the trinitarian economies of revelation and redemption.

My third guiding premise is that retrieval is not replication but a creative looking back for the sake of a faithful moving forward. Accordingly, each of the following chapters begins with a review of what the Reformers said about a particular *sola*. I then consider what they were reacting against in their historical context, and the extent to which Protestants today face the same or different issues. While the proximate cause for a *sola* may have been a negative gesture of protest (which is why Melanchthon could refer to the *solas* as "excluding expressions"[6]), at the heart of each *sola* is a positive insight to the gospel of God and the God of the gospel. Accordingly, the third section in each chapter contributes constructively to the project of retrieval—the appropriation of the *solas* for today—and in particular to the way in which the *solas* address the problem of interpretive authority. Each chapter concludes with four summary theses that draw out the significance of the *solas* for biblical interpretation in the church.

We begin, then, by reviewing what the Reformers wanted to recover by affirming *sola gratia*. Their primary concern was the economy of grace (God's unmerited favor to sinners in communicating life in Christ), but we will also

---

5. Also known as the "Western schism" (1378–1417). The first great schism (1054) separated Rome (Western Catholicism) from Byzantium (Eastern Orthodoxy). See Howard Kaminsky, "The Great Schism," in *The New Cambridge Medieval History*, vol. 6, *c. 1300–c. 1415*, ed. Michael Jones (Cambridge: Cambridge University Press, 2000), 674–98; and Henry Chadwick, *East and West: The Making of a Rift in the Church; From Apostolic Times until the Council of Florence*, Oxford History of the Christian Church (Oxford: Oxford University Press, 2003).

6. See Robert Kolb, "Melanchthon's Doctrinal Last Will and Testament: The *Responsiones ad articulos Bavaricae inquisitionis* as His Final Confession of Faith," in *Philip Melanchthon: Theologian in Classroom, Confession, and Controversy*, ed. Irene Dingel et al. (Göttingen: Vandenhoeck & Ruprecht, 2012), 141–60, esp. 147–48.

examine the ontology and teleology of grace, the presupposition and purpose of the gospel, namely, its origin in the nature of the Triune God and its end in humanity by the Spirit's incorporation of the faithful into God's own triune life. We then move forward with creative fidelity by bringing *sola gratia* to bear on the problem of interpretive authority, especially the problem of determining (1) who has the *authority* to say what the Bible *means* and (2) which, if any, of the many interpretations on offer is authoritative, and why.

Sola Gratia: What the Reformers Meant

The Reformation began as a soteriological question ("How can I obtain salvation?") but quickly led to questions about ecclesiology ("Where is the true church?"). What connects the two is the gospel of the grace of God made flesh in Jesus Christ—the saving Word through which the Triune God shares the divine life and creates the church.[7] The specific theological question ("What is the nature of God?") stayed on the back burner.

Two Theological "Aha!" Moments

Eureka!

Luther's "Aha!" moment came thanks to an exegetical about-face in his understanding of Paul's phrase "the righteousness of God" (Rom. 1:17). In the context of late medieval Catholicism, Luther first understood it to mean the *demand* to make oneself acceptable to God by improving on the infused grace obtained by virtue of one's baptism and the sacraments.[8] What tormented him was the dread that he had not done enough to make himself sufficiently righteous—that is, rightly related to the God who executes justice. It was a terrible burden. After he wrestled with the biblical text for days, the light finally dawned—"Eureka!" He suddenly realized that God's righteousness was not a demand but a donation: a divine gift. The priestly word of absolution ("I absolve you") is not a recognition that a person is deserving of forgiveness but, on the contrary, a speech act that accomplishes what it declares, "an effective,

7. "For Luther, the Church was created by the living presence of Christ through his word the gospel" (Paul D. L. Avis, *The Church in the Theology of the Reformers* [Atlanta: John Knox, 1981], 3).

8. Stated differently: Luther understood Rom. 1:17 in terms of the "active righteousness" (human right-doing) that God demands from us, as opposed to a "passive righteousness" (a result of God's right-doing) that is bestowed on us through faith in Christ's saving work.

accomplishing Word."[9] Luther reports that he felt himself reborn, as if he had "gone through open doors into paradise. The whole of Scripture took on new meaning."[10] Luther had discovered the passive righteousness, and the freedom of the Christian, in the active righteousness, the effective promise of God. Luther had discovered the communicative self-giving that lies at the core of God's being; he had retrieved Paul's (and Augustine's) teaching of *sola gratia*.[11]

EUCHARISTŌ!

For Calvin, the "Aha!" moment was more gradual, coming into focus over the various editions of his *Institutes*. His famous opening statement, about the mutuality of knowing God and knowing oneself, appeared in one form or another in every edition of the *Institutes*, from first (1536) to last (1559). The *Institutes* are "instructions" in *religio*—that is, true worship—and surely it is significant that Calvin calls his greatest work not a *summa theologiae* but a *summa pietatis*. Piety is "that reverence joined with the love of God which the knowledge of his benefits induces."[12] What interests Calvin is the *saving* knowledge of God, and that is what we have in Scripture: the good news that the Father sent his own Son to make us who were by nature children of wrath his own children by adoption. Grace is not God's way of helping us to become obedient children; it is rather God adopting us, unworthy though we are. To know the grace of God is to know oneself as grateful—"Eucharistō!" Indeed, Brian Gerrish argues that Calvin's theology of the Lord's Supper is organically connected to the whole of the *Institutes*. Everything in Scripture and theology concerns God the Father's liberality and his children's answering gratitude: "The holy banquet is simply the liturgical enactment of the theme of grace and gratitude that lies at the heart of Calvin's entire theology, whether one chooses to call it a system or not."[13] Calvin had grasped the freedom of God to adopt us as his own sons and daughters in Christ (Eph. 1:5); he had retrieved *sola gratia*.

9. Oswald Bayer, *Martin Luther's Theology: A Contemporary Interpretation*, trans. Thomas H. Trapp (Grand Rapids: Eerdmans, 2008), 53.

10. Cited in Roland Bainton, *Here I Stand: A Life of Martin Luther* (New York: Mentor, 1950), 49–50.

11. For more on Luther's understanding of the two kinds of righteousness, see Robert Kolb and Charles P. Arand, *The Genius of Luther's Theology: A Wittenberg Way of Thinking for the Contemporary Church* (Grand Rapids: Baker Academic, 2008), 26–29, 35–37.

12. Calvin, *Institutes* I.2.1.

13. Brian A. Gerrish, *Grace and Gratitude: The Eucharistic Theology of John Calvin* (Minneapolis: Fortress, 1993), 20.

Heidelberg Disputation and the Critique of the Theology of Glory

The sixty-second of Luther's famous Ninety-Five Theses states, "The true treasure of the church is the most holy gospel of the glory and grace of God."[14] Luther had reluctantly come to see that the Roman Catholic Church of his day had exchanged its birthright for a mess of lentil stew. The church had exchanged God-given grace for human religiosity: a jury-rigged system for appeasing the divine. This exchange of the truth for a lie—the oh-so-tempting idea that sin is something we can "manage" through our own ritualized practices, a fire we can contain and control—is a perennial problem. Grace contradicts every system of religion precisely because God's free mercy cannot be predicted, calculated, or manipulated. Grace is especially troublesome for control freaks—sinners curved in on themselves, bent on securing their own existence and status.

To misunderstand the grace of God—that it is God alone who, out of his own good pleasure, makes sinners righteous—is to go wrong everywhere in theology. This is the thrust of the twenty-eight theological theses that compose Luther's 1518 Heidelberg Disputation and that compare and contrast the "theology of glory" with the "theology of the cross." The theologian of glory seeks knowledge of God by extrapolating from the visible created world to the invisible realm of the Creator. Rational religion tells us that God will reward our moral striving: God helps those who help themselves. Luther, however, takes his bearings from the cross of Christ alone: *crux sola est nostra theologia* (the cross alone is our theology). The cross contradicts the idea that human freedom can satisfy the law by doing good works. The theology of glory errs in thinking that grace is simply the icing on the cake of natural volition. On the contrary, as Luther says in thesis 16, "The person who believes that he can obtain grace by doing what is in him adds sin to sin so that he becomes doubly guilty."[15]

The stark reality of the cross refutes all "religion." Christianity is not a system for making oneself right before God. It has nothing to do with self-glorification. On the contrary: we are prepared to receive the grace of Christ only when we despair of our natural ability. This is counterintuitive to a species that glories in its accomplishments. (Did you know that there's a Hall of Fame for piano tuners? There is, at the Piano Technicians Guild in Kansas

---

14. Martin Luther, *Martin Luther's Basic Theological Writings*, ed. Timothy F. Lull (Minneapolis: Fortress, 1989), 27.

15. "Heidelberg Disputation" (1518), in ibid., 41.

City, Kansas.) Luther was dealing with a problem that was hardly confined to his historical moment, because pride is endemic to fallen human nature. There is no culture that is righteous, no not one; hence there is no expiration date for the good news of grace alone. We can retrieve *sola gratia* because what Luther discovered as true for him is true for all times and places. "For by grace you have been saved by faith" (Eph. 2:8).

Sola gratia is a necessary truth for a genuinely Christian theology. The Reformers were focused on the economy of grace, but what is ultimately at stake is the theologian's grasp of the reality of God. Theologians of glory extrapolate from what they see in nature to the supernatural being of God. This is natural theology freed from the discipline of revealed theology, an autonomous endeavor whose principal method is the analogy of being. Natural theologians identify God-like properties in creation and then extrapolate and inflate them until they reach infinite proportion, at which point they describe God's being as all-good, all-powerful, together with all the other God-making properties.[16] This is what Ludwig Feuerbach, the nineteenth-century grand master of suspicion, had in mind when he commented that the secret of theology is anthropology. Luther and Feuerbach agree this far: they both view religion—the theology of glory—as idolatrous, ultimately oriented toward nothing more than a human projection, which is to say: *nothing*. Feuerbach calls religion "a dream, in which our own conceptions and emotions appear to us as separate existences, beings out of ourselves."[17] God is the best of humanity writ large—or rather projected—onto a heavenly screen of earthly origin.

Luther contrasts in the starkest terms those who project their own ideas onto God with those who attend to God's self-projection in Christ. Here is thesis 21: "A theology of glory calls evil good and good evil. A theology of the cross calls the thing *what it actually is*."[18] "Religion"—the theology of

16. Reformed theologians display a certain ambivalence about natural theology. Paul speaks of "what can be known about God" (Rom. 1:19) in nature. However, Calvin insists, first, that such knowledge (i.e., of God's existence and power) is not saving, and, second, that such knowledge has been corrupted by sin ("futile thinking," Rom. 1:21) and therefore needs to be corrected by the "spectacles" of Scripture. See further Richard A. Muller, *Post-Reformation Reformed Dogmatics: The Rise and Development of Reformed Orthodoxy, ca. 1520 to ca. 1725*, 2nd ed. (Grand Rapids: Baker Academic, 2003), 1:270–310. Note especially his conclusion: "Supernatural revelation . . . a graciously given way of knowing, provides the context within which all other knowledge must ultimately be understood" (310).

17. Ludwig Feuerbach, *The Essence of Christianity*, trans. George Eliot (Buffalo: Prometheus, 1989), 204.

18. "Heidelberg Disputation," in Luther, *Basic Theological Writings*, 44.

glory—is indeed what Freud says it is: the future of an illusion, namely, the idolatrous preference for one's own thoughts about God.[19] By way of contrast, *sola gratia* represents the theology of the cross, which speaks of God as God really is because it attends to God's free self-revelation in Jesus Christ. The Reformation is first and foremost a recovery of grace: not only that righteousness is a gift of God, but also that God graciously reveals himself in Jesus Christ. The theology of the cross sets forth in speech "what is" in Christ. The Reformers clearly saw and said that what is in Christ is "the grace of God toward sinful humanity."[20] This is not illusion or wish fulfillment; it is historical fact, and the most important truth in the universe. Retrieving *sola gratia* ultimately means retrieving Christian theology as the project of setting forth in speech what faith sees the Triune God is doing in and through Christ and his cross.

Reformation Hermeneutics: A Nose (and Ear) for Grace

The Reformation retrieval of grace was more than a recovery of a neglected or misunderstood biblical theme; it was also a hermeneutical event that led the Reformers to read Scripture in distinct ways to hear and heed the Word of God. The key insight: "God acts by speaking."[21] The words of Scripture are not inert piano keys on which the interpreter displays his or her virtuosity. Rather, God is present and active in his written word (cf. Heb. 4:12). We grasp God because he has first grasped us. Biblical interpretation is *sola gratia* because it rests on three divine communicative initiatives: God the Father's historical initiative to reveal himself to Israel through the words of his servants the prophets; God the Son's historical initiative to reveal the Father by taking on humanity; God the Spirit's ongoing initiative to illumine readers by opening hearts and minds to the living Christ wrapped in the swaddling clothes of Scripture. Jesus is full of grace and truth because he is the culmination of God's communicative initiatives and of God's communicative faithfulness by which he proves his word true in standing by it.[22]

19. Sigmund Freud, *The Future of an Illusion*, trans. and ed. James Strachey (New York: W. W. Norton, 1989).

20. Carl R. Trueman, *Reformation: Yesterday, Today and Tomorrow* (Ross-shire, Scotland: Christian Focus Publications, 2011), 25.

21. Kolb and Arand, *Genius of Luther's Theology*, 175.

22. See Oswald Bayer, "Luther as an Interpreter of Holy Scripture," in *The Cambridge Companion to Martin Luther*, ed. Donald K. McKim (Cambridge: Cambridge University Press, 2003), 76–77.

Grace has both material (i.e., soteriological) and formal (i.e., hermeneutical) significance. The biblical text and its interpreters alike are caught up in a triune economy of communication. Luther resists the idea that Christians read the Bible as they would any other text. Scholars seek to master texts by achieving specialist knowledge and professional skill, but for Luther these things reek of "works." On the contrary, "there is a priority of Scripture itself over its readers and hearers."[23] For Luther, it is not so much that individuals justify this or that interpretation; rather, a theologian "is a person who is interpreted by Holy Scripture, who lets himself or herself be interpreted by it."[24]

NOSE: DISTINGUISHING LAW AND GOSPEL

In order to be a theologian of the cross, and tell it like it is, one must be able to tell the difference between law and gospel. Thesis 26 of the Heidelberg Disputation reads, "The law says, 'Do this,' and it is never done. Grace says, 'Believe in this,' and everything is already done."[25] The reason should be clear: the law enjoins works of human righteousness, but sinners whose wills are in bondage cannot comply. Even to try to comply is to misunderstand the very purpose of the law, which is to convince us of our inability and need for Christ.

Luther teaches that the entire Scripture "is divided in two parts: the commandments and promises."[26] A true theologian knows the difference between law and gospel, a difference all the more important to discern when we discover that law and gospel alike are found in both Testaments. In his "Brief Instruction on What to Look For and Expect in the Gospels" (1521), Luther points out that the Gospels themselves can be (wrongly) read as law if the interpreter depicts Christ as an example of how to live one's life. Readers who make this error make a Moses out of Christ. Simply to ask, "What would Jesus do?" is not yet to proclaim the gospel. On the contrary: to discern the gospel in the Gospels means "that before you take Christ as an example, you accept and recognize him as a gift, as a present that God has given you and that is your own."[27] At the same time, there is a way of reading the books of Moses, and the rest of the Old Testament, as gospel: a promise concerning Christ.

---

23. Bayer, *Martin Luther's Theology*, 69.

24. Oswald Bayer, *Theology the Lutheran Way*, ed. and trans. Jeffrey G. Silcock and Mark C. Mattes (Grand Rapids: Eerdmans, 2007), 36.

25. Martin Luther, "Heidelberg Disputation," in Luther, *Basic Theological Writings*, 16.

26. Martin Luther, "The Freedom of a Christian," in Luther, *Basic Theological Writings*, 600.

27. Martin Luther, "A Brief Instruction," in Luther, *Basic Theological Writings*, 106.

The ability rightly to distinguish between law and gospel is, says Luther, "the highest art in Christendom."[28]

EAR: HEARING THE DIVINE PROMISSIO

There is another aspect to Luther's retrieval of grace that has to do with how God communicates the gift of righteousness in language, an aspect that perhaps best represents the permanent insight accompanying his contextualization of the gospel into his sixteenth-century European context. Luther complains in "The Babylonian Captivity of the Church" that the Mass obscures the gift of Christ, which is bound to the *word*: "Take, eat; this is my body, which is given for you." Everything that matters resides in these words, for it is the saying of these words that constitutes a testament: "a promise made by one about to die, in which he designates his bequest and appoints his heirs."[29] The bequest in question is the forgiveness of sins; the heirs are those who believe the words and thus receive the gift. Luther sees all the promises of God throughout the Bible as foreshadowing this last will and testament. Even in Eden God gave his word of promise to Adam and Eve that their seed would bruise the serpent's head (Gen. 3:15), the first intimation of the gospel's promise.

"Promise" is the operative term, and it led Luther to understand the language of grace in a new way. Take Jesus's statement to the paralytic: "Your sins are forgiven" (Mark 2:5). Jesus is not describing something that has already happened; rather, he is making it happen as he speaks. His words of forgiveness constitute the reality of forgiveness. The scribes listening understood it this way, because they said to themselves, "Why does this man speak like that? He is blaspheming! Who can forgive sins but God alone?" (Mark 2:7). The point is that Jesus, by speaking, is also doing something. That he has the power and authority to do it becomes clear when he next commands the paralytic to walk: "Which is easier, to say to the paralytic, 'Your sins are forgiven,' or to say, 'Rise, take up your bed and walk?'" (Mark 2:9). The miracle gets the attention, but forgiving sins is the greater speech act.[30]

---

28. Martin Luther, "The Distinction between the Law and the Gospel: A Sermon Preached on January 1, 1532," trans. Willard L. Burce, *Concordia Journal* 18, no. 2 (1992): 153.

29. Martin Luther, "The Babylonian Captivity of the Church," in Luther, *Basic Theological Writings*, 294.

30. Oswald Bayer dates Luther's key insight to his *For the Investigation of Truth and for the Comfort of Troubled Consciences* (1518), in which he examined what happens when the

Luther saw the gospel as a similarly powerful word, one that frees sinners as soon as it is spoken. It does not describe a freedom that has already happened; rather, it is the cause and occasion of freedom. The word of the cross frees sinners. The gospel is God announcing and assuring that, in Christ, *our* sins are forgiven. It is a promise that constitutes a relationship, a word that does what it says, like "I do" in the context of a wedding. "This is my body broken for you" is Jesus's "I do" to his disciples. Luther calls the gospel a *verbum efficax*, an efficacious word that does not simply promise freedom but, in promising, actually frees. Oswald Bayer explains: "That the *signum* itself is already the *res*, that *the linguistic sign is already the matter itself*—that was Luther's great hermeneutical discovery, his reformational discovery in the strictest sense."[31] Christ is "really present" in his promise.

In sum, we might say that Luther, and the Reformers in general, experienced grace *verbally*, through the various ways in which the Bible presents Christ—the gift of God. Grace is not simply the content of the gospel but the overarching framework of its communication and reception.

Nature and/or Grace: Other Views

As I noted in the introduction, probably the most surprising, severe, and hurtful criticism of the Reformation was that it unintentionally begat secularization. Indeed, some critics suggest that secularization was virtually foreordained (so to speak) once the Reformers decided to reject the authority of the church magisterium and to deny the sacramental-hierarchical picture of the world that went with it.[32] If this were true, it is only painfully and ironically so, for it would mean that the same movement that recovered God's grace—the absolute priority of God's self-giving initiative for any meaningful human action—ultimately lost it. For what is secularization but the desacralization—the degracification—of the world?[33] Everything depends, however, on what we

---

priest says, "I absolve you of your sins." See the discussion in Bayer, "Luther as an Interpreter of Holy Scripture," 75–76.

31. Bayer, *Martin Luther's Theology*, 52.

32. Some commentators acknowledge that the unraveling of the sacramental tapestry began in the nominalism of the late medieval period but nevertheless fault the Reformers for not doing enough to halt or reverse the process (see, e.g., Boersma, *Heavenly Participation*, chap. 5).

33. See further Charles Taylor, *A Secular Age* (Cambridge, MA: Belknap Press of Harvard University Press, 2007); and James K. A. Smith, *How (Not) to Be Secular: Reading Charles Taylor* (Grand Rapids: Eerdmans, 2014).

mean by "grace" and how it relates to nature in the first place. It is a significant question, pertaining to what Hans Urs von Balthasar calls "the last essential difference" between Catholicism and Protestantism.[34]

Medieval Scholasticism: Grace Perfects Nature (Institutional Mediation)

The relationship of nature and grace is arguably one of the leading themes of Roman Catholic theology. Thomas Aquinas best defines the medieval scholastic view: "Grace does not destroy nature, but perfects it."[35] No other creature can act beyond the limits of its nature, but grace is the gift that allows the human creature to surpass its created capacity insofar as grace is "a certain participation in the divine nature, which surpasses every other nature."[36] For Aquinas, then, nature channels grace, and grace heals and elevates sinful human nature, allowing us to attain our true end of union with God. This, at least, is how certain of his fifteenth- to seventeenth-century commentators read him. For example, Thomas Cajetan introduced the speculative notion of *natura pura*—a state of nature before the fall that had an autonomy and integrity of its own—in order to preserve the gratuity of grace and the very idea of the *super*natural in Aquinas's thought.[37]

Cajetan's interpretation exaggerated Aquinas's indebtedness to Aristotle's notion of nature as having its own intrinsic powers and goals, thus making grace extrinsic to the created order, an add-on to nature (a *donum super-additum*) that allows human beings to obtain the end for which they were created. The sacraments, available only through the Roman Catholic Church, were then viewed as the means that conferred the grace that perfects nature. The Reformers perceived this sacramentalism, and particularly the shortcut to grace afforded by indulgences, as a quasi commodification of salvation that rendered grace subject to the law of supply and demand: "I want more of *that*!"

---

34. The phrase comes from D. Stephen Long's *Saving Karl Barth: Hans Urs von Balthasar's Preoccupation* (Minneapolis: Fortress, 2014), 54. In context, the difference pertains to whether theology works according to an analogy of being (*analogia entis*) or an analogy of faith (*analogia fidei*). What is at stake is the way in which theologians speak of the relationship between Creator and creation.

35. Thomas Aquinas, *Summa Theologiae* I, q. 1, a. 8, *ad* 2. Translations of the *Summa* are from *Summa theologica*, trans. Fathers of the English Dominican Province, 5 vols. (Westminster, MD: Christian Classics, 1981).

36. Aquinas, *Summa Theologiae* I.II, q. 112, a. 1.

37. See Cajetan's *Commentary on Saint Thomas' "Summa theologiae"* (1540).

"Pure Nature": Nature sans Grace

The chief disagreement between medieval Roman Catholics and Protestants concerned the capacities of fallen nature.[38] Scholastics deployed the concept of pure nature to counter the Protestant teaching about the total depravity of fallen human nature. Late medieval / early modern scholastic commentators on Aquinas tended to follow Cajetan, insisting that fallen human nature retained at least the capacity to receive and cooperate with grace. The Reformers countered by insisting that people who are dead in their sins cannot even say, "Please, sir, I want some more (grace)." Catholics then accused Protestants of failing to do justice to nature (and human agency) by affirming "grace alone." This is not the place to delve into the complexities of the discussion. The salient point is that some of these Catholic commentators, in order to preserve the gratuity of grace, postulated a realm of *natura pura* (pure nature) that could exist on its own without grace: "The medieval scholastics and their commentators tended to emphasize the integral autonomy of nature and the natural order."[39] Give nature an inch, however, and it will take a mile. Interestingly enough, it was Henri de Lubac, one of the important figures influencing Vatican II, who first called attention to the trajectory that led from pure self-enclosed nature to modern secularism.[40] This complicates Brad Gregory's account, discussed above, which pins the blame for secularization on the Reformation. Several of the leading Roman Catholic theologians involved in Vatican II themselves lay at least some of the blame on the scholastic and neoscholastic misreadings (on their view) of Aquinas.[41] When nature is viewed as pure or autonomous, grace becomes ontologically "second order," and the result is what Karl Barth rightly described as the "secular misery" of modern theology.[42]

38. See further Gregg R. Allison, *Roman Catholic Theology and Practice: An Evangelical Assessment* (Wheaton: Crossway, 2014), 46–55.

39. Edward T. Oakes, foreword to *Nature and Grace: A New Approach to Thomistic Ressourcement*, by Andrew Dean Stafford (Eugene, OR: Pickwick, 2014), ix.

40. "De Lubac saw that such an emphasis upon an autonomous natural order found a natural home in secularism" (ibid.).

41. Not all contemporary Roman Catholics would agree. Steven A. Long criticizes de Lubac and von Balthasar for abandoning Aquinas's hypothesis that human beings could have been created without supernatural grace or supernatural end. See Long, *Natura Pura: On the Recovery of Nature in the Doctrine of Grace* (New York: Fordham University Press, 2010).

42. Karl Barth, *Church Dogmatics* I/1, ed. G. W. Bromiley and T. F. Torrance, trans. G. W. Bromiley (Edinburgh: T&T Clark, 1975), xiii. In context, the secular misery that Barth has in mind is that form of the knowledge of God associated with the analogy of being (*analogia entis*), according to which we may know God by inferring what he is like from his pale reflection in the entities of creation.

Nouvelle Théologie: *Grace Pervades Nature (Ontological Mediation)*

De Lubac led the Roman Catholic charge against a resurgent modern neo-scholasticism and its notion of pure nature with the publication of his *Surnaturel* in 1946. De Lubac called for a *ressourcement*—a retrieval of the church fathers and a reinterpretation of what Aquinas said about the relationship of nature and grace. For de Lubac, the notion of pure nature is a nonstarter, for planted deep in human nature is a desire for God.[43] Neoscholasticism's view of a supernatural realm "outside and above" nature actually "contributes to the triumph of atheism by making the supernatural superfluous to man's existence."[44] In de Lubac's view, "secular humanism" is a contradiction in terms, for human beings *by nature* have a desire for God, who transcends nature. The idea of a closed order of nature is nothing more than a metaphysical fiction.

De Lubac and the *nouvelle théologie* (French for "New Theology," even though the movement is more a retrieval of patristic theology) held that "natural" being participates in and is oriented toward God, even in its fallenness. They therefore sought to reclaim a sacramental ontology, a view of reality in which grace is the underlying mystery (and reality) of nature.[45] Just as in allegorical interpretation the natural sense "participates" in a spiritual sense, so in a sacramental ontology nature participates in grace. In both cases, the relationship between natural and supernatural is sacramental: "The sacramental interpenetration of sign and reality could also be applied to the relationship between nature and the supernatural."[46] On this view, then, grace is mediated not only by the official sacraments but also by created being in general (hence sacramental *ontology*). The Church nevertheless retains a privileged place in the grand scheme of things, for the grace that nature mediates in general is concentrated particularly, and most fully, in the sacraments: "The Catholic Church [is] the embodiment—the tangible, visible, material, social, concrete manifestation—of the grace of God."[47]

43. Henri de Lubac, *Surnaturel: Études historiques* (Paris: Aubier, 1946).

44. Peter J. Leithart, *Athanasius* (Grand Rapids: Baker Academic, 2011), 106.

45. In the scheme of pure nature, grace is "extrinsic," but according to sacramental-ontological "intrinsicism," everything is always/already graced. Another Roman Catholic theologian, Karl Rahner, proposes the concept of a "supernatural existential" to signify how human beings are constitutionally open to receiving grace, whether or not faith is present.

46. Boersma, Nouvelle Théologie *and Sacramental Ontology*, 7.

47. Allison, *Roman Catholic Theology*, 45. Allison is here closely following Leonardo De Chirico's *Evangelical Theological Perspectives on Post-Vatican II Roman Catholicism* (Bern: Peter Lang, 2003).

The irony is that de Lubac's critics feel that he presses the case against the nature-grace dichotomy too far.[48] If nature participates in grace, then grace is in some sense not extrinsic but intrinsic to nature, and the supernatural grace available in the sacraments is a merely symbolic reminder of a redemption that is always/already the case: "If human nature is so tuned to the divine, grace need not come to us from the *outside*, as it were, in which case this divinization proceeds from *within*; and therefore one need not emphasize the singularity of Jesus Christ."[49] Peter Leithart speaks for many Protestants when, observing this intra-Catholic debate, he comments that the problem is that both neoscholastics and their *nouvelle* detractors appear to chalk up humanity's distance from God to their createdness, not fallenness.[50] On the contrary: the problem is not that God (or the supernatural) is "external" to creation but rather that the whole realm of creation has become alienated from God through sin. Stated differently: the gospel is the good news that men and women can be adopted as children of God, not because human nature has by grace been "elevated," but because human sinners (persons) have by grace been forgiven.

Triune Ontology and the Economy of Salvation

From the perspective of those concerned to recover sacramental ontology—the notion that nature is oriented toward and participates in the supernatural— the Reformation sells nature short in suggesting that grace does not simply perfect or complete but restores and transforms nature. From the perspective of mere Protestant Christianity, however, it is important to distinguish the grace of participation in being (created existence) from the special grace of participation in Christ (covenant existence), and from the further grace associated with the Spirit's illumination. To anticipate: the gospel of Jesus Christ presupposes an ontology of grace, consists in an economy of grace, and continues in a teleology of grace.

48. For a summary of the debate, see Fergus Kerr, *Twentieth-Century Catholic Theologians* (Oxford: Blackwell, 2007), 47–86. See also the discussion in Serge-Thomas Bonino, ed., *Surnaturel: A Controversy at the Heart of Twentieth-Century Thomistic Thought* (Washington, DC: Catholic University of America Press, 2007).

49. Oakes, foreword to Stafford, *Nature and Grace*, x. See also Lawrence Feingold, *The Natural Desire to See God according to St. Thomas and His Interpreters*, 2nd ed. (Washington, DC: Catholic University of America Press, 2004).

50. Leithart, "Residual Extrinsicism," *First Things*, May 28, 2014. http://www.firstthings.com/blogs/leithart/2014/05/residual-extrinicism.

Why introduce ontology—the study of *being*—in a chapter on grace? After all, the Reformers were concerned with soteriology, not questions about God's being, much less being in general. Nevertheless, the present detour into ontology is necessary for three reasons: first, to clarify the deep theological presuppositions undergirding the Reformers' understanding of grace, and thus absolve them of the charge of having unwittingly secularized the world; second, to clarify the nature, purpose, and setting of mere Protestant biblical interpretation; third, to prepare the ground for my later discussion concerning the place of the church in the pattern (economy) of theological authority.

Here I take my cue from Graeme Goldsworthy's observation that *"the Principle of 'grace alone' points us to the ontological priority of God,"*[51] from Bavinck's observation that grace is opposed not to nature but to sin,[52] and above all from Paul's observation in Ephesians 1 that God's grace is the means by which God sums up everything in Christ. "Ontology" may be the watchword, but philosophy is here kept in the backseat; pride of place—the driver's seat— goes to theology: triune self-communication is the overarching framework for theological understanding of God and the gospel. We know the perfect eternal life of God only through its representation (revelation) in the economy of grace. The crux of the argument will therefore be that *sola gratia* has ontological and not merely soteriological significance: first, by helping us better to understand the freedom of God vis-à-vis nature as its Creator; and second, by helping us to see that the Bible, biblical interpretation, and biblical interpreters refer not to natural entities and processes but to elements in an economy of grace. We are *not* to read the Bible like any other book, as if it were an element in the immanent economy of natural reason, but rather with eyes and ears opened by grace, open and operative in the communicative domain of the Triune God.[53]

Communicative Ontology: The Triune Grounding of Grace

How does the principle of grace (*sola gratia*) point us to divine aseity, the priority of God's being? How do we move from soteriology to ontology? Paul

51. Goldsworthy, *Gospel-Centered Hermeneutics*, 47.

52. Herman Bavinck, *Reformed Dogmatics*, ed. John Bolt, trans. John Vriend (Grand Rapids: Baker Academic, 2003), 1:361.

53. So John Webster: "The Bible, its readers and their work of interpretation have their place in the domain of the Word of God, the sphere of reality in which Christ glorified is present and speaks with unrivalled clarity . . . and by his Spirit bestows powers of mind and will so that they may be quickened by that summons to intelligent life under the Word" (*The Domain of the Word: Scripture and Theological Reason* [London: Bloomsbury T&T Clark, 2012], viii).

in Ephesians 1 provides a telling clue: it is to the praise of God's glorious grace that he has chosen us in Christ "before the foundation of the world" (1:4). In Christ, through the Spirit, the saints get a share in God's own life, becoming co-heirs with the Son of the Father's wealth: "In him we have obtained an inheritance" (1:11), a treasure made up of "every spiritual blessing in the heavenly places" (1:3). What exactly do we obtain? All the privileges of sonship, everything that the Father shares with the Son, thanks to the "Spirit of adoption" (Rom. 8:15).

We move from grace to ontology because in order to explain the salvation by grace that we have in Christ, we first must talk about the free (i.e., uncaused) self-communicative action of the Triune God: "Salvation comes from the Trinity, happens through the Trinity, and brings us home to the Trinity."[54] Salvation comes *from* the Trinity: what we receive in Christ are the light, life, and love that characterize the eternal life of the Triune God. In John Webster's words: "The external works of the Holy Trinity are the orderly enactment of the absolutely original and antecedent purpose of God the Father."[55] Salvation happens *through* and brings us home *to* the Trinity: the good news is that through the work of the Son and Spirit, those who are not God are adopted into the divine life and given the privilege of calling God "Father." In Jesus's high-priestly prayer in the Gospel of John, he says to his Father, "You loved me before the foundation of the world" (John 17:24). This is crucial. Contrary to what a number of contemporary theologians believe, God did not *need* the world in order to have something to love. God is love (1 John 4:8)—always has been, always will be. God *is* love, a ceaseless interpersonal self-giving of Father to Son and Son to Father in the Spirit. Eternal personal relations—that's trinitarian ontology.

The eternal life of God in himself is perfect, made up of lively personal relations: the Father's *begetting* the Son, the Son's *being begotten*, and the Spirit's *proceeding* from the Father and the Son. These relations of eternal origination—paternity, filiation, spiration—identify God's perfect life.[56] These are the "movements" in the immanent Trinity that ground the work of the Son and Spirit in the history of salvation. The technical term is "procession," a divine self-communication *ad intra* (in contrast to the "missions"

54. Sanders, *Deep Things of God*, 10.
55. Webster, *Domain of the Word*, 7.
56. See John Webster, "God's Perfect Life," in *God's Life in Trinity*, ed. Miroslav Volf and Michael Welker (Minneapolis: Fortress, 2006), 143–52.

of Son and Spirit, which are self-communications *ad extra*). But there are other interpersonal communications in the Godhead in addition to relations of origin. In the first place, the Son enjoys the Father's love in eternity too. Second, the Son shares the life of the Father: "For as the Father has life in himself, so he has granted the Son also to have life in himself" (John 5:26). And third, the Son shares the Father's light and has communicated it to his followers by giving (breathing on) them the Holy Spirit (John 20:22). Again the high-priestly prayer: "Father, glorify me in your own presence with the glory that I had with you before the world existed" (John 17:5).

Theologians do well not to speculate about God's immanent being. Yet Scripture authorizes a degree of ontological inference in stating that God *is* light, life, and love from before the foundation of the world. There is biblical warrant for thinking that light, life, and love characterize God's eternal being—that is, what Father, Son, and Spirit have in common in spite of their differential interpersonal relations. Let us call the sharing of God's love, life, and light triune *communication*.[57] Scripture depicts the life of the Father, Son, and Spirit as a *doing* than which nothing greater can be conceived, a ceaseless activity of free and loving communication whose beginning and end is triune communion—eternal intercourse. This is the deep ontological background of the gospel message that God has incorporated a human people into his own life.

God was under no compulsion to create a world. God was fully God—fully actualized in his divine three-personed being—without the created order. We preserve the gratuity of grace in this first sense of divine communication only by affirming the antecedent perfection of God's inner life (i.e., the immanent Trinity). This, I believe, is what Goldsworthy has in mind when he says that *sola gratia* points us to the ontological priority of God. The universe, including space and time, exists only because of the grace of creation, a free initiative of the Triune God, who was already complete in himself. This free self-giving—this act of primordial love—is the deep presupposition of the gospel.

Scripture often speaks of "the grace of God" but never says, "God *is* grace" the way it says, "God is love" or "God is light." This omission raises an intriguing question: Is God gracious toward himself? Clearly, God is the sum total of his perfections. Like providence, however, grace has reference only to what is external to God. What, then, is grace? On one level, with a view

---

57. For discussion of the concept of triune communication in much greater detail, see Kevin J. Vanhoozer, *Remythologizing Theology: Divine Action, Passion, and Authorship* (Cambridge: Cambridge University Press, 2010), 259–71.

to God's act of creation, grace is God's free communication of his light, life, and love to what would otherwise not exist at all. In being gracious, God is being fully himself *toward undeserving others*. John Stott defines grace as "love that cares and stoops and rescues."[58] Here is the ontological point: grace is not some third thing between God and human beings, a supernatural substance or power that gets infused into nature to perfect it. Rather, grace is the gift of God's beneficent presence and activity—that is, the communication of God's own light, life, and love to those who have neither the right to them nor a claim on God.[59] Grace is God giving what is not owed. Grace is God in communicative action *ad extra*. Grace is the economic Trinity, the means by which God extends himself toward others, first in creation and later in redemption. Put simply, grace is the Triune God—God sharing his Fatherly love for creation in the Son through the Spirit.

Covenantal Economy: The Historical Outworking of Grace

What was predestined in Christ to the praise of God's grace involves more than creation and was made known by the plan set forth in Christ, "a plan [*oikonomia*] for the fullness of time" (Eph. 1:10). The "economic" Trinity refers to the work of the Father, Son, and Spirit to execute, in time, the plan conceived in eternity.[60] Whereas creative grace is the love of God *ad intra* being poured out in creative activity, saving grace is the life of God *ad intra* being freely poured out *ad extra* in redemptive activity. The mystery of redemption, made known in Christ, is that God graciously shares his own perfect life with those who are not perfect. Biblical theology traces the economy of redemption and focuses on the unfolding of God's plan of salvation in history via the various covenants through the agency of the Son and Spirit.

The economy—the works of the Triune God in world history—corresponds to the immanent being of God. For example, the missions of Son and Spirit enact in time the eternal begetting and proceeding that characterize the immanent Trinity. Elsewhere I have described this in dramatic terms: *God's*

58. John R. W. Stott, *Christ the Controversialist: A Study in Some Essentials of Evangelical Religion* (Downers Grove, IL: InterVarsity, 1970), 214.

59. Compare John Barclay's observation on the nature of "gift": "A gift can be *unconditioned* (free of prior conditions regarding the recipient) without also being *unconditional* (free of expectations that the recipient will offer some 'return')" (*Paul and the Gift* [Grand Rapids: Eerdmans, 2015], 562).

60. J. I. Packer describes the economy as God's "single, huge, mind-blowing plan" (*Taking God Seriously: Vital Things We Need to Know* [Wheaton, IL: Crossway, 2013], 36).

mighty acts in history theatrically represent the perfections of God's nature and the outworking of God's decree.[61] The missions of the Son and Spirit are the acting out, in the history of Jesus, of what has been going on in God's triune life eternally, namely, the communication of God's light, life, and love: "God *enacts* his perfection."[62] God shares his eternal life, light, and love with those who have no claim on him out of his sheer goodness, his unsearchable freedom and love. It is in this manner that the Trinity, and its communicative ontology, serves as the proper and necessary basis for the gospel. God's grace means that God, while remaining fully himself, freely takes the initiative to share or communicate himself with those who had turned their backs on him.

In an important sense, the economy of grace begins with creation itself because, as we have seen, God was under no compulsion to create. Furthermore, everything that God does is the joint work of Father, Son, and Spirit. That everything was made through the eternal Word is already a work of divine self-giving: creation begins by God's sharing his light (Gen. 1:3–4; John 1:3–4). According to Jonathan Edwards, the end for which God created the world was *self-communication.*[63] Creation was an excuse, as it were, for God to share with creatures his own life—his knowledge, love, and joy. Creation is fundamentally a theater for God's glory, a place where God can be seen to be God by those who are not God. Creation is the condition for the appearance of grace—triune communication, divine self-giving—in human history.

God's grace is God communicating himself to others according to a plan that culminates in the mystery of Jesus Christ (Eph. 3:9). However, after Adam's fall, grace takes on an additional sense. It is no longer simply a matter of God's self-communicative activity, because sinners cannot endure the presence of a holy, righteous God (Isa. 6:5). For the unholy to come into contact with perfect holiness is to incur divine wrath, and ultimately destruction (2 Sam. 6:6–7). We need, therefore, to define grace as involving more than mere communicative activity: grace is God's undeserved and unmerited self-giving. It is indeed wonderful to participate in being (creative grace), but it is something even more marvelous when fallen creatures participate in Christ (redemptive grace).

---

61. Kevin J. Vanhoozer, *Faith Speaking Understanding: Performing the Drama of Doctrine* (Louisville: Westminster John Knox, 2014), 75–82.

62. Webster, "God's Perfect Life," 147.

63. Edwards, *The Works of Jonathan Edwards*, vol. 13, *The "Miscellanies,"* ed. Thomas A. Schafer (New Haven: Yale University Press, 1994), 277.

The history of grace in a fallen world takes the form of a series of personal initiatives by the Triune God to human creatures. If I belabor the point, it is to contrast what I am calling a communicative ontology with a sacramental ontology. For the latter, creatures are related to God, and his grace, simply by virtue of existing. There is an element of truth to this, of course. Creatures depend on God's sustaining grace each moment for their continued existence. However, this being-there is not yet what Scripture calls "life." God's life-giving presence is not merely a matter of metaphysical sustenance (preserving our generic being-there) but is an active being-for-us. Scripture recounts the story of God making communicative initiatives to particular persons who, because of sin, had forfeited their proper relationship to God. To put it simply: fallen creatures are sustained in being-in-general by God but do not enjoy the covenantal communion for which they were created and which is now available only by being in Christ. Grace comes into its own—that is, into the more familiar Reformation sense of "undeserved favor"—just here, for Scripture tells us that God has not abandoned his human creatures but instead has made further life-giving communicative initiatives: "and the Word became flesh and dwelt among us" (John 1:14). To be "in Christ" is to be graciously included in the communicative activity of the Father and the Son through the Spirit, the triune life.

Many of the most important communicative initiatives were *covenants*, solemn oaths that established familial relationships between the Lord and a particular people who would otherwise be estranged from God. Yet the most important triune communication is the Word made flesh: "The incarnation offers greater grace, the grace of deeper participation in the communion of the Triune God."[64] The covenant of grace involves "a king who *rules*, a people who are *ruled*, and a sphere where this rule is *recognized* as taking place."[65] If creatures share in the light, life, and love of God, it is not simply because they exist in the animal kingdom, as a robust sacramental ontology might suggest, but rather because they have responded to God's gracious communicative initiatives with faith in Christ and have thus been transferred into the kingdom of the Son (Col. 1:13). Christians do not simply participate in being; they participate in Christ. According to sacramental ontology, humans participate, as do all entities, in God's being on a sliding scale: faith and obedience bring

64. Leithart, *Athanasius*, 111.
65. Graeme Goldsworthy, *Gospel and Kingdom: A Christian Interpretation of the Old Testament* (Exeter, UK: Paternoster, 1981), 53.

one closer to what one already has. We need here to distinguish physical life (being in general) from the spiritual life (being in Christ) given to those who respond to God's Word in faith and trust. Human beings exist and even flourish for a time because of common grace, but this should be biblically and theologically distinguished from the special favor (saving grace) that attends being in Christ: "If anyone is in Christ, he is a new creation" (2 Cor. 5:17).

The economy of redemption reveals God's ontological perfections. We begin to understand who God is in eternity from what he does in time. His covenant-making and covenant-keeping actions in particular reveal that God *is* faithful and true (Exod. 34:6–7). God's love *is* his self-giving; God's righteousness *is* his right-doing; God's faithfulness *is* his word-keeping. In similar fashion, let me suggest that God's grace is his *face-shining*. This phrase captures grace's dual character as both disposition and activity.

First, disposition. One of the most frequent Hebrew terms for "grace," *ḥēn*, connotes the favor that an inferior finds in the eyes of a superior. The term is found forty-three times in the idiom "to find favor in the eyes of so-and-so" (e.g., "But Noah found favor in the eyes of the LORD" [Gen. 6:8]). The Septuagint uses the Greek word for "grace," *charis*, to translate it. Numbers 6:25 brings out the second aspect of grace, its activity: "The LORD make his face to shine upon you and be gracious to you." The face represents God's presence—the shining, the graciousness of his presence.[66] Psalm 80 corroborates the connection in its thrice-repeated line, "Let your face shine, that we may be saved!" (Ps. 80:3, 7, 19). God's triune presence and activity are light-giving. God is light (1 John 1:5); Jesus Christ is the light of the world (John 8:12); the Spirit is the shining of the light of the gospel upon human minds and hearts (2 Cor. 4:6). Moses's face was shining when he came down from Mount Sinai "because he had been talking with God" (Exod. 34:29). The face of God not only shines but also speaks: the Lord said to Abram, "I will make of you a great nation, and I will bless you" (Gen. 12:2). This Abrahamic promise lies at the heart of the covenant of grace, and it is associated with a second Hebrew term, *ḥesed* (steadfast love), God's special covenant kindness. Calvin points out that this promise is "gratuitous," and that this grace is foundational (i.e., ontologically prior) to faith.[67]

God was under no obligation to make his face shine upon the earth. To be sure, after six days of creating he pronounced the world "very good," and it is

66. In Scripture, to "see the face" of someone is to be in or come before a person's presence (see Gen. 32:20; Esther 1:14; Acts 20:25).

67. Calvin, *Institutes* III.2.24.

safe to infer that he smiled upon the first family (Gen. 1:28), but soon thereafter there was little to smile about. Sin led Adam and Eve to hide from the presence of the Lord (3:8), and the final consequence of sin was banishment from the Lord's garden-temple, hitherto a place of divine-human meeting and conversation. But there was further distancing from God. Cain, after murdering his brother, laments, "From your face I shall be hidden" (4:14), and two verses later we read, "Then Cain went away from the presence of the LORD" (4:16). A scant two chapters later we hear this chilling verdict: "Now the earth was corrupt in God's sight" (6:11). Even the children of Abraham—Israel, his treasured possession—and her kings repeatedly did "what was evil in the sight of the LORD" (Deut. 9:18; Judg. 2:11; 1 Kings 14:22). This is not secularization but insurrection. Yes, there are also pathetic attempts at ingratiation, but it is impossible for sinners to curry God's favor. Grace is the one thing that we cannot get with our own resources only, no matter how hard we strive.

Sola gratia. God freely sets in motion both creation and redemption, the latter a process of self-communication that would prove to be unsurpassingly costly. For Jesus Christ is the gratuitous promise of God made flesh, the steadfast love, the shining face and Word of God, up close and personal, "full of grace and truth" (John 1:14; cf. Exod. 34:6–7). Thanks to the Son's saving work, what was his by nature is the believer's by grace. It is in Christ that God smiles on us as adopted children. What Christ communicates is his filial status and relationship, something that we could never have attained through our own dint of effort. We know that, because Israel tried to live up to that status but could not: "Out of Egypt I called my son" (Hosea 11:1). In sum, the grace that God communicates is ultimately himself, and he does so by uniting people to Christ through the Spirit. The Trinity is thus the ontological presupposition of the gospel of grace. Grace points us to the ontological priority of God, the priority of God's presence and activity: his shining face.

Scripture also speaks of grace "to describe a particular gift of God that enables human beings to do and be things that, left to themselves, they seem hardly able to do and be."[68] Protestants are sometimes squeamish about talking like this, especially if it suggests that grace is something that can be infused into the soul with which people then cooperate. Nevertheless, there are too many instances where one cannot simply substitute "undeserved good favor"

68. Peter Groves, *Grace: The Cruciform Love of God* (London: Canterbury, 2012), 4.

and make sense of the text. For example, when Paul arrives in Achaia, he "greatly helped those who through grace had believed" (Acts 18:27). God's unmerited favor here works a change in people.

This is not the place to provide an inventory of every kind of grace that theologians have seen fit to describe (e.g., converting, prevenient, effectual, cooperating). Suffice it to say that the economy of grace includes not only undeserved favor but also gifts that make us more like Christ. The most important of these gifts is the Holy Spirit (Acts 2:38; 10:45), himself the giver of life, and of further spiritual gifts (1 Cor. 12:4–11; Heb. 2:4). In the final analysis, God's grace refers both to the communicative initiatives that establish a covenant relationship and "to the gifts that allow that relationship to be sustained."[69] Grace is the gift of God that enables us to grow more like God.

Jesus Christ is the shining face of God, in whose light (and through whose Spirit) the church lives and moves and has its being. Grace presupposes the triune ontology: the perfect life of Father, Son, and Spirit sharing their light, life, and love among themselves. Grace is this perfect life of God directed outward, toward creation and the church, in order to draw them inward, into God's own life. Augustine, the Doctor of Grace, said that it takes two forms: the light in our minds and the love in our wills—or in trinitarian terms, the Word, who directs our knowing, and the Spirit, who directs our doing. Augustine was particularly fond of Romans 5:5: "God's love has been poured into our hearts through the Holy Spirit who has been given to us."[70] This love in our hearts unites us to the one who is love, and it allows us to live out God's love in loving our neighbors as ourselves.

In sum, grace in this second redemptive and economic sense is God's gift of his own life. The gospel is the good news that the Father adopts children of Adam as his own by uniting them to Christ through the Holy Spirit. The immanent Trinity is thus the ontological presupposition of the gospel, and the gospel is the proclamation of the economic Trinity.[71]

---

69. Ibid., 16.

70. See Augustine, *A Treatise on the Grace of Christ and on Original Sin*, trans. Dr. Holmes (London: Aeterna, 2014), book 1, chap. 27.

71. Walter Kasper makes a similar point about the ontology and economy of grace: "Only if God in himself is self-communicating love can he communicate himself externally as the one who he already is. . . . In God's mercy, the eternal, self-communicating love of the Father, Son, and Holy Spirit is mirrored and revealed" (*Mercy: The Essence of the Gospel and the Key to Christian Life* [New York: Paulist Press, 2013], 93).

Communion: The Final Purpose of Grace

By grace we have been created, and "by grace you have been saved" (Eph. 2:5). We who were dead in our sins have been made alive—thank God!—but to what end? Goldsworthy rightly reminds us that the gospel "is not simply 'forgiveness of sin' and 'going to heaven when you die.' The gospel is a restoration of relationships between God, man and the world."[72] According to Jonathan Edwards, "The great thing purchased by Jesus Christ for us, is communion with God, which is only in having the Spirit."[73] We can link this to Dietrich Bonhoeffer's observation that "the church is God's new will and purpose for humanity."[74] What connects all three answers is the idea of *communion*. The final purpose of God's gracious communicative initiatives is interpersonal communion, the supreme covenant blessing: "I . . . will be your God, and you shall be my people" (Lev. 26:12). In covenantal communion, each person is for the other.

Communion is essentially a *sharing in union*.[75] The purpose of God's grace is to establish a unitive relationship: the *telos* of the plan—the end of the *oikonomia*—is "to unite all things in him [Christ], things in heaven and things on earth" (Eph. 1:10). Peter O'Brien identifies cosmic reconciliation (things in heaven) and the new humanity in Christ that reconciles Jew and gentile (things on earth) as the central message in Ephesians.[76] In Christ, there is "one new man in place of the two" (Eph. 2:15). In Christ, God is establishing his kingdom on earth: one holy nation made up of what used to be two peoples, a new people that is being built into a living temple (2 Cor. 6:16; 1 Pet. 2:5), a people who are the place where God now rules. Alfred Loisy's famous observation that "Jesus announced the Kingdom and what came was the Church" implies a discrepancy between the two.[77] However, if the people are the place where God rules, we can see the church as a sign or, perhaps better,

72. Goldsworthy, *Gospel and Kingdom*, 122.

73. Edwards, "Miscellany No. 402," in *Works of Jonathan Edwards*, vol. 13, *The "Miscellanies,"* 466.

74. Dietrich Bonhoeffer, *Sanctorum Communio: A Theological Study of the Sociology of the Church*, ed. Clifford J. Green, trans. Reinhard Krauss and Nancy Lukens, Dietrich Bonhoeffer Works 1 (Minneapolis: Fortress, 1998), 141.

75. For further discussion, see Vanhoozer, *Remythologizing Theology*, 283–88.

76. Peter T. O'Brien, *The Letter to the Ephesians*, Pillar New Testament Commentary (Grand Rapids: Eerdmans, 2009), 58, 62. Chrys Caragounis suggests that the powers represent "the things in heaven," while the church represents "the things on earth" (*The Ephesian Mysterion: Meaning and Content* [Lund: Gleerup, 1977], 144–46).

77. Loisy, *L'Évangile et l'Église*, 2nd ed. (Bellevue, 1903), 155.

a *parable* of the kingdom. The church's mission is to communicate to the ends of the earth the good news that Jesus has made it possible for sinners to be reconciled, and to commune, with God.

The important point is that salvation involves restored relationships with God and other people, and that the church is where salvation should be on conspicuous display. The grace of God's self-communicative activity results in the grace of communion: a communion of the Trinity, but also of the saints. It is the special task of the Holy Spirit to create a "fellowship of differents"—rich and poor, male and female, Jew and gentile—by uniting them to Christ.[78] The mystery of grace is the Triune God working in perfect communion *in se* (in himself) to extend this communion *ad se* (beyond himself). One way that God extends his communion to the saints is by conforming us to the image of Jesus Christ, so that we share the mind and heart of Christ. This is the Holy Spirit's special task: so to minister Christ's life as to make believers like him, so to minister God's Word that it dwells richly in our hearts (Col. 3:16). As we will see below, the special illuminating grace associated with the Spirit is to consummate a face-to-face communion with the risen Christ, a communion that sets our faces aglow and enlightens the eyes of our heart (Eph. 1:18).

Finally, we should observe that the communion that is the *telos* of the gospel has a more concrete expression: the end of the *oikonomia* (the plan of God) is the *oikos* (the house of God). The Septuagint uses the Greek term *oikos* more than two thousand times, and many of these pertain to the tabernacle or temple, the dwelling place or "house of the Lord" (e.g., Exod. 23:19; 1 Sam. 3:15; 1 Kings 8:11). As Greg Beale and others have pointed out, kings often built temples in order to commemorate their victories.[79] Jesus's victory on the cross results in a temple made of living stones (1 Pet. 2:4–5). The church, far from being a parenthesis or appendix in God's plan, is instead its centerpiece. Paul calls the church "the household of God" (1 Tim. 3:15). Jesus is its cornerstone and master (Heb. 3:6). Again, the whole point of the *oikonomia* is for the Triune God to build a holy temple where the Spirit joins believers together in Christ to make them a fit dwelling place for God (Eph. 2:19–22). But this is not all. As we will see in later chapters, the church is not simply the end of God's gracious economy but a means of continuing

---

78. See Scot McKnight, *A Fellowship of Differents: Showing the World God's Design for Life Together* (Grand Rapids: Zondervan, 2014).

79. G. K. Beale, *The Temple and the Church's Mission: A Biblical Theology of the Dwelling Place of God* (Downers Grove, IL: IVP Academic, 2004).

grace. In particular, overseers of the church function as stewards of God's house (Titus 1:7; cf. 1 Pet. 4:10). The teaching ministry of the church is itself a gift of the risen Christ, an important part of the economy of grace (Eph. 4:11–14). To retrieve *sola gratia* is to appreciate again the church and her teaching ministry as a gift of grace.

Sola Gratia for Bible, Church, and Interpretive Authority

We can now draw some morals for how a retrieval of *sola gratia* may be brought to bear on the problem of interpretive authority for reading the Bible in the church. Remember what retrieval does: it looks back in order to move forward. The *solas* are resources, something on which we draw to resolve problems and continue our mission more effectively—"a very present help in trouble" (Ps. 46:1). In particular, we are looking back at what the Reformers meant by *sola gratia* in order to move forward creatively and so respond to the problem flagged by both Brad Gregory and Christian Smith: that secularization was an unintended consequence of the Reformation. The basic criticism, again, is that the Reformation's emphasis on *sola scriptura* and the priesthood of all believers desacralized the church, eliminating the ecclesial middlemen, and made every individual an independent interpretive authority when it came to determining what the Bible means.

The present work addresses the contemporary critique of the Reformation in several stages. *Sola gratia* addresses the charge of secularization by locating biblical interpreters and interpretation in the all-encompassing economy of triune communicative activity. *Sola fide* and *sola scriptura* address the charge of skepticism by focusing on the principle and pattern respectively of what I will describe as the economy of theological authority. *Solus Christus* addresses the charge of schism by focusing on the royal priesthood of all believers, and this is the proper context for understanding *sola ecclesia*. Finally, *soli Deo gloria* returns to the scene of the crime—Protestant division over the Lord's Supper—in order to address the challenge of hyperplurality and interpretive disagreement in the church.

As previously mentioned, I view the *solas* not as doctrines in their own right as much as theological insights into various facets of the ontology, epistemology, and teleology of the gospel. The focus in the present chapter has been on redemptive history (the economic Trinity) as a faithful expression of the perfect life of the Triune God (the ontological Trinity). I have distinguished three distinct movements of divine grace: the primordial grace of creation, the redemptive grace that unites us to Christ, and the sanctifying grace that conforms us to Christ's image. I now conclude by drawing out some implications of the triune ontology and economy of redemption for the issue that lies at the center of our inquiry: the conflict of biblical interpretations and interpretive authorities.

I offer four theses, organized under two headings: first, implications of *sola gratia* understood as a material principle that specifies the content of Scripture; second, implications of *sola gratia* viewed as a formal principle that enables right reading of Scripture. The theses describe the interpretive practice of "mere Protestant Christians," a set whose contents I do not further specify at this point. My hope is that the profile will have been sufficiently filled out by the end of this book for readers to ascertain whether or not, when these saints go marching in, they want to be in their number.

Grace as the Focus of Biblical Interpretation (The Material Principle: Reading to Learn Christ)

   1. Mere Protestant Christians agree that the many forms of biblical discourse together make up a single unified story of God's gracious communicative initiatives.

Sola gratia emphasizes divine communicative initiatives, God's free and loving acts of self-giving and mercy. As such, *sola gratia* specifies what Christianity is all about. Christianity is not primarily a system of ideas but an account of how the Creator has reached out with both hands, Son and Spirit, to lift up a fallen world in a loving embrace. These acts span the Testaments and provide a unified identity description of the Triune God: the God who brought Israel out of Egypt is also the one who raised Jesus from the dead, and both acts are instrumental in executing the plan of salvation. Scripture is essentially a narrative account of God's gracious self-communicative activity in the histories of Israel and Jesus Christ whereby the Father adopts a people by uniting them to his Son through his Spirit.

Mere Protestant Christians agree on the persons and events that make up the story: this is a point of fundamental importance, especially in light of disagreements over various doctrinal issues. Mere Protestant Christians may differ over precisely how to read the story and what it means, but not about the main persons and events. The distinction is important. It is one thing to differ over this or that aspect of a story, but something else to differ about what the story is. As we have seen, the story concerns the loving initiatives of the Triune God to share his life with human creatures. There is one gospel (Gal. 1:6–7), but four Gospels, just as there is one mere Protestant Christian understanding of the gospel story but several denominational interpretations as to its precise meaning. Even the New Testament authors tell the story of Jesus in different ways, yet they all tell the story of Jesus. This is the sine qua non of Christian theology.

Mere Protestants may differ to some extent over the meaning and significance of God's words and deeds, then, *but not to the point of changing the story*. This is what the deceivers mentioned in 2 John did in refusing to confess "the coming of Jesus Christ in the flesh" (2 John 7). To deny the incarnation is to delete an essential event in the story, effectively changing the story into something other than God's self-communication, and thereby short-circuiting the economy of grace. Everything depends on the distinction between story and interpretation, which in turn depends on a distinction between doctrines of differing dogmatic rank, an issue to which we will return in a later chapter. The basic point here is that the great dogmas of the faith preserve the integrity of the story of salvation by specifying the ontological identity of the divine dramatis personae. Who is Jesus? He is the eternal Son in human form and nature, yet of the same nature as God the Father. On such fundamental truths there is universal consent. By way of contrast, the major Protestant confessions not only preserve the integrity of the story but also elevate certain doctrinal matters that distinguish them from other Protestant groups, and in so doing sometimes give the impression that second-order doctrines are of first-order importance.[80]

2. Mere Protestant Christians agree that the Bible is fundamentally about grace in Jesus Christ.

This may sound trite, but we should not underestimate its significance, especially in light of what I said above about deceivers. It is no little thing to achieve interpretive consensus as to what a text is fundamentally about. Luther

---

80. I am aware that one person's (or denomination's) second-order doctrine is another's cherished first-order truth. Interestingly, for Paul the things "of first importance" included Jesus dying for our sins and being raised on the third day (1 Cor. 15:3–4)—events in a story rather than particular interpretations of these events. Yet I also recognize that certain doctrines, such as justification by faith, play an important role in guarding against misinterpretations of the story. I will return to the question of dogmatic rank in mere Protestant Christianity below.

says, "Unless one understands the things [*res*] under discussion, one cannot make sense of the words [*verba*]."[81] What these first two theses highlight is the function of the *solas* as "gathering places," topics or themes that provide crucial insights into the biblical story and on which there is widespread agreement.[82] It is worth observing that in viewing the Bible as fundamentally a discourse about the mystery of God's grace revealed in Christ, we are following the interpretive lead of Jesus himself, who consistently explained his person and work by reference to the Old Testament, as the fulfillment of previous divine communicative initiatives: "And beginning with Moses and all the Prophets, he interpreted to them in all the Scriptures the things concerning himself" (Luke 24:27). *Sola gratia* is a permanent reminder that at the heart of Christianity is good news—the story of what the Triune God is doing in Jesus Christ.

Grace as the Framework of Biblical Interpretation (The Formal Principle: Reading in the Economy of Grace)

> 3. Mere Protestant Christians believe that the Bible, the process of interpretation, and interpreters themselves are all parts of the triune economy of grace.

The Bible is the living and active Word of God, not inert matter or a dead body on which interpreters perform exegetical autopsies. To rely on one's own native interpretive powers is to succumb to the temptation of a "hermeneutics of glory"—that is, the expectation that one can discover God's Word through one's own natural exegetical abilities.

Many in the modern academy read the Bible, in the words of the nineteenth-century Oxford biblical scholar Benjamin Jowett, "like any other book,"[83] so much so that Michael Legaspi links the modern rise of biblical studies, a specialist discipline, with the "death" of Scripture.[84] In the academy, biblical interpretation is largely a descriptive endeavor whose aim is to describe what the biblical authors meant in their (often reconstructed) historical contexts.

---

81. Cited in Martin H. Franzmann, "Seven Theses on Reformation Hermeneutics," *Concordia Journal* 36, no. 2 (2010): 120.

82. I will deal with interpretive disagreements in chap. 5, where we will see that mere Protestant Christianity is a unity-in-diversity. See further W. David Buschart, *Exploring Protestant Traditions: An Invitation to Theological Hospitality* (Downers Grove, IL: IVP Academic, 2006), esp. 255–75.

83. Benjamin Jowett, "On the Interpretation of Scripture," in *The Interpretation of Scripture and Other Essays* (London: George Routledge & Sons, 1907), 1–76.

84. See Michael C. Legaspi, *The Death of Scripture and the Rise of Biblical Studies* (Oxford: Oxford University Press, 2010).

Modern biblical scholars have created an "academic Bible"—a stitched-
together collection of texts, shorn of all scriptural properties, that tell us
more about the people who wrote, edited, and collected them and their times
than they do anything else.[85] Hans Frei describes the change from Scripture
to academic Bible as a "great reversal" in hermeneutics: "Interpretation was
a matter of fitting the biblical story into another world with another story
rather than incorporating that world into the biblical story."[86] To read the Bible
through the lens of an interpretive framework derived from elsewhere than
Scripture is to insert both text and interpreter into a this-worldly economy
of criticism (nature) rather than a triune economy of revelation (grace).[87] It
is this practice, I submit, not mere Protestant Christianity, that has most
contributed to secularizing the biblical text and its interpretation.

Mere Protestants acknowledge the Bible as what it is: the result of a divine
initiative and a means of continuing divine communicative action. Mere
Protestants acknowledge the Bible as a divine address, and themselves as
addressees. This too is grace—God freely communicates himself in words to
us in order to establish covenantal relations—and the warrant for thinking
in terms of communicative ontology. John Piper asks why Paul begins his
thirteen letters with "grace *to you*" but concludes with "grace *be with you*"
(or some variation thereof). The answer: because Paul believes that "God's
grace is being mediated to the readers by the words, the truth."[88] The process
of interpretation is from grace to grace: it is by grace alone that the Word
is spoken and received, and it is by grace alone that the Word dwells richly
within us (Col. 3:16). It is not that grace *perfects* natural interpretive acts,
making our innate interpretive abilities that much better (as one might expect
of grace in a sacramental ontology), but rather that it *restores* interpretive
agents to right-mindedness and right-heartedness and *reorients* interpretive
acts to their proper end: receiving Christ into our hearts and minds.

To recognize Scripture as God's gracious address is to view biblical interpretation less as a procedure that readers perform on the text than a process of

85. Ibid., 7.

86. Hans W. Frei, *The Eclipse of Biblical Narrative: A Study in Eighteenth and Nineteenth
Century Hermeneutics* (New Haven: Yale University Press, 1974), 130.

87. See further Mark Alan Bowald, *Rendering the Word in Theological Hermeneutics: Mapping Divine and Human Agency* (Aldershot, UK: Ashgate, 2007), chap. 1.

88. John Piper, "Feed the Flame of God's Gift: Unashamed Courage in the Gospel (2 Timothy
1:1–12)," in *Entrusted with the Gospel: Pastoral Expositions of 2 Timothy*, ed. D. A. Carson
(Wheaton: Crossway, 2010), 19.

spiritual formation that takes place in the readers: "God's employment of the words of Scripture to be an instrument of his own communicative presence, by which process they are made holy, has its goal and essential counterpart in God's formation of a holy people."[89] God speaks new hearts into being, energizing and orienting them to heaven.

To read in the economy of grace is to let what the Bible is govern the way one approaches it. The Bible is Holy Scripture; upon reading it, we step onto holy ground, namely, the domain of the revelatory and redemptive presence of the risen and ascended Christ. John Webster decries the ways in which the study of Scripture has been "uncoupled" from divine activity and ecclesial life. It is far better, because more accurate, to view readers as denizens in the "domain of the word." The accent is not on hermeneutics—our principles for right reading—but on what God does to form right readers. For example, the clarity of Scripture is a function not of "the clarifying powers of the standardly rational reader"[90] on the text but of the work of the Holy Spirit in the reader. This means that we must give our full attention to what the Lord is saying to us in Scripture rather than try to discover what we wish he had said. In the economy of grace, mere Protestant Christians ought to be all ears.[91]

Mere Protestant interpreters are part of the economy of grace as members of the church, the domain on earth of Christ's risen presence: "Scripture interpretation is rational activity under this rule."[92] The various Protestant houses (interpretive communities) are the place where right habits of theological interpretation are best formed and where the fruit of these habits is best exhibited. Both habits and fruit are a function of Scripture's intended effect, which is to help transfer readers from their former existence in the domain of darkness to enter into the realm of reconciliation: the kingdom of God, a kingdom of light. The mention of light brings us to a last thesis.

> 4. Mere Protestant Christians are interpreters who themselves are caught up in the triune economy of light and who therefore read the Bible as children of light.

89. Murray Rae, "On Reading Scripture Theologically," *Princeton Theological Review* 14, no. 1 (2008): 23.

90. Webster, *Domain of the Word*, 23.

91. So Webster: "Whatever the church does with Holy Scripture, its acts of reading, construing and interpreting, have value only insofar as they are modes of attention" (ibid., 45).

92. Ibid., 47.

Everything that I have previously said about the ontology, epistemology, and teleology of the gospel (all of which are implicit in *sola gratia*) can be restated in terms of light. This is a rich topic to which I can here do only scant justice. First, "God is light" (1 John 1:5), dwells "in unapproachable light" (1 Tim. 6:16), and said, "Let there be light" (Gen. 1:3). This was the most basic communicative initiative—the grace of creation itself—a sharing of God's own light via the making of a world. That humans enjoy physical and spiritual light owes everything to its ontological source in the triune grace of God.

Second, "light" refers to the redemptive grace of God made known in Jesus Christ. Jesus is both the "true light, which gives light to everyone" (John 1:9), in the sense that he gives life to everyone who comes into the world, and "the light of the world" (John 8:12; 9:5), the shining face of God who smiles upon his set-apart people, those who are his treasured possession.[93] In Christ, the light who is also Logos (Word), the Father makes himself known. Revelation in Christ is the high point in the economy of enlightenment. The Bible too is part of the economy of enlightenment, a creaturely attestation of the light of the world and a means of advancing the dominion of that light. Paul speaks of "the light of the gospel of the glory of Christ" (2 Cor. 4:4), a light that shines in our hearts "to give us the light of the knowledge of God's glory" (2 Cor. 4:6).

Light enlightens; it communicates knowledge. However, Calvin speaks of a "twofold enlightening": "[God] shines forth upon us in the person of his Son by his Gospel, but that would be in vain, since we are blind, unless he were also to illuminate our minds by his Spirit."[94] This brings us to the particular work of the Spirit in yet a third moment of grace: the grace of illumination. The Spirit shines the light of Christ into our hearts and minds, removing the veil of ignorance (2 Cor. 3:12–18) and making us "children of light" (Eph. 5:8; 1 Thess. 5:5). The whole economy of grace is thus an economy of light inasmuch as it concerns the shining of God's face, in Christ, through the Scriptures and the Spirit, who illumines them, into the hearts of those who themselves become a kingdom of light (cf. Col. 1:13). The economy of light is therefore the gracious way God administers knowledge and understanding from light to light through light. The triune economy of light refers to both

93. As with grace, we need to distinguish the ontology, economy, and teleology of God's light.

94. Commentary on 2 Cor. 4:6, in John Calvin, *The Second Epistle of Paul the Apostle to the Corinthians and the Epistles to Timothy, Titus, and Philemon*, trans. T. A. Small (Grand Rapids: Eerdmans, 1996), 57.

the making common of the knowledge of God (the history of revelation) and the way God delivers us from the domain of darkness and transfers us to his kingdom of light (the history of redemption). The Triune God is Lord of his lighting. Grace is what accounts for the life and light of God *ad intra* being poured out *ad extra* on undeserving sinners.

And the Lord has been gracious. Light proceeds from the Father, through the Son, and attains its end in people's hearts and minds by the Spirit. The Spirit's role in the economy of light is crucial: he inspires the Scriptures; he assures us that Scripture is God's Word; he opens hearts and minds so that people can *see* the light (i.e., understand the Scriptures).[95] The traditional term is "illumination," which refers to "the ways in which the operation of creaturely intelligence is caused, preserved and directed by divine light, whose radiance makes creatures to know."[96] Simply put: the Spirit enables right reception of God's communication (1 Cor. 2:11–16). Less simply put (in John Owen's terminology): the Spirit is the principal efficient cause of our understanding God's mind as revealed in Scripture. According to Owen, "Men may have a knowledge of *words*, and the *meaning* of propositions in the Scripture, who have no knowledge of the *things themselves* designed in them"[97]—until, that is, the Spirit brings that knowledge about. Owen thinks that the Spirit's *way* of causing us to understand involves our own mental faculties, and that the *means* of our coming to understand include not only grammars and lexicons but also, more importantly, church teachers and church tradition—a point to which I will return in chapter 3.

To read in the economy of grace is to read with faces exposed to the face of God shining on us through the text. "For God, who said, 'Let light shine out of darkness,' has shone in our hearts to give the light of the knowledge of the glory of God in the face of Jesus Christ" (2 Cor. 4:6). According to Jonathan Edwards, "There is a difference between having a rational judgment that honey is sweet, and having a sense of its sweetness."[98] The Spirit's illu-

95. See further Kevin J. Vanhoozer, "The Spirit of Light after the Age of Enlightenment: Renewing/Reforming Pneumatic Hermeneutics via the Economy of Illumination," in *Spirit of God: Christian Renewal in the Community of Faith*, ed. Jeffrey Barbeau and Beth Felker Jones (Downers Grove, IL: InterVarsity, 2015), 149–67.

96. Webster, *Domain of the Word*, 50.

97. John Owen, *Causes, Ways, and Means of Understanding the Mind of God*, ed. Thomas Russell, Works of John Owen 3 (London: Richard Baynes, 1826), 418.

98. Jonathan Edwards, "A Divine and Supernatural Light," in *The Sermons of Jonathan Edwards: A Reader*, ed. Wilson H. Kimnach, Kenneth P. Minkema, and Douglas A. Sweeney (New Haven: Yale University Press, 1999), 126.

mination communicates not simply the sense but the sweetness of the grace that is in Christ. Moreover, the light that emanates from the face of Christ shining in the Scriptures makes our faces shine as well: "The Spirit's role—or goal—in interpretation is to allow the interpreter to understand the text in such a way that the text transforms the interpreter into the image of Christ."[99] The Spirit's illumination communicates the gospel so thoroughly that what is in Christ begins to be what is in us too.

The Word of God is "a lamp shining in a dark place" (2 Pet. 1:19). Calvin's comment is apt: "Without the word nothing is left for men but darkness."[100] The only reason we are not in darkness is that God, in his grace, has spoken. And, through the word he has spoken, we are being called "out of darkness into his marvelous light" (1 Pet. 2:9). Mere Protestant Christians read Scripture in the economy of grace in order to be drawn higher up, and further into that light. The Spirit illumines the faithful, opening eyes and ears to see and hear the light of the world, the Word of God dazzling in the canonical fabric of the text: God's unmerited favor toward us shining in the face of the biblical Jesus.

---

99. Gary L. Nebeker, "The Holy Spirit, Hermeneutics, and Transformation: From Present to Future Glory," *Evangelical Review of Theology* 27, no. 1 (2003): 47.

100. Commentary on 2 Pet. 1:19, in John Calvin, *Commentaries on the Catholic Epistles* (Edinburgh: Calvin Translation Society, 1855), 388.

2

Faith Alone

The Mere Protestant Principle of Authority

In the previous chapter I argued that retrieving "grace alone" attunes us to the way in which the Triune God shares his own light, life, and love with us in Jesus Christ through the Spirit. Mere Protestant exegetes and theologians do not simply bring their own natural powers to bear on Scripture but rather participate in the economy of grace (and, as we will see, in an economy of interpretive authority). My main claim was that *sola gratia* effectively rebuts the charge that the Reformers "naturalized" biblical interpretation. That was the point of examining Luther's contrast of a theology of glory with the theology (and hermeneutics) of the cross. What illumines Scripture is not the light of autonomous reason but the light that originates from the Father, radiates in the Son (Heb. 1:3), and penetrates to hearts and minds through the Spirit. One cannot therefore lay the blame for secularization at the Reformers' doorstep.

We turn now to the charge that the Reformation unintentionally begat skepticism, the crisis in knowing (epistemology). In particular, we will examine Richard Popkin's charge that Luther's new criterion for knowledge was "that which conscience is compelled to believe on reading Scripture."[1] Mere

1. Popkin, *History of Scepticism*, 5.

Protestant Christians need to do more than "always let their conscience be their guide": Scripture is sufficient, as we will see in the next chapter, but we cannot say as much for this Jiminy Cricket approach to hermeneutics.[2] What, then, is the role of faith in biblical interpretation, and how does it relate to the dictates of conscience? Does faith sanctify subjectivity, give us access to a special kind of objectivity, or open up a space of intersubjectivity? How does faith alone compensate for the loss of external authority (the church magisterium) in biblical interpretation? Here too Graeme Goldsworthy helpfully identifies the theological stakes: "*The principle of 'faith alone' points us to the ontological inability of the sinner and the epistemological priority of the Holy Spirit.*"[3] As salvation is by grace alone, so too is knowledge of God, through faith. The burden of the present chapter is to argue that the Reformers anticipated, even if they did not fully develop, what we may call a "modest testimonial foundationalism" of a kind that has come to fruition only recently in, for example, the work of the mere Protestant Christian philosopher Alvin Plantinga.

Sola Fide: What the Reformers Meant

The Basic Insight: Saved through Faith

"For by grace you have been saved through faith. And this is not your own doing; it is the gift of God, not a result of works" (Eph. 2:8–9). "The just shall live by faith" (Rom. 1:17 KJV). Luther's insight into the meaning of justification, and salvation, was arguably the crucial catalyst of the Reformation. Luther initially understood this according to late medieval Christendom's teaching that although God gives grace, people have to take it and run (work) with it—make efforts to improve on grace to merit even more. Alas, Luther was never quite sure if he had run fast or far enough. As is well known, the crucial turning point came when Luther discovered that our works do not "make righteous" but that God "declares righteous" (i.e., innocent) those who through faith trust in what God has done for them in Christ, rather than in what they can do for themselves. Luther came to believe that the main purpose of the law was to convict us of our utter helplessness as concerns the project of making ourselves acceptable to God. Anything that gives us confidence

2. For Disney-deprived readers, the reference is to the song in the film *Pinocchio*.
3. Goldsworthy, *Gospel-Centered Hermeneutics*, 50 (emphasis original).

in ourselves is ultimately a work of the law. This includes our intellectual efforts, "works" of the mind, an insight that led twentieth-century Lutheran theologians like Rudolf Bultmann (see below) to posit a connection between two senses of justification: soteriological and epistemological.

Lutheran theologians came to view justification as "the article by which the church stands or falls."[4] Philip Schaff calls justification by faith the "material principle" of the Reformation and the sum of the gospel.[5] It is essentially the retrieval of Paul's doctrine that God declares us righteous on the merits of Christ alone through faith alone. There has been much ferment over the doctrine of justification of late. This is not the place to rehearse debates over who gets Paul most nearly right: the Reformers or the New Perspective theologians. I have been there, done that.[6] What we can say is that Paul is addressing not a Jewish legalism narrowly conceived but the more radical and widespread tendency of sinners to justify themselves, either morally or intellectually. In nontheological contexts, "justification" means "to show or prove oneself right or reasonable." There is an inveterate human tendency to try to vindicate one's beliefs and behaviors through works, especially the work of rationalization. Luther's early attempt to make himself righteous before God was a paradigmatic case of rationalization, which we may safely associate with the theology of glory.

Justification by faith is not simply a doctrine but a key moment in the story of how God forgives sin and restores right relations with fallen human creatures. As such, justification is a key moment in the economy of grace. According to John Barclay, God's activity in Christ is sheer gift (2 Cor. 9:15).[7] Justification is not about having to become righteous, much less a reward for achieved righteousness, but, as it were, an *awarding* of righteousness (right-standing or right-relatedness): an undeserved divine gift that overturns and dismisses every scheme and concept of worth, be it human moral striving (the traditional

4. The phrase so worded comes from Johann Heinrich Alsted's *Theologia scholastica didacta* (Hanover, 1618). Luther said something very similar: *quia isto articulo stante stat Ecclesia, ruente ruit Ecclesia*, "Because if this article [of justification] stands, the church stands; if this article collapses, the church collapses" (*D. Martin Luthers Werke: Kritische Gesamtausgabe* [Weimar: H. Böhlau, 1883–2009], 40/3:352.3 [hereafter WA]).

5. Schaff, *Principle of Protestantism*, 80.

6. See Kevin J. Vanhoozer, "Wrighting the Wrongs of the Reformation? The State of the Union with Christ in St. Paul and Protestant Soteriology," in *Jesus, Paul, and the People of God: A Theological Dialogue with N. T. Wright*, ed. Nicholas Perrin and Richard B. Hays (Downers Grove, IL: IVP Academic, 2011), 235–58.

7. Barclay, *Paul and the Gift*, 6.

Lutheran view of the works of the law) or ethnicity (the New Perspective).[8] Barclay argues that Paul's theology of grace is oriented not simply toward individual transformation but toward the formation of communities. The primary concern in the present context is not with justification per se but with *sola fide* and, in particular, the role of faith vis-à-vis Word and Spirit in debates about the locus of authority and truth. The salient point is that Christ is the gift of God, and that this gift—being in Christ—is received by faith alone.[9]

Faith is the means by which believers personally appropriate the benefits of Christ's work; it is the way we lay hold of Christ, the way that everything he is and has done becomes ours. Calvin defines faith as "a firm and certain knowledge of God's benevolence toward us, founded upon the truth of the freely given promise in Christ both revealed to our minds and sealed upon our hearts through the Holy Spirit."[10] Faith does not derive from anything in us—as if credulity were a virtue that God then rewards—but is rather a response to the message of the gospel, effected by Word (gospel proclamation) and Spirit (1 Cor. 12:3; 1 Thess. 2:13). Indeed, faith "is the principal work of the Holy Spirit."[11] The Spirit uses human means to create faith: "So faith comes from hearing, and hearing through the word of Christ" (Rom. 10:17). *Sola fide* thus refers to the way Christians come to know and appropriate the gift of Jesus Christ via the human words of Scripture.

The Authority of the Word: Grammatical-Historical Philology

In his classic textbook *Protestant Biblical Interpretation*, Bernard Ramm sets out what he calls the "Protestant system of hermeneutics." He identifies inspiration as the foundation and edification as the goal, and under method, he discusses theological presuppositions such as the clarity of Scripture, progressive revelation, and the analogy of faith—no surprises here. However, he goes on to devote sixty pages—by far the longest section of the book (not counting his survey of "historical schools" of interpretation)—to the "philological principle."[12] By "philology" he means the "total program in understanding a

---

8. Ibid., 2.
9. Note that "being in Christ" encompasses both what traditional Reformation and New Perspective theologians want to affirm: individual salvation and a new faith community.
10. Calvin, *Institutes* III.2.7.
11. Calvin, *Institutes* III.1.4.
12. Bernard Ramm, *Protestant Biblical Interpretation*, 3rd rev. ed. (Grand Rapids: Baker, 1970), 113–63.

piece of literature."[13] It is a matter of bringing all the grammatical-historical procedures characteristic of good scholarship to bear on Scripture with the aim of discovering the original meaning.

Luther was indeed a philologist, and, like the Renaissance humanists, he sought to return *ad fontes* (to the sources): the original languages. Roland Bainton, Luther's biographer, explains that the breakthrough in Luther's wrestling match with Romans 1:17 was a function of his insight into the exact shades of meaning in Paul's text: "One understands why Luther could never join those who discarded the humanist tools of scholarship."[14] It was thanks to Erasmus's critical edition of the Greek New Testament that Luther discovered that the original Greek *dikaioō* (to *declare* righteous) in Romans 3:28 and elsewhere had been translated in the Vulgate with the Latin verb *iustificare* (to *make* righteous). Luther added the word "alone" (German: *al-lein*) to Paul's thesis statement in Romans 3:28 in his 1522 translation ("For we hold that one is justified by faith *alone* apart from the works of the law"), as if to put an exclamation point on the uselessness of works, and he defended his addition on the grounds that it brought out Paul's meaning.[15]

Luther's appeal to the original text—an exercise in philology—overturned the tables of Scripture's Latin translators. At first, Luther was unaware that he had unleashed a conflict over interpretive authority; he was convinced that his critique of indulgences would receive papal support. His critics quickly disabused him of his notion that philology trumps papal authority, and Luther eventually (and somewhat reluctantly) came to see with increasing clarity that the real issue underlying everything else was the locus of authority—the source of authoritative statements of the truth of the gospel.

Rupert Davies, in his study of the problem of authority at the time of the Reformation, wonders whether it was philology or psychology that led Luther to his insight about faith alone. Davies suggests that Luther's powerful realization of the gift-like nature of justification may have led to his affirming Romans "the purest Gospel of all"[16] and to his dismissal of the book of James as worthless because it contains no syllable of gospel. Davies grants that Luther set up Scripture as an objective standard with which to test and correct human interpretations, yet he judges Luther's attempt to provide a stable authority to

13. Ibid., 114.
14. Bainton, *Here I Stand*, 49.
15. Luther defended his decision in "Open Letter on Translating" (1530).
16. Cited in Davies, *Problem of Authority*, 35.

have failed because it does not reckon with the necessity to interpret the Word of God. Davies depicts Luther's situation in terms of a dilemma: "The great majority of Christians must either say that in theory they submit themselves to the Word of God, but that as they do not clearly know what that Word says they can make only provisional decisions . . . , or they must submit to the Word of God *as interpreted by someone more learned than themselves*."[17] This second alternative, the one usually taken, introduces a fatal note of subjectivity at a crucial juncture. Why, in the face of an authoritative translation/interpretation (the Latin Vulgate), does Luther prefer his own?[18]

The Testimony of the Spirit: Subjectivity and/or Certainty?

How ought mere Protestant Christians reply to the oft-mentioned criticism that "the 'principle of private judgment' is the very essence of Protestantism"?[19] Robert McAfee Brown calls this accusation one of the four "false images" of Protestantism.[20] Still, it's a good question. Luther appealed to Scripture against certain human traditions of the Roman Catholic Church, though eventually he had to contend with challenges to his own interpretations of Scripture (which his opponents called "opinions"). For example, Zwingli, in his 1522 treatise "The Clarity and Certainty of the Word of God," agreed with Luther that the Bible was authoritative and self-interpreting, but he disagreed with Luther over the interpretation of Jesus's words "This is my body" (Matt. 26:26). This was ground zero of what Alister McGrath dubs "Christianity's dangerous idea": "The question was not simply whether Luther or Zwingli was right: it was whether the emerging Protestant movement possessed the means to resolve such questions of biblical interpretation."[21] Is there no authoritative balm in Gilead?

17. Ibid., 57 (emphasis added).
18. According to Harriet Harris, this element of subjectivity is also a blind spot for evangelicals insofar as they identify God's Word with their interpretations: professing themselves wise (possessing objective philological knowledge), they became fundamentalists (possessing subjective psychological certainty only). See Harriet A. Harris, *Fundamentalism and Evangelicals* (Oxford: Clarendon, 1998).
19. Clifford Howell, *Of Sacraments and Sacrifice* (Collegeville, MN: Liturgical Press, 1953), 131.
20. Brown, *Spirit of Protestantism*, 8–11. The other three false images are that Protestantism is essentially a protest, a diluted Catholicism, and a matter of the intellect only (faith as assent to particular truths).
21. McGrath, *Christianity's Dangerous Idea*, 70. See also Gregory, *Unintended Reformation*, 86–96.

Enter the Holy Spirit. Pentecost marks the gift of the Holy Spirit, the ultimate author of Scripture, and thus the ultimate authority of its interpretation.
We are discussing *sola fide*, and for Calvin, "faith is the principal work of the
Holy Spirit."[22] Can an appeal to the Holy Spirit redeem the principle of private judgment? Is it because Luther and Calvin had the Holy Spirit that they
were in a position to arbitrate between interpretive options—for example, to
decide "when the Fathers conformed to Scripture and when they did not"?[23]
Is the Holy Spirit the principle of interpretive authority? Or does appealing
to the Holy Spirit simply relocate the problem of the locus of interpretive
authority to a different level, leaving Protestants to discern which interpretive
community the Spirit is actually guiding? It will be important to keep in mind
both levels of the conflict of interpretations: private and public.

According to Bernard Ramm, "*the Holy Spirit speaking in the* Scriptures . . . *is
the principle of authority for the Christian church.*"[24] Ramm contrasts this with
what he calls the "abbreviated Protestant principle," which he associates with
William Chillingworth's famous comment: "The Bible, I say the Bible only, is the
religion of Protestants."[25] It is abbreviated because although it correctly identifies
the *external* principle, it omits the *internal* principle: the witness of the Spirit.
Calvin is the clear hero in Ramm's *The Witness of the Spirit.*[26] Calvin avoids
both the Romanist error of positing an infallible church and the "Enthusiast"
(i.e., radical Anabaptist) error of founding certainty on an immediate revelation
of Scripture that was not bound to the contents of Scripture (remember Anne
Hutchinson). Calvin's mediating third way calls for preserving the union of
Word and Spirit, and he goes so far as to say that to separate them is "detestable
sacrilege"—this in a chapter entitled "Fanatics, Abandoning Scripture and Flying
Over to Revelation, Cast Down All the Principles of Godliness."[27]

That Calvin's notion of the internal witness of the Spirit stops short of
resolving the problem of interpretive authority becomes apparent when one
realizes that for him the primary function of the Spirit's testimony is to assure

22. Calvin, *Institutes* III.1.3.

23. Susan E. Schreiner, *Are You Alone Wise? The Search for Certainty in the Early Modern
Era* (Oxford: Oxford University Press, 2011), 82.

24. Bernard Ramm, *The Pattern of Religious Authority* (Grand Rapids: Eerdmans, 1957),
28 (emphasis original).

25. Cited in ibid., 29. The original quotation may be found in *The Works of William Chillingworth*, 10th ed. (London, 1742), 354.

26. Bernard Ramm, *The Witness of the Spirit: An Essay on the Contemporary Relevance of
the Internal Witness of the Holy Spirit* (Grand Rapids: Eerdmans, 1959), 12.

27. Calvin, *Institutes* I.9.1.

us *that* the Bible is God's Word (a witness to divine origin). The *testimonium* of the Spirit does not indicate *which* of the many interpretations on offer is the correct one (a witness to divine meaning). Calvin says that we recognize the Spirit in his agreement with Scripture: "He is the Author of the Scripture: he cannot vary and differ from himself."[28] Of course, what Scripture means is precisely what is at issue. Geneva, we have a problem.

Kathryn Tanner helpfully sets out the two sides of a "split understanding" of how the Spirit works.[29] Those on one side of the split stress the immediacy of the Spirit's work in human subjectivity: "the Spirit showed me"—a claim to self-evident divine validation that is hard for others to refute without getting into a schoolyard dispute ("Did not!" "Did so!"). To claim such divine inspiration for one's interpretation risks making one's hearing of the Spirit the trump card, rather than Scripture itself. Appealing to an experience of the Spirit is "an attack on the authority of all communally and socially validated forms of intellectual, religious, and moral achievement that take their rise from long, slow processes of training or learning."[30] Direct appeals to the Spirit's authority are shortcuts that lead back to another kind of abbreviated Protestant principle, where Spirit effectively eclipses Word.

On the other side of the split are those who emphasize the mediate nature of the Spirit's work in the course of ordinary human history. The Spirit's authority is not over and above other sources but at work in, under, and through them. Instead of resting in subjective certainty, those who take this view engage in a discerning process: "But test the spirits to see whether they are from God" (1 John 4:1). Stated positively: this view sees reason, study, grammar books, and so forth as what the Westminster Confession of Faith calls "the ordinary means" the Spirit uses to guide us into all truth (John 16:13).[31] And this is the crucial point: determining how the Spirit exercises his authority and leads the church into all truth. Here we may recall Luther's pointed retort, in his treatise "On the Bondage of the Will," to Erasmus citing interpretive disagreement as evidence of Scripture's lack of clarity: "The Holy Spirit is no skeptic."[32]

---

28. Calvin, *Institutes* I.9.2.

29. Kathryn Tanner, *Christ the Key* (Cambridge: Cambridge University Press, 2010), 274–301 (chap. 7, "The Working of the Spirit").

30. Ibid., 287.

31. Westminster Confession of Faith 1.7.

32. Martin Luther, "On the Bondage of the Will," in *Luther and Erasmus: Free Will and Salvation*, ed. E. Gordon Rupp and Philip S. Watson, Library of Christian Classics (Philadelphia: Westminster, 1969), 109.

If *sola fide* emphasizes the epistemological priority of the Spirit, should we locate the Spirit's work in individuals, the community, or both? The present chapter is primarily concerned to get the *principle* of authority right. In the next chapter I will consider in more detail the *pattern* of authority.

Faith and/or Criticism: Other Views

Sola fide means both that Christians are saved apart from works and that saving faith is occasioned only by the hearing of the Word of God in the power of the Spirit. What lies behind the Reformers' confidence that they were hearing the gospel correctly? More pointedly: What *authorizes* mere Protestant Christianity? The answer, I suggested, has something to do with philology and pneumatology—with the Spirit using words to effect faith. Before exploring this further, it will be helpful to examine three other strategies for understanding the relationship between faith, philology, and understanding.

Medieval Allegorizing

Luther inherited an ancient tradition of biblical interpretation, distilled and refined by Augustine, that valued allegorical interpretation because, no matter how obscure or apparently mundane the text, one could always find something to edify one's faith. According to the popular medieval rhyme, "The letter shows us what God and our fathers did; the allegory shows us where our faith is hid." One might have expected Luther to show some sympathy for this approach to the extent that he believed that the Bible ultimately presented the mystery of Christ in and through the history of Israel.[33] What concerned Luther was his perception that allegorizing could easily become a Trojan horse with which one could smuggle all sorts of mischief into the Scriptures. Luther worried that the authoritative Word of God was being overlaid, and thus distorted, by fanciful interpretations that imported human doctrines. In the hands of certain allegorizers, Scripture became the proverbial "nose of wax." Luther objected to the kind of allegorizing that undermines the philological principle inasmuch as it makes the Bible

---

33. On the difference between allegory and typology (the more Protestant way of reading for the spiritual or christological sense), see Kevin J. Vanhoozer, "Ascending the Mountain, Singing the Rock: Biblical Interpretation Earthed, Typed, and Transfigured," *Modern Theology* 28, no. 4 (2012): 781–803.

mean something other than what it says. Allegory locates the "real" (i.e., spiritual) meaning elsewhere than the literal sense, as the etymology of the Greek term suggests (*allos* [other] + *agoreuō* [I speak]). Ramm's verdict is succinct: "The Bible treated allegorically becomes putty in the hand of the exegete."[34] Clearly, allegorizing locates the principle of authority somewhere other than in the text.

Modern Historical Criticism

Whereas medieval scholars believed that faith was the key to unlocking the meaning of Scripture, the tendency of modern biblical scholars is to think that faith either is unnecessary or actually impedes the historical and "scientific" investigation of the biblical text. Spinoza lays down the rule of no-faith: "The rule of [biblical] interpretation must be nothing more than the natural light of reason which is common to all men, and not some light above nature or any external authority."[35] The ideal exegete, on this view, is the historian; whether or not the historian is a person of faith is merely incidental.

The tug-of-war between Christian faith and historical criticism dominated the debate over biblical interpretation for much of the modern era, culminating in the nineteenth and twentieth centuries.[36] "Liberal" biblical scholars claimed to discover historical errors in Scripture: after all, to be critical is to be aware that the reality (i.e., what actually happened) may be different from appearances (i.e., what the Bible said happened). "Conservative" biblical scholars argued that the same critical tools, when wielded by persons of faith, could equally well be used to prove the Bible true.[37] Many biblical scholars thus found themselves "between" faith and criticism.[38]

A few twentieth-century biblical scholars retrieved *sola fide* in a surprising new way that has as much to do with epistemological as soteriological

34. Ramm, *Protestant Biblical Interpretation*, 30.

35. Benedict de Spinoza, *Theological-Political Treatise*, ed. Jonathan Israel, trans. Michael Silverthorne and Jonathan Israel (Cambridge: Cambridge University Press, 2007), 116.

36. For a handy collection of the seminal texts, see Darren Sarisky, ed., *Theology, History, and Biblical Interpretation: Modern Readings* (London: Bloomsbury T&T Clark, 2015).

37. See, for example, James K. Hoffmeier and Dennis R. Magary, eds., *Do Historical Matters Matter to Faith? A Critical Appraisal of Modern and Postmodern Approaches to Scripture* (Wheaton: Crossway, 2012).

38. See Mark A. Noll, *Between Faith and Criticism: Evangelicals, Scholarship, and the Bible in America*, 2nd ed. (Vancouver: Regent College Publishing, 2004); Christopher M. Hays and Christopher B. Ansberry, eds., *Evangelical Faith and the Challenge of Historical Criticism* (Grand Rapids: Baker Academic, 2013).

justification. For these scholars, faith is necessary, not to perceive the mystery hidden in redemptive history, as in allegorizing, nor to prove the historical worth of the biblical narrative, but rather, and on the contrary, to demystify history, as in demythologizing. Rudolf Bultmann believed that he had inherited the Reformers' exegetical mantle: "Indeed, de-mythologizing is a task parallel to that performed by Paul and Luther . . . the radical application of the doctrine of justification by faith to the sphere of knowledge and thought."[39] Like justification by faith, demythologizing "destroys every longing for security."[40] Bultmann views faith as radical insecurity, epistemological as well as existential, and thus the demand to abandon every effort to make our existence, or our knowledge of God, secure.[41]

Gerhard Ebeling, one of Bultmann's students, went even further, arguing that the historical-critical method is the hermeneutical counterpart of *sola fide*, and hence a distinctly Protestant form of biblical interpretation. In Ebeling's hands, historical criticism becomes a crucial aspect of faith's abandonment of trust in "works of the flesh" (i.e., inherited tradition): "The *sola fide* destroys all secretly docetic views of revelation which evade the historicalness of revelation by making it . . . a sacred area from which the critical historical method must be anxiously disbarred."[42]

Postmodern Pragmatism

Christians today inhabit a situation in which there are not only multiple biblical interpretations but also multiple *ways of reading* the Bible jostling for position in the academy (less so in the church, where inductive Bible study remains strong). Brad Gregory and Christian Smith are correct at least in this: we live in a time of pervasive interpretive plurality. Protestants are coping in different ways. Some continue to pursue the way of criticism, but with believing rather than agnostic presuppositions. For these conservatives, objective knowledge is still the goal of faith's search for textual and historical understanding.

39. Rudolf Bultmann, *Jesus Christ and Mythology* (New York: Scribner, 1958), 84.
40. Ibid.
41. Although Bultmann bears superficial resemblance to a fideist (i.e., one who holds that faith needs no rational justification), Wolfhart Pannenberg says that the better way to understand him is in terms of his insistence on "the self-authenticating Word of God which demands obedience" (*Revelation as History*, [London: Macmillan, 1968], 9).
42. Gerhard Ebeling, "The Significance of the Critical Historical Method for Church and Theology in Protestantism," in Sarisky, *Theology, History, and Biblical Interpretation*, 213–14.

More recently, some theologians have appealed to *sola fide* to support not historical criticism but pragmatism. They argue that the idea of "believing criticism" is still in thrall to modern philosophy and its ideal of the omnicompetence of universal reason. They acknowledge that believing criticism seems preferable to an anything-goes hermeneutical relativism, yet they also think that the Reformation's search for the "plain sense" created a two-headed hermeneutic monster: "a proliferation of interpretations and the multiplication of interpretive communities."[43]

According to its postmodern critics, the tempter in the garden of modernity is the ideal of objective knowledge, personified by E. D. Hirsch, a hermeneutic theorist who holds out the forbidden fruit of authorial intention: the possibility that interpreters can manage the conflict of interpretations, gain objective knowledge, and thus gain control of what would otherwise be an unmanageable hermeneutical chaos. What's so bad about biblical exegetes striving for objectivity in interpretation? The problem, as Merold Westphal sees it, is that human interpretation requires acts of "faith," by which he means the acceptance of beliefs and practices whose rightness cannot be established from some neutral or objective point of view. The one indubitable fact about biblical hermeneutics is that its interpreters do not agree on what the text means. Consequently, what begins as faithful criticism ends in interpretive pride, and often violence: "Anxiety about relativism morphs into arrogance."[44] James K. A. Smith, a philosopher at Calvin College, agrees: the knee-jerk reaction to relativism is to seek absoluteness, but the claim to have absolute or even objective knowledge comes close to claiming that one knows as God knows. Smith thinks that we need to come clean and acknowledge the finitude and contingency of our creaturehood, and thus the relativity of our perspectives and interpretations, of texts and everything else.

If individual interpreters cannot achieve objectivity through philology, what stops the slide into interpretive relativism? The short answer: faith community traditions.[45] Westphal draws on the philosopher Hans-Georg Gadamer to remind us that we are not autonomous but rather *traditioned* individuals,

43. James K. A. Smith, foreword to *Whose Community? Which Interpretation? Philosophical Hermeneutics for the Church*, by Merold Westphal, The Church and Postmodern Culture (Grand Rapids: Baker Academic, 2009), 10.

44. Westphal, *Whose Community?*, 47.

45. So James K. A. Smith: "If pragmatism helps us understand the conditions of our finitude, then our trajectory should be 'catholic'" (*Who's Afraid of Relativism? Community, Contingency, and Creaturehood* [Grand Rapids: Baker Academic, 2014], 18).

members of communities that shape the way we see, think, and talk about things.[46] This position is postmodern because it rejects the autonomy of modern liberal individualism, and pragmatist because what bears authority is not universal reason but community practice. The basic idea is that of the philosopher Ludwig Wittgenstein. Meaning is use, and we learn how to speak about things by participating in the language games associated with a community's form of life: "We make our way in the world on the basis of a know-*how* that is acquired through practice, absorbed from our immersion in a community of practice that 'trains' us how to grapple with the world rather than 'mirroring' reality."[47] For example, one learns the meaning of "googly" by participating in the game of cricket, either by playing or by watching a game with someone who understands it (I still do not).

There is much to appreciate in this postmodern retrieval of community tradition. Yet the problem—the conflict of interpretations and interpretive communities—remains: for if our grasp of meaning and truth, and our sense of what makes for a "good" interpretation, depends on the faith community to which we happen to belong, then for all intents and purposes what bears authority is the interpretive community. But *which one?* It is highly ironic that Protestants, of all people, are now appealing to *sola fide* in support of the authority of interpretive communities. Moreover, it is far from clear how postmodern pragmatists could explain Martin Luther, or any person who launches a prophetic critique against the tradition of the interpretive community that formed him or her. We need to go back to the drawing board, which in this case means the Reformers' retrieval of Scripture, if we are rightly to understand the relationship of faith, interpretation, and authority.

The Principle of Authority

Faith can refer both to believing trust (faith's subjective disposition) and to that which is believed (faith's objective deposit). In Luther's case, he came by faith to the conclusion that justification by faith is the article on which the church stands or falls. Luther appealed to the Spirit's impress of the written word upon his conscience: "Here I stand." While it is probably too simplistic to draw a straight line between Luther's appeal to conscience and the modern

---

46. Westphal, *Whose Community?*, 74.
47. Smith, *Who's Afraid of Relativism?*, 105.

ideal of individual autonomy, the critics of the Reformation whom we have examined nevertheless see a shared tendency toward self-reliance: call it the haughtiness of the lone Protestant interpreter. The postmodern explosion (deconstruction) of the myth of the detached knowing subject has swung the pendulum back toward authority and tradition. Yet, in the final analysis, is not the appeal to communal tradition as potentially pluralistic as the appeal to individual conscience? Remember those thirty-eight thousand denominations tallied by the *Atlas of Global Christianity.*

Is interpretive authority located in the individual's conscience (whose?) or the community's tradition (which one?)? Luther took his stand as an individual against the authorized community tradition of his day. In order to respond to the charge that the Reformation loosed interpretive skepticism (and relativism) upon the world, I want now to examine the *principle* of interpretive authority that is part and parcel of mere Protestant Christianity. I do so in three steps, asking: (1) What is authority? (2) How does it relate to rationality? (3) What role does it play in the process of interpretation? Then, after clarifying the principle of authority, the next chapter turns to *sola scriptura* and the *pattern* of interpretive authority, giving special attention to the role the interpretive community plays.

The Principle of Authority: The Triune God

Authority presently gets little respect. A 2014 Gallup poll showed that public faith in the US Congress had reached a historic low, with just 6 percent of Americans approving, which is lower than their faith in those who sell used cars. People today often associate authority with the abuse of power or with constraints on personal freedoms. People resent authority most when it is felt to be an oppressive power that impinges from the outside on one's own power to believe or act as one likes. It is a top-down imposition of force, either of the state or of the empire—in any case, something powerful enough to crush the individual, body and soul. Yet this is only the pathological face of political authority, distorted into a coercive authoritarianism. A biblical-theological analysis of authority views things quite differently.

Divine Authority: The Triune Lord

Authority is rightful say-so, the power to commend belief and command obedience. Authority is linked to authorship, for who has more right to say-so over something than the one who conceived and originated it? "For there is no authority except from God, and those that exist have been instituted by God" (Rom. 13:1). God is originator of the created order, the Creator of all things, the "Maker of all things visible and invisible" and hence the Author of being in general: God "calls into existence the things that do not exist" (Rom. 4:17). God also initiates covenantal relationships and institutions: "I will establish my covenant with you" (Gen. 6:18); "On that day the LORD made a covenant with Abram" (Gen. 15:18). He is the Lover of a set-apart people, his "treasured possession" (Exod. 19:5; Deut. 7:6), and the Lord of the covenant that binds them together.[48] All three persons of the Trinity are involved in everything that God does, creating and covenanting alike: *omnia opera trinitatis ad extra indivisa sunt* (all the external works of the Trinity are indivisible).[49] This includes exercising authority.

The authority principle in Christianity is the Triune God in verbal communicative action: what bears authority is the voice of God communicating the Word of God to the creatures and people of God. Authority (rightful say-so) must be *said* because there is nothing to be believed or obeyed apart from meaningful content. Authority involves *rightful power* because God knows everything that he has made. As Maker of heaven and earth (including human beings), God has constituted the essential nature of things, determined their proper function, and ordered their final purpose. God has the right to command human obedience because he is the Author of human freedom.

In the beginning God's creative Word instituted created order (e.g., "let there be light"; "let the earth sprout vegetation"). "The earth is the LORD's, and everything in it" (Ps. 24:1 NIV). The Lord God is the authority (the rule maker and referee) because he is the originator of the game. Without rules, we could not play chess. The same is true of any other game, and of more serious human activities and institutions, like marriage. It follows, then, that authority—rightful say-so—is not a coercive force but an enabling condition of free play.

God knows the end for which we were created, and his authoritative words are intended for our good. Far from constraining human freedom, authority

48. For a helpful discussion of God's authority as an aspect of his covenant lordship, see John M. Frame, *The Doctrine of God* (Phillipsburg, NJ: P&R, 2002), 83–89.

49. This was a classic formula of patristic theology. Philip Cary calls it "Augustine's Rule" ("On Behalf of Classical Trinitarianism: A Critique of Rahner on the Trinity," *Thomist* 56 [1992]: 368).

is a necessary condition for human flourishing. Why is there something rather than nothing? Because God freely chose to share his own life with what is not God and thereby enlarge what was already a perfect fellowship. Divine authority and human answerability are two sides to the same covenantal relationship. Authority is not something negative (coercive force); nor is it part of the punishment for Adam's fall. Authority is rather part and parcel of God's good created order, an enabling condition, like wisdom, for freedom's flourishing. To anticipate: *Biblical authority orients freedom to the new reality that is in Christ Jesus.* Oliver O'Donovan writes, "Authority is the objective correlate of freedom. It is what we encounter in the world which makes it meaningful for us to act."[50] Think again of the chess game: the rules of chess are precisely what make the game susceptible of so many fascinating variations. It has been said that chess is war, but I say unto you: chess is authorized action, regulated freedom.

DIVINE AUTHORIZATION: THE HUMAN CREATURE

"Authorization" is the key term. "To be an authority is to be authorized by someone or something beyond oneself."[51] Listen again to Paul: "There is no authority except from God, and those that exist have been instituted by God" (Rom. 13:1). The Greek word translated as "instituted" (*tassō*) means "to assign to a position, to appoint." What authority authorizes is an office: "To have authority is to exercise an office and to do so because someone has authorized it."[52] All true authorities—all authorizing agencies—are divinely appointed to their respective offices. A special concern of the present book is the "office" of biblical interpretation. Who are the Bible's authorized interpreters, and who/what authorizes them?

The theme of authority appears early in the biblical story. God created Adam and Eve in his image and then instituted them as ruled rulers: "Fill the earth and subdue it, and have dominion over the fish of the sea and over the birds of the heavens and over every living thing that moves on the earth" (Gen. 1:28). No sooner do humans appear on the scene than God appoints

---

50. Oliver O'Donovan, *Resurrection and Moral Order: An Outline for Evangelical Ethics* (Grand Rapids: Eerdmans, 1986), 122.

51. Victor Lee Austin, *Up with Authority: Why We Need Authority to Flourish as Human Beings* (London: T&T Clark, 2010), 141–42.

52. David T. Koyzis, *We Answer to Another: Authority, Office, and the Image of God* (Eugene, OR: Pickwick, 2014), 138.

them his vice-regents on earth: "The most basic office we hold is indeed that of divine image."[53] Human beings have been divinely authorized to act as authorities in the world—to have dominion over acreage in Eden—and we image God when we exercise authority rightly.

Adam and Eve were authorized and answerable agents, charged with ruling the earth in God's place. They were free to do what they wanted as long as they respected the belief-guiding and action-guiding words of God. Authority over earth has nothing to do with imposing one's will to power on creatures or creation. On the contrary, God authorized the first couple "to accomplish a particular task, to act in a particular capacity, to seek a particular end."[54] The creation mandate authorized Adam and Eve to preserve the integrity and develop the potential of the created order. In short: they were *authorized to exercise a kind of dominion over a particular domain for a particular duration.*[55]

God's Word authorizes certain ways that human beings are to live together before him in order to flourish. This is worth pondering: the primary purpose of authority is to provide persons with what is needed to help others to flourish. Imagine a sinless symphony orchestra, a musical society, made up of many members.[56] Would an orchestra made up of only saints and no sinners need authority or not in order to flourish? The answer should be obvious: of course it would! One person must stand over, or at least in front of, the others and decide how to, well, *conduct* this society—for example, how fast to go and how loud or soft to play. For there is seldom one right answer: decisions have to be made between equally legitimate options. It is not because the musicians are selfish that the conductor has to exercise authority; rather, the conductor's authority is simply a necessary condition of the musicians playing together and thus realizing a good that, without the conductor, would be beyond their grasp. Authority is essentially *"the power in charge of unifying common action through rules binding for all."*[57] This social aspect of authority will loom large when we consider the role of biblical interpretation in the church.

---

53. Ibid.

54. Jonathan Leeman, *The Church and the Surprising Offense of God's Love: Reintroducing the Doctrines of Church Membership and Discipline* (Wheaton: Crossway, 2010), 140.

55. The resemblance to Goldsworthy's description of the kingdom as God's *people* in God's *place* under God's *rule* is intentional. See Goldsworthy, *Gospel and Kingdom*, 53.

56. This example comes from Austin, *Up with Authority*, 16–19.

57. Yves R. Simon, *A General Theory of Authority* (Notre Dame, IN: University of Notre Dame Press, 1980), 47.

Divine Authority Usurped: Autonomous Adam

We see, then, that divine authority provides the framework for meaningful human action and the possibility for freedom to flourish. Because God knew and desired what was best for Adam and Eve, their consistent response ought to have been Mary's "Let it be to me according to your word" (Luke 1:38). Instead of being empowered by the divine authorization, as God intended, our human parents rebelled. Authority became disordered when Adam and Eve decided to do something for which they were not authorized. The primal sin, however, was Adam's failure to exercise oversight: the fall was both a violation of the law and an *abdication of office*.

It was also a spectacular failure in interpretation. The serpent (an unauthorized interpreter) first misquotes the divine prohibition not to eat of one tree and instead makes it a blanket prohibition (Gen. 3:1). Eve corrects him as to the wording, so the serpent questions, then contradicts, the meaning of the words, making them say something that God did not say. And the evening and the morning were the first day of the hermeneutics of suspicion.

A false picture of freedom—"You will be like God" (Gen. 3:5)—took Eve captive. The serpent's claim was not ordered to reality: it was a lie, and falsehood always fails to deliver on its promise. Though Adam and Eve were already God-like, created in God's image, they reached for more and were left clutching thin air. There is no true freedom in refusing the created order or denying reality. Such is the fruit of autonomy, the attempt to authorize one's own authority and order. Adam and Eve were the first heretics (I use the word in the sense of its Greek verbal derivation, *haireomai*, "to choose for oneself"). To pick and choose which words to heed and which to ignore is effectively to deprive those words of authority. The problem today, as Peter Berger describes it, is that the world is characterized by a pluralization of interpretive traditions such that "picking and choosing become imperative."[58] Hence the title of his book: *The Heretical Imperative*. As we have seen, Brad Gregory lays this heretical imperative—the condition of having to choose between a hyperplurality of interpretive options without a clear criterion—at the Reformers' doorstep. But Adam's usurpation of divine authority is hardly the end of the biblical story.

---

58. Peter L. Berger, *The Heretical Imperative: Contemporary Possibilities of Religious Affirmation* (Garden City, NY: Anchor, 1979), 25.

DIVINE AUTHORITY RESTORED: JESUS CHRIST, *SUMMA AUCTORITAS*

Several passages in the Gospels have an important bearing on our under-standing of authority, especially the risen Christ's stunning claim: "All au-thority in heaven and on earth has been given to me" (Matt. 28:18). Paul says something similar about the ascended Christ, seated at God's right hand in the heavenly places, "far above all rule and authority and power and domin-ion" (Eph. 1:20–21). There is no limit to the domain of dominical authority.

Jesus sums up in his person the offices of prophet, priest, and king by which God administered his covenant with Israel, offices that had provided the nation with a structure of authority. All three offices served the function of authorizing life under God's rule. God's Spirit, who came upon those who were anointed, was with Jesus from the moment of his conception, and all the offices that define human being converge and are fulfilled in him. Jesus's authority is distinct because no officer before him—neither prophet, priest, nor king—could have said, "L'état, c'est moi" the way Jesus could, for the kingdom of God came in his own person and proclamation. *God the Father authorized Jesus to instantiate the kingdom of heaven on earth.*

Jesus fulfills his priestly office by serving as the tabernacle of God made flesh (John 1:14), the lamb of God (John 1:29), the high priest superior to the order of Aaron (Heb. 7:11), and by exercising authority to forgive sins (Matt. 9:6// Mark 2:10//Luke 5:24). He exercises the prophetic office by speaking the truth, authoritatively interpreting the law: "For he taught them as one who had author-ity, and not as the scribes" (Mark 1:22).[59] And he exercises his kingly office when he rebukes some rogue waves, prompting those with him to say, "Who then is this, that even the wind and sea obey him?" (Mark 4:41). An even better example is the story of Jesus's healing of a centurion's servant. The centurion does not want to bother Jesus to come all the way to his house, so he sends friends with a message for Jesus: "But say the word, and let my servant be healed. For I too am a man set under authority, with soldiers under me: and I say to one, 'Go,' and he goes; and to another, 'Come,' and he comes; and to my servant, 'Do this,' and he does it" (Luke 7:7–8). The centurion understands the nature of authority and perceives that Jesus has been divinely authorized. Indeed, Jesus responds, "I tell you, not even in Israel have I found such faith" (Luke 7:9).

59. Note that Satan challenges Jesus's authority by twisting and denying God's Word and Jesus's interpretation of it (see Matt. 4:1–11//Luke 4:1–13). So has it always been with the "father of lies" (John 8:44) and "deceiver of the whole world" (Rev. 12:9).

The authority principle in Christianity, I have said, is the Triune God in communicative action. Jesus Christ is the Son of God, the Word who was with God and was God, made flesh—one of us. The Son sees, is, and does everything the Father sees, is, and does, with one exception: the Father eternally begets the Son; the Son is eternally begotten.[60] Jesus alone is thus both able and authorized to reveal the Father: he is the image of the invisible God (Col. 1:15). Stated differently: Jesus is God's personal and eternal Word made human and historical. He is the eternal divine communicative activity—the light and life of God—become incarnate (Heb. 1:2). This explains why all authority in heaven and on earth has been given to him: he is the divine Son in and through whom all things have been made (Col. 1:16) *and remade*—that is, made right and rightly ordered.[61]

Divine Authority Delegated: Apostolicity

"All authority in heaven and on earth has been given to me" (Matt. 28:18). In light of such a claim, it is easy to understand why some theologians want to locate all authority in Christ. For example, P. T. Forsyth locates authority not so much in the Bible as in the gospel, alluding to William Chillingworth's famous phrase even as he turns it against him: "The Gospel, and the Gospel alone, is the religion of Protestants."[62] Perhaps Ramm had Forsyth in mind when he wrote, "The difficulties of a single principle of authority (rather than a pattern of authority) appear clearly in discussions of the authority of Jesus Christ. Frequently the authority of Christ and the authority of the Scriptures are opposed."[63]

This opposition of *sola scriptura* and *solus Christus* is deeply to be regretted—and studiously to be avoided. The Gospels show Jesus *delegating* his authority to others. In Matthew 10 Jesus gives the twelve disciples the authority to heal disease and exorcise demons, authorizing them to do the same

---

60. See John 5:19 ("For whatever the Father does, that the Son does likewise") and the extended reflection on this passage in Kevin J. Vanhoozer, "At Play in the Theodrama of the Lord: The Triune God of the Gospel," in *Theatrical Theology: Explorations in Performing the Faith*, ed. Trevor Hart and Wesley Vander Lugt (Eugene, OR: Cascade, 2014), 1–29.

61. See O'Donovan, *Resurrection and Moral Order*, 140–62 ("The Authority of Christ").

62. P. T. Forsyth, "The Cross as the Final Seat of Authority," in *The Gospel and Authority: A P. T. Forsyth Reader*, ed. Marvin W. Anderson (Minneapolis: Augsburg, 1971), 159. Chillingworth wrote, "The Bible, I say the Bible only, is the religion of Protestants" (*Works of William Chillingworth*, 354).

63. Ramm, *Pattern of Religious Authority*, 46.

kinds of things he had been doing in the two previous chapters. They have a share in Jesus's own authority: "He *appointed* twelve (whom he also named apostles)" (Mark 3:14). The number "twelve" is surely symbolic, alluding to the twelve tribes of Israel. Jesus is here authorizing a new community, with new officers (cf. Eph. 2:19–20). They are commissioned officers or "envoys": "ones sent" (Gk. *apostolos*) with a purpose.[64] Jesus commissions the apostles not only to do the kinds of things he has done but also to preach (Mark 3:14) and "proclaim the kingdom of God" (Luke 9:2). He not only appoints but also promises to *anoint* the apostles with the Holy Spirit, thereby fully empowering them for their office, in particular, to be Jesus's witnesses (Acts 1:8)—this in accordance with Jesus's earlier promise to send his disciples a "Helper" from the Father (John 15:26). The Spirit will guide them into all truth, for the Spirit "will not speak on his own authority, but whatever he hears he will speak" (John 16:13).

Jesus sends his apostles to teach others to observe what Jesus has commanded his disciples (Matt. 28:20). They are his appointed spokesmen, his delegated authorities who, with his Spirit, will speak his truth. Jesus notes the parallel between his own commission from the Father and his commissioning of his apostles: "As the Father has sent me, even so I am sending you" (John 20:21). *The apostles are authorized interpreters of Jesus's person and work, inscribers of the meaning of the Christ event whose written discourse is part and parcel of the triune economy of communicative action.*[65] It therefore makes no sense to pit the authority of the gospel against apostolic authority.

Paul too is an apostle who has received his authorization from the risen Lord. The salient point is that Jesus delegates his authority, and that "apostleship" refers to an office that authorizes publication of the Christ event.[66] What characterizes the apostolic office is an authorization to transmit eyewitness testimony as to the meaning and significance of the gospel. This is the

64. On the origins of the term, see J. B. Lightfoot, "The Name and Office of Apostle," in *The Epistle of St. Paul to the Galatians*, 10th ed. (London: Macmillan, 1986), 92–101; F. H. Agnew, "The Origin of the NT Apostle-Concept: A Review of Research," *Journal of Biblical Literature* 105 (1986): 75–96.

65. Though I cannot argue the point here, I believe that "inspiration" qualifies not the disciples as persons but their written discourse. See further Kevin J. Vanhoozer, "The Apostolic Discourse and Its Developments," in *Scripture's Doctrine and Theology's Bible: How the New Testament Shapes Christian Dogmatics*, ed. Markus Bockmuehl and Alan J. Torrance (Grand Rapids: Baker Academic, 2008), 191–207.

66. See John Howard Schütz, *Paul and the Anatomy of Apostolic Authority* (Cambridge: Cambridge University Press, 1975).

status—"apostle of Christ" (1 Thess. 2:6)—that Paul is so concerned to defend vis-à-vis his detractors at Corinth: "Am I not an apostle? Have I not seen Jesus our Lord?" (1 Cor. 9:1). At issue in Corinth is precisely Paul's apostolic authority, namely, his authorization to hand on the truth of Jesus Christ on Christ's behalf and at Christ's behest. Paul knows of no higher appeal than Jesus's authorization of his apostolic ministry (2 Cor. 10:8).

Epistemic Authority: Self-Reliance versus Trust in Others

Apostolicity is one of the four traditional marks of the church, along with oneness, holiness, and catholicity. Minimally, apostolicity means that a church in whatever place and time must be in line with the apostles if it is to be considered genuinely Christian.[67] The apostolic office was that of faithful transmission, either by recording eyewitness testimony or by transmitting received tradition (1 Cor. 15:3). The apostles were not authors in the sense of originators of a new teaching; rather, their office was to hand on what they had witnessed for themselves or received from Jesus. Søren Kierkegaard distinguished the apostle from the genius: the genius discovers what she knows through unaided reason; in contrast, the apostle discovers what he knows by being told.[68] What about us, their readers? How do we discover the meaning of what we have been told? I will briefly consider three possibilities before offering my own account.[69]

EPISTEMIC ACCESS TO APOSTOLIC AUTHORITY: THREE UNSATISFYING OPTIONS

By "epistemic access" I mean a method for coming to know something—in this case, the meaning of the authoritative apostolic message. The traditional Roman Catholic answer is to appeal to apostolic succession: as Jesus handed on his authority to the apostles, so the apostles handed on their authority to others, often by literally laying hands on them. Authority

67. There are two possible meanings of "in line with" the apostles: a literal lineage (i.e., apostolic succession) or a consistency with the apostles' teaching. In this context I mean the latter.

68. Søren Kierkegaard, "On the Difference between a Genius and an Apostle," in *The Present Age; and, Two Minor Ethico-Religious Treatises*, trans. Alexander Dru and Walter Lowrie (Oxford: Oxford University Press, 1940). See also Kevin J. Vanhoozer, "The Trials of Truth: Mission, Martyrdom, and the Epistemology of the Cross," in *First Theology: God, Scripture, and Hermeneutics* (Downers Grove, IL: IVP Academic, 2001), 337–73.

69. These three correspond roughly to the medieval, modern, and postmodern options for relating faith and criticism examined above.

on this view is a function of an unbroken chain of communication. However, as Herman Bavinck pointedly notes, "there is not a word in Scripture about such an apostolic succession."[70] Further, as we will see in the next chapter, this view fails to preserve sufficiently the distinction between inspired (infallible) apostolic writing and noninspired (fallible) postapostolic interpretation.

Second, and on the other end of the spectrum, is the scholarly option, which locates authority with the expert. We live in an age of specialization, and today the only authorities that many people respect are those who have gained technological sophistication in their field (including biblical scholarship). Does having knowledge—epistemic authority—replace being appointed to an office? Stated differently: Does superior intellectual knowledge—of ancient Near Eastern archaeology, for example—constitute scholars as *authorized* biblical interpreters? Interestingly, Jesus himself was unimpressed by a kind of biblical scholarship that knew the Scriptures but not him (Matt. 22:29// Mark 12:24; John 5:39).

The third option is fundamentalism. Fundamentalists refuse to bow the knee either to popes or to modern biblical scholarship, emphasizing instead the exclusive authority of the Bible—as read by fundamentalist leaders. Well, they don't say that exactly, but this is precisely the concern of both evangelicals like Bernard Ramm and liberals like James Barr.[71] They worry that fundamentalism is an interpretive community that covers its own presuppositional tracks. Their leaders proclaim, "The Bible says," but then they deliver their own tradition-bound interpretations (of course, fundamentalists are not the only ones guilty of that). Kathleen Boone here evokes Stanley Fish, for whom interpretive communities "are made up of those who share interpretive strategies not for reading (in the conventional sense) but for writing texts, for instituting their properties and assigning their intentions."[72] Boone criticizes fundamentalists for encouraging community traditions that authorize their own interpretations and then identify them with Scripture: "Thus pastors are seen not as authorities in their own right, but as conduits of the text."[73] She notes the irony of the fundamentalist position: "Fundamentalists are caught

70. Bavinck, *Reformed Dogmatics*, 4:324.

71. See esp. Ramm, *Witness of the Spirit*, 123–27; and James Barr, *Fundamentalism* (London: SCM, 1981).

72. Fish, *Is There a Text?*, 171.

73. Kathleen C. Boone, *The Bible Tells Them So: The Discourse of Protestant Fundamentalism* (Albany: State University of New York Press, 1989), 87.

in the very trap they try to avoid. They must resort to some form of institutional authority, unless they want to grant authority to the interpretations of any reader whatsoever who espouses the inerrancy doctrine."[74] Regardless of the accuracy of Boone's description, the danger of conflating God's Word with our interpretation of it is real—and not for fundamentalists only. What is worrisome to Boone about fundamentalists in particular, however, is their apparent blind spot to the fact that they *are* interpreting: "Only by concealing their role as interpreters are fundamentalist authorities able to wield their immense power over ordinary believers."[75]

Each of the aforementioned approaches locates authority in a particular interpretive community: the Vatican (the magisterium of the Roman Catholic Church); the Society of Biblical Literature (the professional organization of biblical scholars); independent institutions run by (often self-appointed) ecclesial magnates (fundamentalism). Each of these interpretive communities in different ways appropriates for itself the authority that attaches to the biblical text. Put differently: each of these interpretive communities assumes authority over the text by authoring or "overstanding" it (i.e., saying what it means).[76] What, then, should an ordinary believer do? Whose interpretation of the apostolic testimony is authoritative, and why? Two texts from Ephesians will help to guide us through these epistemological thickets.

Epistemic Self-Reliance

"Let no one deceive you with empty words" (Eph. 5:6). Taken out of context, Paul's warning might be used by some as a justification for systematic doubt. "Let no one deceive you" is the mantra of those who need to see or prove everything for themselves, people who are so afraid of being taken in that they take nothing on trust, people who are happy only when they serve as their own authority principles.[77]

---

74. Ibid., 72.

75. Ibid., 95.

76. To state the issue in yet another way: each of the three interpretive communities examined resembles a social constructivist epistemology in which what counts as knowledge (i.e., the meaning of the biblical text) is constructed by the scientific or interpretive community. The challenge that accompanies such claims (in this case, that God's Word is community dependent) is knowing how to guard against a relativism of both knowledge and truth. See further Peter L. Berger and Thomas Luckmann, *The Social Construction of Reality: A Treatise in the Sociology of Knowledge* (Garden City, NY: Doubleday, 1966).

77. As I will argue below, the reality is more complex: the question is not whether or not to trust—some trust in something beyond ourselves is inevitable—but rather *what* or *whom* to trust.

Is Paul recommending a policy whereby we systematically doubt what others tell us? Is the apostle Paul a first-century Cartesian rationalist? May it never be! The context of Paul's caution about not being deceived is intended not as a general epistemological maxim but rather as a warning to the Ephesians not to be influenced by the surrounding pagan culture characterized by sexual immorality and other types of disobedience.

Even so, how do we explain a figure like Martin Luther? Is there something about mere Protestant Christians that predisposes them to be epistemological lone rangers—always protesting, but never coming to tradition? When it comes to individual knowers, it is important to distinguish epistemic autonomy from epistemic responsibility. In what follows I am borrowing liberally but not uncritically from Linda Zagzebski's *Epistemic Authority: A Theory of Trust, Authority, and Autonomy in Belief.*

Zagzebski analyzes the attitude of what she calls the "extreme epistemic egoist": a person who refuses to take anything on authority.[78] Interestingly, extreme epistemic egoists can be either rationalists or fideists: they can stubbornly rely either on their own reasoning or on their own believing, independent of any reasons. While it may be tempting to associate fideism with *sola fide*, it would also be a mistake, at least in the present context. As commonly used, "fideism" refers to a reliance on faith *against* reason. Alvin Plantinga defines "fideism" as "the exclusive or basic reliance upon faith alone, accompanied by a consequent disparagement of reason."[79] By way of contrast, *sola fide*, when rightly understood, is compatible with a kind of rationality, as we will soon see.[80]

The problem with extreme epistemic egoism of either variety is that it does not do away with but simply relocates trust, namely, in oneself—a dubious prospect, especially for Christians who affirm total depravity. Zagzebski makes a compelling argument that individuals have a responsibility to be epistemically conscientious: to use their faculties to the best of their abilities in order to get the truth.[81] What counts here is not just an individual's

78. An extreme epistemic egoist "refuses to take the fact that someone has a given belief as a reason to believe it herself" (Zagzebski, *Epistemic Authority*, 52).

79. Alvin Plantinga, "Reason and Belief in God," in *Faith and Rationality: Reason and Belief in God*, ed. Alvin Plantinga and Nicholas Wolterstorff (Notre Dame, IN: University of Notre Dame Press, 1983), 87.

80. "Fideism" is often used as a pejorative term. I am using it in a technical sense in contrast to "rationalism" in order to highlight two different ways a person can exercise trust in oneself.

81. Zagzebski, *Epistemic Authority*, 48.

conscience but *conscientiousness*: "When I am conscientious I will come to believe that other normal, mature humans have the same natural desire for truth and the same general powers and capacities that I have."[82] Unless I succumb to extreme epistemic egoism—the belief that I am epistemologically holier than thou—there is no reason to think that other readers of Scripture are being less conscientious in their interpretations of the Bible than I am. More pointedly, it is irrational—less than epistemically conscientious—to trust one's own epistemic faculties and *not* those of others.[83] Individuals cannot avoid epistemic responsibility, but epistemic responsibility need not lead to individual autonomy. Indeed, the rationality that begins with self-reliance, if it is honest and consistent, ends with trusting others. And this, I submit, is the epistemological significance of Luther, who exemplified not individual autonomy (the authority of private conscience) but epistemic trust in an apostolic word that was not his own (the rationality of personal conscientiousness).

Epistemic Trust in Others

There is no shame in accepting what one is told: "Our trust in the word of others is fundamental to the very idea of serious cognitive activity."[84] This is in sharp contrast to those modern thinkers who say that we need sufficient reason or evidence before we can rightly believe testimony. If we suspend belief until we have verified what others have told us or experience it for ourselves, we would have a greatly reduced stock of knowledge. Believing what we are told is as important a source of knowledge as are perception and memory. According to the eighteenth-century philosopher Thomas Reid, God designed the human mind to believe the deliverances of memory, perception, *and testimony* unless we have good reason to think otherwise.[85] Even secular philosophers now acknowledge the significance of testimony for accounts of human knowledge: like memory and perception, testimony "can constitute

82. Ibid., 55.

83. See Richard Foley's case for acknowledging the intellectual authority of the opinion of others in *Intellectual Trust in Oneself and Others* (Cambridge: Cambridge University Press, 2001).

84. C. A. J. Coady, *Testimony: A Philosophical Study* (Oxford: Clarendon, 1992), vii. Cf. Augustine's treatise *De utilitate credendi* (On the Usefulness of Belief).

85. Thomas Reid, *Essays on the Intellectual Powers of Man*, ed. Derek R. Brookes (University Park: Pennsylvania State University Press, 2002). See also Nicholas Wolterstorff, *Thomas Reid and the Story of Epistemology* (Cambridge: Cambridge University Press, 2001), esp. chap. 7, "The Epistemology of Testimony" (163–84).

a noninferential, cognitive 'connection' between the subject and an objective fact."[86]

Alvin Plantinga provides what we could call a mere Protestant Christian epistemology that explains why it is rational to trust apostolic testimony: "A belief is rational if it is produced by cognitive faculties that are functioning properly and successfully aimed at truth (i.e., aimed at the production of true belief)."[87] Plantinga's Aquinas/Calvin (AC) model of epistemology stipulates that God has created human beings with certain reliable belief-producing faculties, including perception, memory, the *sensus divinitatis*, and human testimony.[88] Plantinga's model shows its distinctly Protestant colors, however, when he goes on to elaborate Calvin's doctrine of the Holy Spirit's *internal testimony*, which involves "the production in us human beings of the gift of *faith*, that 'firm and certain knowledge of God's benevolence towards us.'"[89] Faith comes by the Spirit impressing the truths of the gospel upon our minds and hearts as believers read Scripture.

The first thing faith believes is that Scripture is the Word of God (2 Tim. 3:16); that is, in reading Scripture we are hearing God's own speech. A Christian "proves" that the Bible is God's Word not by amassing reams of historical evidence but by attending to its claims. It is as if reading Scripture evokes in the reader a more focused *sensus divinitatis*: "The highest proof of Scripture derives in general from the fact that God in person speaks in it."[90] Calvin used the term *autopistos* to refer to Scripture's self-authenticating testimony that needs no external demonstration, not even from the institutional church, but only the internal confirmation of the Spirit who authored it.[91]

What is the nature of this self-authenticating testimony? It is not the claim that the truth of Scripture is self-evident, like $2 + 2 = 4$. Nor is it the claim

---

86. Mats Wahlberg, *Revelation as Testimony: A Philosophical-Theological Study* (Grand Rapids: Eerdmans, 2014), 138. Wahlberg is here summarizing John McDowell's understanding of testimonial knowledge as set forth in his essay "Knowledge and the Internal," in *Meaning, Knowledge, and Reality* (Cambridge, MA: Harvard University Press, 1998), 395–413.

87. Alvin Plantinga, *Knowledge and Christian Belief* (Grand Rapids: Eerdmans, 2015), 46.

88. Plantinga notes that both Aquinas and Calvin concur on the claim that there is a natural knowledge of God, though he goes on to acknowledge that his model is "based on Calvin's version of the suggestion" (*Warranted Christian Belief* [Oxford: Oxford University Press, 2000], 170), which features "the Bible, the internal testimony of the Spirit, and faith" (242).

89. Plantinga, *Knowledge and Christian Belief*, 48.

90. Calvin, *Institutes* I.7.4.

91. Calvin, *Institutes* I.7.5. For more on Calvin's understanding of *autopistos* as involving both truth and trustworthiness, see Henk van den Belt, *The Authority of Scripture in Reformed Theology: Truth and Trust* (Leiden: Brill, 2008), 93–116.

that Scripture provides evidence for itself from which one can infer its truth.[92] Neither is it the fideist claim that we simply have to believe Scripture in spite of evidence or reasons to the contrary. It is rather the threefold claim that (1) believing testimony in general is rational; (2) in this case only, the primary person whose (inspired) testimony we believe is divine; and (3) the Spirit uses testimony to produce certain knowledge: "Now faith is the assurance of things hoped for, the conviction of things not seen" (Heb. 11:1).

The beliefs about the gospel that the Spirit impresses on hearts and minds are justified or have "warrant" (Plantinga's preferred term for rational legitimacy) not because they have been shown to be reliable but because they are the product of a God-given, reliable belief-producing process: the internal (personal) testimony of the Spirit to the meaning and truth of Scripture. What faith knows through Word and Spirit is immediate: "For the person with faith . . . the great things of the gospel seem clearly true, obvious, obviously compelling."[93] The Spirit's work is thus "a special case of the pervasive process of testimony."[94] The Triune God is the primary testifier: agent, content, and efficacy alike.[95]

It is noteworthy that Plantinga identifies the content of faith with "the central teachings of the gospel"[96] rather than with particular doctrinal (and denominational) definitions. He here follows Jonathan Edwards's emphasis on "the great things of the Gospel."[97] In particular, Plantinga maintains that the propositional object of faith "is the whole magnificent scheme of salvation God has arranged."[98] The emphasis is on the story, not its possible interpretations.[99] Better: the emphasis is on giving interpreters enough of a cognitive grasp of the meaning of the story to enable them to become active participants in the story.[100]

92. Plantinga, *Warranted Christian Belief*, 260–61.
93. Ibid., 264.
94. Plantinga, *Knowledge and Christian Belief*, 61.
95. Mention here should be made of Kevin Diller's case for reading Alvin Plantinga and Karl Barth together as making a common case for theological knowledge as proceeding from triune revelation: "Warrant for theological knowledge is . . . conveyed by means of a self-confirming, Spirit-enabled, belief-producing process that transforms cognitive capacities" (*Theology's Epistemic Dilemma: How Karl Barth and Alvin Plantinga Provide a Unified Response* [Downers Grove, IL: IVP Academic, 2014], 172).
96. Plantinga, *Knowledge and Christian Belief*, 59.
97. Plantinga, *Warranted Christian Belief*, 80.
98. Ibid., 248.
99. Note too that Plantinga insists that Christian belief about the gospel is warranted simply on the basis of hearing/reading the biblical testimony, quite apart from historical evidence or argument (*Knowledge and Christian Belief*, 65).
100. See further Vanhoozer, *Faith Speaking Understanding*.

In light of the preceding, it therefore seems that the all-too-common tendency to tar Protestant Christianity with the brush of epistemic autonomy is seriously misguided. *Sola fide* is not a hammer with which to reinforce the authority of one's own private judgments. It accords better with Zagzebski's thesis about the importance of trusting others: "The authority of a person's testimony is justified by my conscientious judgment that I am more likely to satisfy my desire to get true beliefs and avoid false beliefs if I believe what the authority tells me than if I try to figure out what to believe myself."[101] Consider how 1 John 2:27 might bear on our discussion: "But the anointing [i.e., the Holy Spirit] that you received from him [Christ] abides in you, and you have no need that anyone should teach you." In context, this verse likely concerns the threat from gnostics who claimed to have access to secret teaching. John is not giving his reader a blanket assurance that the gift of the Holy Spirit makes individuals into infallible interpreters; he is rather encouraging them to abide in what they have heard—from others—from the beginning (1 John 2:24).

The pertinent question remains: *Which* others? The apostles, of course, because their testimony is that of Spirit-guided eyewitnesses. But *whose interpretation* of the apostolic message? No one can serve two martyrs (from Gk. *martys*, "witness"). No one can avoid placing one's faith in *some* authority, whether oneself or another. This is what Paul implies too when he says, "That is not the way you learned Christ!—assuming that you have heard about him and were taught in him" (Eph. 4:20–21). Nowhere else in the Greek New Testament or extrabiblical literature of the time do we encounter the phrase "to learn a person."[102] F. F. Bruce thinks that to be "taught in [Christ]" means being taught "in the context of the Christian fellowship."[103] Paul's Ephesian readers learned Christ in the community of his followers—itself "a creature of the Word" (Luther). And this leads directly to my next point.

Interpretive Authority and Fiduciary Framework

An epistemically conscientious person will admit, "Other normal, mature humans have the same natural desire for truth and the same general powers and capacities that I have."[104] When it comes to biblical interpretation, the question

101. Zagzebski, *Epistemic Authority*, 133.
102. O'Brien, *Letter to the Ephesians*, 324.
103. F. F. Bruce, *The Epistles to the Colossians, to Philemon, and to the Ephesians*, New International Commentary on the New Testament (Grand Rapids: Eerdmans, 1984), 357.
104. Zagzebski, *Epistemic Authority*, 55.

is whether other normal, mature humans are also being guided into all truth. Stated differently: Are all interpretive communities created—and redeemed— equally? Obviously, I cannot examine every Christian interpretive community. It will suffice to distinguish those communities that nurture a primary trust in their own authorized interpreters and interpretations and those that nurture a primary trust in Scripture's self-interpreting authority. The dividing line between the two types of communities concerns the nature and necessity of the church's authoritative mediation between biblical text and believing faithful.

Scripture as Primary Factor in the Fiduciary Framework

"The fear of the Lord is the beginning of knowledge" (Prov. 1:7). All knowing begins with what Michael Polanyi calls a "fiduciary framework" (fiduciary = pertaining to *fides*, "involving trust"): an interpretive framework that one takes initially on faith until it proves itself by yielding a harvest of understanding.[105] Polanyi emphasizes the personal (and interpersonal) nature of knowledge by calling attention to the communal dimension of a fiduciary framework. To espouse a fiduciary framework is to inhabit a tradition of inquiry and to be apprenticed to its senior practitioners. In particular, to inhabit a fiduciary framework is to indwell a language. Lesslie Newbigin explains: "We do not look at the language as an object over against us; we think *through* the language. By indwelling it we are able to make contact with the world around us."[106] Finally, fiduciary frameworks are ultimately grounded on assumptions about the way things are.

If Polanyi is right, Christian theology is no worse off than modern science. Everyone has to have faith in something to get the knowing process started. Polanyi did not, as far as I know, address the question of the Christian fiduciary framework. While it would be easy to assume that Polanyi would have jumped on board the postliberal cultural-linguistic bandwagon that accords authority to interpretive communities, a good case could be made for making Scripture the Christians' default fiduciary framework, the source and norm of theological knowledge and wisdom.[107] After all, Calvin refers to the Scriptures

105. Michael Polanyi, *Personal Knowledge: Towards a Post-Critical Philosophy*, corrected ed. (Chicago: University of Chicago Press, 1962), 266.

106. Lesslie Newbigin, *Proper Confidence: Faith, Doubt, and Certainty in Christian Discipleship* (Grand Rapids: Eerdmans, 1995), 40.

107. "Cultural-linguistic" refers to George Lindbeck's proposal for a postliberal theology that makes the church's language and practices the framework for making sense of Scripture rather than viewing them, with liberals, as expressions of a more fundamental religious experience.

as the "spectacles of faith."[108] Moreover, faith itself is evoked, governed, and nurtured by the authoritative testimony to Christ written in the Scriptures, which is why Paul can refer to "the foundation of the apostles and prophets" (Eph. 2:20). This is the Scripture principle, which I will examine further in the following chapter. Suffice it to say that the fiduciary framework of the Bible is the beginning of theological knowledge: it is primarily by one's Spirited indwelling of the biblical text—its metaphors, its overarching narrative, its several literary genres—that one comes to trust the apostolic testimony and to encounter the reality "which was from the beginning, which we have heard, which we have seen with our eyes, which we looked upon and have touched with our hands, concerning the word of life" (1 John 1:1)—Jesus Christ.

Church and Church Tradition as Secondary Factor in the Fiduciary Framework

There is an economy of authoritative testimony: God the Father makes himself known in and through Christ; Christ makes himself known to the apostles; the apostles make Christ known to us; the Spirit enables people of faith to receive the apostolic testimony. Where does this leave the church, the interpretive community of the faithful?

Paul says to the Ephesians, "When you read this, you can perceive my insight into the mystery of Christ" (Eph. 3:4). Faith comes by hearing the Word, understanding by reading it. Paul is not advocating a hermeneutics of *ex opere operato* (lit., "by the work worked"—i.e., by the reading read/ grasped), though it would be nice if we could understand texts simply by reading them. As we have seen, while testimony can be a means of knowledge, only the Holy Spirit can give the certainty that accompanies faith that the apostolic testimony makes personally known the risen Christ. But we need to distinguish the Spirit as the *cause* of our knowing from the various *means* the Spirit may use to bring about this knowledge.[109] Paul probably is referring to the practice of having his letters read in church meetings. If so, then the Ephesians are getting insight into the mystery of Christ, not as isolated individuals, but as members of the household of faith.

See Lindbeck, *The Nature of Doctrine: Religion and Theology in a Postliberal Age* (Philadelphia: Westminster, 1984).

108. Calvin, *Institutes* I.6.1.

109. See further Vanhoozer, "Spirit of Light." I take the distinction between "cause" and "means" of understanding from John Owen.

Polanyi says that scientists learn from other persons, like apprentices: "To learn by example is to submit to authority."[110] To what extent is biblical interpretation like being apprenticed to a tradition of inquiry? Polanyi uses the theologically loaded term "indwelling" and suggests that scientists work by indwelling community traditions (i.e., the tradition of the Western scientific community). Polanyi is not saying that any fiduciary framework is as good as another, but only that they are inevitable, and that some frameworks allow us to make contact with reality in ways that others do not (i.e., they yield insights). Modern biblical critics belong to academic interpretive communities and work with a fiduciary framework too; the only question is whether it allows them to make contact with divine reality. I have argued that the Triune God constitutes the Bible as its own fiduciary framework.

"Faith alone" means that individual interpreters had best attend to the authoritative apostolic testimony (the primary fiduciary framework) as read in the context of the church (a secondary fiduciary framework). The church is not like other interpretive communities. Its reading must not be a function of this or that interpretive interest; the church must not "use" the text for its own purposes. For the church is "a creature of the Word"—an interpretive community that exists not to have its way with the text but to let the Word have its way with the interpreters. John Webster rightly states, "The reading of Holy Scripture is thus a field of divine activity; it is not simply human handling of a textual object. And that divine activity is God's speech to which we are, quite simply, to attend."[111] What kind of authority does the church have? This is the key question. The church is neither a voluntary association of autonomous individuals nor an interpretive community that, like other such communities, is bound together by a set of arbitrary interests and conventions. Calvin likens church to a mother who guards and guides her children with "motherly care until they mature and at last reach the goal of faith."[112] One of the most important tasks of mother church is homeschooling: "The church is a mother that teaches her children to trust the truth."[113]

---

110. Polanyi, *Personal Knowledge*, 53.

111. John Webster, *Word and Church: Essays in Christian Dogmatics* (Edinburgh: T&T Clark, 2001), 93.

112. Calvin, *Institutes* IV.1.1.

113. Van den Belt, *Authority of Scripture*, 325.

The purpose of the church's nurture is to form people into a holy nation and royal priesthood, where every individual bears an appointed office: citizen of the gospel. To be justified by grace through faith is to be incorporated into a kingdom with Christ as head and authorized to interpret the charter of that kingdom. To be justified is to be declared righteous—right with God—and with this status comes other rights of the new covenant, including adoption and citizenship. These implications of justification have horizontal as well as vertical significance, incorporating the justified into one body—a body politic. To put one's faith in Jesus is to confess him as Lord, not just of oneself but also of the world, particularly of the new-covenant community. *Sola fide* promotes, then, not individualism but a righteous *polis*: a city and citizenship of the gospel, an interpretive community whose mandate is to profess and perform a word that it indwells yet that also stands over against it, a word to which the church must measure up.[114] Justification carries with it appointment to an office that authorizes those who have been justified to serve as "ambassadors for Christ" (2 Cor. 5:20). But we are getting ahead of ourselves.

"A society which wants to preserve a fund of personal knowledge must submit to tradition."[115] With the mention of tradition we reach the end of this inquiry into the principle of authority and stand at the threshold of our next topic: the pattern of interpretive authority. Tradition will indeed have a place in my account of *sola scriptura*. Yet in the Father's household there are many Protestant mansions, making the question "*Which* tradition?" inescapable.

Sola Fide for Bible, Church, and Interpretive Authority

I began this chapter by examining the charge that the Reformers unintentionally paved the way for modern skepticism by refusing the authority of the church and preferring their own private judgment as to what the apostle Paul really meant by justification. I now wish to conclude this chapter with four more theses, three of which retrieve implications from *sola fide* that overturn this common caricature. I begin, however, with a thesis that restates the authority principle of mere Protestant Christianity.

114. For the main idea in this paragraph I am indebted to Jonathan Leeman, *Political Church: The Local Assembly as Embassy of Christ's Rule* (Downers Grove, IL: IVP Academic, 2016), chap. 6 ("The Politics of the Kingdom").

115. Polanyi, *Personal Knowledge*, 53.

5. The authority principle of mere Protestant Christianity is the say-so of the Triune God, a speak-acting that authorizes the created order and authors the Scriptures, diverse testimonies that make known the created order as it has come to be and to be restored in, through, and for Jesus Christ.

Divine authority, deriving from divine authorship, is at the core of the universe. God's Word makes distinctions and connections, thus creating a meaningful structure out of the formless void.[116] Divine authority—rightful say-so—is "what we encounter in the world which makes it meaningful for us to act."[117] God's law enables purposive freedom; God's gospel restores and transforms it. God's say-so justifies, both in soteriology, where God's declaring sinners righteous makes them so, and in epistemology, where God's testimony warrants belief. The authority principle in Christian theology is the Triune God in communicative action: simultaneously initiator, conveyor, and guarantor of the Word that generates and governs faith.

6. As persons created in God's image and destined to be conformed to the image of God's Son, mere Protestant biblical interpreters believe that the Spirit both summons them to attend and authorizes them to respond to the voice of the Triune God speaking in the Scriptures to present Christ.

God calls human persons into existence, conferring on them the privilege and responsibility of answerability. Because there is no place on heaven or earth that the Word of God is not, we cannot avoid responding to it. "Believe the gospel"; "repent and be baptized": there is no alibi for not answering. Faith is a gift of the Holy Spirit by which we are enabled to lay hold of the Christ we meet in the Spirit-given Scriptures. The Spirit enables Christ to dwell in our hearts through faith, but this does not mean that we are trapped in subjectivity. On the contrary, the Spirit's witness is always to the risen Christ—the *res* that the *verba* of Scripture are ultimately about. To have Christ dwell in our hearts means that he "exercises his rule over all that we are and do."[118] To the extent that we respond to his lordship, an external authority, we become freer to act as his authorized agents on earth, thus fulfilling the promise of our created

116. This includes "veracious" authority, the authority of truth: "If the laws of thought are not established by God, whose veracity is originative and constitutive of reality and of its legitimate representation, there can be no distinction between truth and error" (Auguste Lecerf, *An Introduction to Reformed Dogmatics* [London: Lutterworth, 1949], 365).

117. O'Donovan, *Resurrection and Moral Order*, 122.

118. O'Brien, *Letter to the Ephesians*, 259.

image. In faith, informed by the Word and framed by Spirit-guided tradition, we confess *what is* "in Christ." In Christ we see that freedom and authority go hand in hand, and that we are made to flourish as "ruled rulers." What must not be missed is the Spirit's role in bringing about a genuine hearing that objectively relates us to, and gives us knowledge of, something real: the gospel of body and blood.

> 7. Mere Protestant biblical interpreters believe that they will have a better under-
>   standing of what God is saying in Scripture by attending to the work of other
>   interpreters (and communities of interpreters) as well as their own community's
>   work.

Philology—the love of biblical language and literature—is part and parcel of mere Protestant Christianity. At the same time, Ramm is right to caution us against the abbreviated Protestant principle: to ignore the internal witness of the Spirit is to put asunder what God joined together (i.e., Word and Spirit). Biblical study alone can become one more variation on the theme of justification by works—scholarly works. It is equally misguided to appeal to the Holy Spirit as an interpretive shortcut, like some get-out-of-hermeneutical-jail-free card. "Faith alone" was never meant to encourage epistemic egoism. *Sola fide*, properly understood, neither blesses nor confers the "right of private judgment." Rather, faith is the means by which the Spirit unites persons to Christ. And, because God has created men and women as social beings who learn from others, faith—trusting in the words of apostolic others—is eminently rational. Because nothing is more important than answering God's address, epistemically conscientious biblical interpreters will be open to learning what others have understood God to say, especially when the "others" in question are those whom the Spirit has also united to Christ. To anticipate the next chapter: we best come to understand the testimony of the apostles in the context of the catholic church.

> 8. Mere Protestant Christians believe that faith enables a way of interpreting
>   Scripture that refuses both absolute certainty (idols of the tower) and rela-
>   tivistic skepticism (idols of the maze).

Every interpreter indwells some fiduciary framework or another and belongs to some interpretive community or another, whether we define it broadly (e.g., the community of women) or more narrowly (e.g., an academic approach like the Tübingen school or dispensationalism). People inhabit more than one interpretive community at the same time (e.g., a professional society, a social class, a denomination, a local church, a gender).

Regardless of one's location, there are two temptations that beset every interpretive community: on the one hand, to think too highly of one's particular reading (interpretive pride); on the other, to think too little of one's particular reading (interpretive sloth). Pride in the "assured results" of critical reason is the besetting temptation of modern biblical scholarship; sloth is the temptation for postmodern interpreters to the extent that their attention is focused more on exposing the situatedness of what passes for objective exegesis than on the text itself. Pride and sloth are the two ends of the spectrum of deadly interpretive sins. All sin is a denial of reality—that is, a refusal of the Creator and his created order.[119] In different ways, both pride and sloth deny our creaturehood, the one by denying our finitude, the other by denying our responsibility.

Pride and sloth are ultimately denials of God's authority insofar as each in its own way refuses to accept the divine testimony, perhaps because they each deny its meaningfulness, clarity, or truth. Pride and sloth are also ways of denying our divinely authorized status as interpretive agents: persons designed to understand and respond to other persons and ultimately to God. Justification by faith, rightly understood, is a license for neither complacency nor despair; it is rather God's reauthorization for us to image him as ruled rulers, and to speak and act as citizens of his kingdom. Biblical interpretation is best undertaken in the context of the community of the justified (the church), where individuals learn from one another how to become virtuous (i.e., righteous) interpreters: right-minded and right-hearted readers. In interpretation, as in all areas of the Christian life, we must counter pride with proper confidence, and sloth with due diligence—twin fruits of faith alone.

In conclusion: *sola fide* is the answer to skepticism, for faith yields knowledge but is not a "work." Faith is, rather, perseveringly confident, patiently attentive, and properly basic[120]—a warranted epistemic trust in biblical testimony. What do we know that we have not received? True faith has to do

---

119. Oliver O'Donovan observes, "Sin is always 'against,' since it is constituted as refusal of some aspect of good reality, and all sins are against God, the creator, sustainer, and redeemer of all good reality" (*Ethics as Theology*, vol. 2, *Finding and Seeking* [Grand Rapids: Eerdmans, 2014], 18).

120. Plantinga's term for a belief that does not need to be justified or inferred from any other belief in order to be deemed rational (*Warranted Christian Belief*, 175–79).

not with an anti-intellectual fideism or private judgment, then, but rather with testimonial rationality and public trust, the trust of God's people in the testimony of God's Spirit to the reliability of God's Word. Could it be that the Reformation begat not epistemological skepticism but its only effective antidote: epistemic (and spiritual) trust?

3

Scripture Alone

The Mere Protestant Pattern of Interpretive Authority

The previous chapter set forth the authority principle of mere Protestant Christianity: *the say-so of the Triune God that authorizes the created order by speaking it into existence and authorizes the prophets and apostles to make known how in Jesus Christ God has made creation new.* The Reformers retrieved this authority principle, insisting that only in Scripture does the church have God's say-so in written (and thus permanent) form. Principles need to be put into practice, however, and often the way people apply a principle helps us understand what they mean by it. "Justice" remains something of an abstraction, for example, until we begin to see how a particular society works it out. Something similar may pertain to *sola scriptura*. The present chapter therefore continues to focus on the epistemology of the gospel, turning from the principle to the practice of biblical authority. Chapters 4 and 5 then focus on different aspects of the teleology of the gospel.

Sola scriptura is perhaps the most challenging of the *solas* to retrieve. Even many Protestant theologians now urge its abandonment on the grounds that, in insisting on Scripture *alone*, it overlooks or even excludes the importance of tradition, the necessity of hermeneutics, and the relationship between Word and Spirit.[1] Moreover, according to a common way of telling the story of the Reformation, *sola scriptura* marks the spot where Protestantism falls apart.[2] Protestants subscribe to the formula but use it to underwrite different, often contrasting, projects. We have already encountered the objection: "No honest religious historian can deny that the result of *sola scriptura* has been doctrinal chaos."[3] I'm not a religious historian (though I hope that I'm honest), but I would like respectfully to demur. While it is true that a certain degree of doctrinal chaos came after the Reformation, it is fallacious to argue that *sola scriptura* was the primary reason. Neither individualism nor pluralism was inherent in *sola scriptura*. One cannot infer that one event *caused* another simply because the alleged cause *came before* the alleged effect.[4] Simplistic rebuttals will not work, however. If we are to extract successfully a normative Protestantism from the ruins of historical Protestantism, and absolve *sola scriptura* as "the sin of the Reformation,"[5] we need to situate the principle of biblical authority in the broader pattern of theological authority.

When people say that they regret the Reformation, then, it is often *sola scriptura* that they have in mind, for they draw a straight cause-and-effect line from *sola scriptura* to church divisions. Let me briefly recall two hostile witnesses to the stand to summarize the prosecution's case. Christian Smith argues that *sola scriptura* (he calls it "biblicism") is an "impossible" principle, because even those who agree with the principle disagree about its results, and hence, appeals to the Bible's authority have settled nothing. If we were to judge *sola scriptura* by its fruits, says Smith, then we must judge it a practical failure.[6] Brad Gregory charges *sola scriptura* with unintentionally creating the conditions for the hyperpluralism in Western society today: not only did the Reformers disagree over things like the Lord's Supper; they also disagreed

---

1. So Henk van den Belt, "Problematic Character of *Sola Scriptura*."

2. According to Robert W. Jenson, *sola scriptura* is the most problematic Reformation slogan and, in his judgment, "cannot finally be salvaged for any significant use" (*Lutheran Slogans: Use and Abuse* [Delhi, NY: American Lutheran Publicity Bureau, 2011], 63). Jenson reads the *sola* as intended to exclude something, and he says that what is typically excluded is the authority of tradition. The present chapter approaches things differently in locating tradition in the pattern of interpretive authority rather than excluding it altogether.

3. Rose, *Protestant's Dilemma*, 87.

4. The technical term of this logical mistake is the *post hoc* fallacy: *post hoc ergo propter hoc* (after this, therefore because of this). The mistake is to confuse chronology with causality. The categories are not interchangeable.

5. Georges Florovsky, *Bible, Church, Tradition: An Eastern Orthodox View* (Belmont, MA: Nordland, 1972), 48.

6. Smith, *Bible Made Impossible*, xi.

over the criterion for distinguishing what was essential from the inessential, and these exegetical and doctrinal and methodological disagreements turned into ecclesial divisions.[7] *Sola scriptura* turned out to be not a uniter but a divider. That, at least, is the prevailing narrative on the academic street.

It is precisely here that the wisdom of treating the *solas* together becomes apparent. For, properly understood, "Scripture alone" does not mean "Scripture abstracted from the economy of grace" or "Scripture apart from the community of faith" or even "Scripture independent of church tradition." What I therefore propose to do in this chapter is locate *sola scriptura* in relation to its sibling *solas* in order to understand it as an element—a unique and essential element, to be sure, but an element nonetheless—in the pattern of authority, a pattern, I hasten to add, that is itself biblical.[8]

Sola Scriptura: What the Reformers Meant

In light of objections past and present, it is important to determine what the Reformers originally meant by *sola scriptura*. In particular, in what sense is Scripture *alone*? The legitimacy of the Reformation stands or falls on Luther's judgment that Scripture alone contains all things necessary for salvation, communicates them effectively, compels one's conscience, determines doctrinal truth, and commands the church's allegiance above all other earthly powers and authorities, including councils and popes. To anticipate: it is not that Scripture is alone in the sense that it is the sole source of theology; rather, Scripture "alone" is the *primary* or *supreme* authority in theology. "Scripture alone" excludes rivals such as the teaching office of the church and church tradition when it comes to the role of *infallible* (magisterial) authority. It does not eliminate other sources and resources of theology altogether. The challenge for those who wish to maintain *sola scriptura* is to locate it rightly in the broader pattern or economy as the *primal* and *final*, but not the sole, authority.

Luther did not initially realize the implications of his attack on indulgences (he expected the pope to side with him), but official response to his Ninety-Five Theses quickly focused his attention on what was fundamentally at stake:

7. Gregory, *Unintended Reformation*, 368.
8. Arnold Huijgen remarks, "*Sola scriptura* should be understood as inherently related to the other solas, for if this perspective is lost, the specter of the dilemma of Biblicism or postmodern relativism looms large" ("Alone Together").

Sylvester Prierias wrote, "Whoever does not hold fast to the teachings of the Roman Church and of the Pope as the infallible rule of faith, from which even Holy Scripture draws its strength and authority, is a heretic."[9] In responding to this direct attack, Luther did not invent the concept of Scripture's supreme authority, but his circumstances forced him to make explicit what had been implicit for centuries in the early church. In God's providence, falsehood is often a goad to greater understanding and doctrinal development. The Reformers had Rome to the right of them and enthusiasts to the left of them; they therefore had to hammer out their understanding of Scripture's authority against those who exaggerated human tradition, on the one hand, and those who exaggerated the immediate revelations of the Spirit, on the other.

What needed to be understood at the time of the Reformation, and today, is the locus of interpretive authority: Whose say-so speaks for God's say-so? Luther had a suggestion: the Spirit speaking in the Scriptures is his own interpreter. In addition, the Word is in a certain sense its own best interpreter: "Scripture interprets Scripture." The problem with slogans is that they can sometimes take on a life of their own. *Sola scriptura* has not escaped its share of semantic slippage. Before we retrieve it, then, it may help briefly to summarize what it meant for the Reformers.[10]

Clarity

Sola scriptura presupposes clarity. Just as the sound of a bugle, if indistinct, will fail to call for battle (1 Cor. 14:8), so too will an unclear text fail to command the conscience. The solemn Protestation of the Diet of Speyer (1529) sets out the Protestant position: "This holy book is in all things necessary for the Christian; it shines clearly in its own light."[11] There are things in Scripture that are "hard to understand" (2 Pet. 3:16), but the Reformers insisted that (1) the Spirit illumines our minds; (2) clearer portions of Scripture illumine passages that are less clear; (3) the deficiency is not with Scripture but with our knowledge of its vocabulary and context; and (4) for

9. Sylvester Prierias, *De potestate papae dialogus* (1518), cited in Thompson, *Sure Ground*, 250–52.

10. See further Matthew Barrett, *God's Word Alone: The Authority of Scripture; What the Reformers Taught . . . and Why It Still Matters* (Grand Rapids: Zondervan Academic, 2016), esp. chap. 1.

11. Cited in Timothy George, *Reading Scripture with the Reformers* (Downers Grove, IL: IVP Academic, 2011), 119.

those who have been enlightened, it is impossible to miss the light (meaning) of the gospel shining out from its pages. Calvin speaks of the Scriptures as "spectacles"—canonical corrective lenses—that help bring our dim eyesight into sharper focus.[12]

Scripture's clarity does not mean that reading works *ex opere operato*, as if simply pronouncing the words magically yields understanding. Nor does clarity mean that Scripture wears doctrines like the Trinity on its sleeve. Rather, it means that those whose eyes of the heart (Eph. 1:18) have been opened by the Spirit cannot miss the main story: the good news about Jesus Christ. In Francis Turretin's words, "The Scriptures are so plain in things essential to salvation . . . that without the external aid of tradition or the infallible judgment of the church, they may be read and understood profitably by believers."[13] While there are indeed a variety of interpretations, especially about *how* salvation happens, mere Protestant Christians agree about *what* happened and *who* did what (e.g., Father, Son, and Spirit). This explains both why mere Protestants practice baptism *and* why they do not all practice it the same way.[14] It is important to remember the polemical context in which the Reformers affirmed the clarity of Scripture so as not to use it as an interpretive carte blanche.

We have a better sense of what clarity means if we think of it not in terms of the conceptual precision so valued by contemporary analytic philosophers but rather in the properly theological terms of God's self-communication: "There are no insurmountable obstacles to God's communicative purposes."[15] The unfolding of God's Word gives light (Ps. 119:130), and the agency of the unfolding and light-giving is not the church or academic scholarship apart from the triune economy but rather the Spirit speaking (not just having spoken) in the Scriptures (and through the church and, sometimes, academy). It is God's own communicative action that is a lamp unto our feet, not some magisterium—or our subjective opinion. Mark Thompson's observation is apt:

12. See further Mark D. Thompson, *A Clear and Present Word: The Clarity of Scripture* (Downers Grove, IL: InterVarsity, 2006).

13. Francis Turretin, *Institutes of Elenctic Theology*, vol. 1, *First through Tenth Topics*, trans. George Musgrave Giger, ed. James T. Dennison Jr. (Phillipsburg, NJ: P&R, 1992), 2.17.7.

14. Timothy Ward notes that it is tempting but not necessary to assume that the clarity of Scripture means that all Bible-believing Christians will agree on everything the Bible says. This is not what the Reformers meant by the clarity of Scripture. See Timothy Ward, *Words of Life: Scripture as the Living and Active Word of God* (Downers Grove, IL: IVP Academic, 2009), 123–24.

15. Thompson, *Clear and Present Word*, 165.

"It is this conviction that Scripture is clear which precludes us from viewing [Luther's] stand as simply the imposition of private judgment."[16]

Sufficiency

Sola scriptura also implies the sufficiency of Scripture, though the abstract concept begs the question, sufficient for what? To answer that Scripture is sufficient for *everything*—stock market investments, leaky faucets, clogged arteries—is to saddle it with unrealistic expectations, and eventually to succumb to naïve biblicism and the quagmire of pervasive interpretive pluralism.

Let us rather say, with Isaiah, that Scripture is *sufficient for everything for which it was divinely given*: "[My word] shall not return to me empty, but it shall accomplish that which I purpose, and shall succeed in the thing for which I sent it" (Isa. 55:11). Paul tells Timothy that Scripture is "profitable *for* teaching, *for* reproof, *for* correction, and training in righteousness" (2 Tim. 3:16). These verses help us see what sufficiency means and does not mean. The Bible is sufficient for the use that God makes of it, not for every use to which *we* may want it put. In John Webster's words: "Scripture is *enough*. This is because Scripture is what God desires to teach."[17] Scripture is "enough" to learn Christ and the Christian life.

We can unpack "enough" in two ways. First, Scripture is *materially* sufficient ("enough") because God has communicated everything we need to know in order to learn Christ and live the Christian life: "all things that pertain to life and godliness" (2 Pet. 1:3). Article VI of the Church of England's Thirty-Nine Articles makes exactly this point: "Holy Scripture containeth all things necessary to salvation."[18] The material sufficiency of Scripture excludes any possibility of Scripture needing an external supplement in order to achieve the purpose for which it was sent. The Westminster Confession forbids adding any new content to Scripture, "whether by new revelations of the Spirit, or traditions of men," thereby echoing statements in Scripture itself, such as Revelation 22:18: "I warn everyone who hears the words of the prophecy of this book: if anyone adds to them, God will add to him the plagues described

16. Thompson, *Sure Ground*, 239. For a fuller discussion of Luther's position, see Thompson, *Clear and Present Word*, 143–50.

17. Webster, *Domain of the Word*, 18.

18. Compare the Westminster Confession of Faith: "The whole counsel of God concerning all things necessary for his own glory, man's salvation, faith and life, is either expressly set down in Scripture, or by good and necessary consequence may be deduced from Scripture" (1.6).

in this book." What God has authored is adequate for his communicative purpose: "Scripture is materially sufficient for the bearing of propositional content (the presentation of Jesus Christ as the means of salvation) and for the conveying of illocutionary force (the call or invitation to have faith in him)."[19] But this is not the same as Scripture being able to authorize its own interpretation, or to adjudicate between rival interpretations.

There is, therefore, second, the question of Scripture's *formal* sufficiency, and this concerns the authority by which Scripture is interpreted. For the Roman Catholic Church, the interpretive authority is the magisterium. Rome decides what churches elsewhere must believe—hence, *Roman* catholicity. It is this second sense of sufficiency that is of special interest to us, and it is important enough to deserve a further heading of its own: "Scripture Interprets Scripture." The burden of my discussion will be to argue that Protestants, in addressing the problem of interpretive authority, have retrieved the *unabbreviated* principle of true catholicity, according to which the church is present where the gospel is rightly proclaimed in word and sacrament.[20] To anticipate: God in his grace has given his children the church—a fellowship of saints; a teaching ministry; a tradition of interpretation; a table of communion—as a means of grace, a precious external aid in the proper reception of his Word. Because the church is a creature of the Word—the preached gospel of God's grace—we must say that canonicity generates and governs catholicity: "Wherever that gospel is taken seriously . . . there is the Church."[21]

"Scripture Interprets Scripture"

Does Scripture's sufficiency mean that Scripture contains not only all the ingredients for a feast but also the recipe for preparing it? The concern of the Roman Catholic Church at the time of the Reformation, and of many

19. Timothy Ward, *Word and Supplement: Speech Acts, Biblical Texts, and the Sufficiency of Scripture* (Oxford: Oxford University Press, 2002), 205.

20. Vincent of Lérins addresses the formal sufficiency of Scripture when he formulates his own "canon"—that is, his rule that we ought to believe "that which has been believed everywhere, always, and by all men. For that is truly and rightly 'catholic'" ("The Commonitory," in *Early Medieval Theology*, ed. George E. McCracken and Allen Cabaniss [London: SCM, 1957], 38). The present work challenges the way in which Rome has appropriated Vincent's "canon of (cultural-linguistic) catholicity" by contrasting it with a Protestant "canonical catholicity"—that is, a canonical-linguistic catholicity in which agreement with the Scriptures, and churches that affirm the supreme authority of the Scriptures, is more important than agreement with Rome.

21. P. T. Forsyth, *The Church and the Sacraments* (1917; repr., Eugene, OR: Wipf & Stock, 1996), 34–35.

non-Catholic Christians today, is that this notion is a recipe for ecclesial disaster. Whereas friends of *sola scriptura* think "Scripture interprets Scripture" follows from it the way the second line of a psalm expands upon the first, its critics view these two slogans more like two electrical wires that, though both are connected to the battery of biblical authority, must be kept from touching, lest the user suffer risk of chemical explosion, serious injury, and even death (if the instructions for my battery backup sump pump are to be believed). The worry, again, is that every individual will read Scripture in a way that is right in his or her own eyes and then claim that it is the authorized interpretation. It is no minor concern.

The Reformers insisted that Scripture not be taken captive either by Roman tradition or by Radical enthusiasm. Neither custom nor experience determines the Bible's meaning, for each is too fickle. This is obvious with regard to experience (there are so many), less so with tradition, yet Luther is insistent: "Tell me, if you are able, by whose judgment is the question settled if the statements of the fathers are in conflict with one another? Scripture ought to deliver this judgment, which cannot be delivered unless we give to Scripture the principal place in all things, which is acknowledged by the fathers."[22]

To say "Scripture interprets Scripture" is to say more (but not less) than "The parts interpret the whole and the whole interprets the parts" and "The parts that are less clear must be read in light of those that are more clear." These are crucial principles, but they apply to the interpretation of any text. We must be careful not to let "Scripture interprets Scripture" become an excuse for naïve biblicism. The Reformers never meant to imply that the Bible does not need human interpreters. To be sure, the Bible itself provides textual clues and directions for putting the pieces of the canon together in the right order and in the right sense; but, it is one thing to say that Scripture provides the overarching metanarrative and hermeneutical framework for understanding its parts, and quite another to say that the Bible alone authorizes or adjudicates between rival interpretations. The Bible does not run by itself apart from the Spirit, who speaks in it and illumines readers. Scripture's sufficiency is not simply a formal textual property. Even the demons believe in general hermeneutics.

Luther, then, is doing more than formulating a theory of textuality. He is referring to something altogether more active, and theological: "that [Scripture] is interpreting itself [*sui ipsius interpres*], testing, judging and illuminating all

22. Luther, WA 7:97.19–24.

things."[23] Stated simply: it is not that the church interprets Scripture but that Scripture interprets the church. The church understands its nature and function only in the light of Scripture. Elsewhere I have explained this by saying that biblical interpreters are *apprentices* to the canonical practices of the Bible itself:

> The primary conversation that leads to understanding, then, is the Spirit-enabled conversation that takes place within and between the canonical books themselves. . . . Good theological judgment is largely, though not exclusively, a matter of being apprenticed to the canon: of having one's capacity for judging (a capacity that involves imagination, reason, emotion, and volition alike) formed and transformed by the ensemble of canonical practices that constitute Scripture.[24]

Gerhard Forde makes a similar point: "The interpreter does not remain standing simply as subject over against the text as object to be interpreted. Rather . . . it is the scripture that comes to interpret the exegete. It is the task of the exegete to allow the Spirit of the scripture, the matter itself, to speak."[25]

These quotations begin to sketch what is involved in the economy of interpretive authority: the Triune God employs various means to minister the gospel in ways that build up the body of Christ. Strictly speaking, Scripture is not "alone," because it is an ingredient in a triune economy of communication. When we examine further what Scripture says about this economy, we will see that Scripture is sufficient to play its designated part as the supreme authority of theology, but again, not alone or independently of the Holy Spirit, or of the church and its teaching ministry. "Scripture interprets Scripture" is therefore a truism not about texts in general but about one particular text—the Bible—and its place in the economies of revelation and redemption. For the Reformers, it is the Spirit speaking *Christ* in the Scripture, in the context of the household of God, who finally authorizes an interpretation, not an external magisterium or an internal revelation. Finally, as we will see in later chapters, the Spirit speaks in Scripture by way of ordained ministers of the Word and the whole royal priesthood of believers. These too play a part in the pattern of interpretive authority.

23. Ibid.
24. Vanhoozer, *Drama of Doctrine*, 331.
25. Gerhard O. Forde, *A More Radical Gospel: Essays on Eschatology, Authority, Atonement, and Ecumenism*, ed. Mark C. Mattes and Steven D. Paulson (Grand Rapids: Eerdmans, 2004), 71 (from Forde's essay "*Scriptura sacra sui ipsius interpres*: Reflections on the Question of Scripture and Tradition").

Scripture and/or Tradition: Other Views

In this regard, what should we make of the Ethiopian eunuch who was reading the prophet Isaiah when the Holy Spirit told Philip to approach his chariot: "So Philip ran to him and . . . asked, 'Do you understand what you are reading?' And he said, 'How can I, unless someone guides me?'" (Acts 8:30–31)? If Scripture is self-interpreting, what was Philip doing in that chariot? There are at least three possibilities for understanding what Philip represents: (1) the sharing of oral tradition (Acts 8:35); (2) a strategy for reading the text (typologically, canonically, and christologically); (3) the teaching office of the church. These three options are related to three ways of viewing the relationship between Scripture and the ongoing life of the church. Will the real Philip please stand up?

Roman Magisterium (Tradition II)

The Roman Catholic critique of *sola scriptura* is simply stated: Scripture alone is not enough to determine the correct interpretation. For that, Philip is necessary—in this case, the authorized interpretation of the church's teaching office as determined by apostolic succession.

The Council of Trent (1545–63)—the showpiece of the sixteenth-century Roman Catholic Counter-Reformation—was called to reaffirm the church's main tenets and to show Protestants the errors of their ways.[26] The decree on the Scriptures said that saving truth is contained "both in the written books and the unwritten traditions."[27] Heiko Oberman dubs this position—that there is a second source of authoritative revelation—"Tradition II," in distinction from "Tradition I" (the view of most church fathers), where the "I" stands for the "one source" theory that tradition transmits the same revelatory content as contained in the Scriptures.[28] Irenaeus's view is a good example of Tradi-

---

26. For a study of what went on behind the scenes, as it were, see John W. O'Malley, *Trent: What Happened at the Council* (Cambridge, MA: Belknap Press of Harvard University Press, 2013), 89–102.

27. Earlier drafts of the decree had said that revelation came "partly" (*partim*) through Scripture and "partly" (*partim*) through tradition. According to Yves Congar, the final statement contains vestiges of this "two-source" view (*Tradition and Traditions: An Historical and a Theological Essay* [New York: Macmillan, 1967], 167).

28. Heiko A. Oberman, *Forerunners of the Reformation: The Shape of Late Medieval Thought*, trans. Paul L. Nyhus (London: Lutterworth, 1967), 58. We can further distinguish between the "coincidence view" ("strong" Tradition I), which assumes tradition always gets it right, and an "ancillary view" ("weak" Tradition I) that views tradition as a helpful external aid to right biblical interpretation, but not an infallible one. See further Anthony N. S. Lane, "Scripture, Tradition, and Church: An Historical Survey," *Vox Evangelica* 9 (1975): 37–55, esp. 42–44.

tion I. For him, true tradition is simply a summary of what the apostles passed on in their biblical writings: "The Church, though dispersed throughout the whole world, even to the ends of the earth, has received from the apostles and their disciples this faith."[29] In other words, Tradition I simply means that the catholic church ("dispersed throughout the whole world") shares the same fundamental understanding of the canon. As to Scripture being its own interpreter, Trent deemed it formally *insufficient*. The teaching authority or magisterium of the church was also necessary: "It decrees that no one relying on his own judgment shall . . . presume to interpret [the Holy Scriptures] contrary to the sense which holy mother Church, to whom it belongs to judge of their true sense and interpretation, has held and holds."[30]

The nineteenth century saw an increase in papal authority, marked by lengthy encyclicals and culminating with the dogma of papal infallibility at the First Vatican Council (1869–70).[31] Pope Pius IX claimed papal supremacy, namely, the ability to assert jurisdiction over the church, including the college of bishops. In his own words: "I, I am Tradition, I, I am the Church."[32] One is sorely tempted here to speak not of *sola scriptura* but of *sola Roma*.

Vatican II (1962–65) nuanced the relationship between Scripture and tradition, making clear that the two "make up a single deposit of the word of God,"[33] just as clergy and laity make up a single people of God. This is a far cry from *sola scriptura*, however, as section 9 from *Dei Verbum*, the "Constitution on Divine Revelation," perhaps the most important document of Vatican II, makes clear: "The Church does not derive her certainty about all revealed truths from Sacred Scripture alone. Both Sacred Scripture and sacred tradition must be accepted and honored with equal sentiments of devotion and reverence."[34] Nothing essential has therefore changed with regard to Rome's *sola magisterium* since the Reformation.[35] As section 10 of *Dei Verbum* states,

29. Irenaeus, *Against Heresies* 1.10.1 (translation from *Ante-Nicene Fathers* 1:330).

30. In H. J. Schroeder, trans., *The Canons and Decrees of the Council of Trent* (Rockford, IL: Tan Books, 1978), 19.

31. See Francis A. Sullivan, *Magisterium: Teaching Authority in the Catholic Church* (New York: Paulist Press, 1983), 79–118 (chap. 5, "The Infallibility of the Magisterium in Defining Dogmas of the Faith").

32. Cited in Owen Chadwick, *A History of the Popes, 1830–1914*, Oxford History of the Christian Church (Oxford: Oxford University Press, 1998), 210.

33. Vatican II, *Dei Verbum* §10.

34. Vatican II, *Dei Verbum* §9 (cf. *Catechism of the Catholic Church* §82).

35. See Richard R. Gaillardetz, *Teaching with Authority: A Theology of the Magisterium in the Church* (Collegeville, MN: Liturgical Press, 1997); Gaillardetz, *By What Authority? A*

"The task of giving an authentic interpretation of the Word of God, whether in its written form or in the form of Tradition, has been entrusted to the living teaching office of the Church *alone*."[36] Even if Oberman may have been hasty in attributing a two-source theory to Trent, Tradition II rightly calls attention to Rome's insistence on the necessity to read Scripture through the lens of the tradition of its magisterial papal pronouncements.[37]

Fundamentalist Biblicism: "Solo" Scriptura (Tradition 0)

According to Oberman, the Reformers affirmed Tradition I: the notion, common in the church fathers, that the Rule of Faith provided a "single exegetical tradition of interpreted Scripture"[38] that took its bearings from Scripture itself rather than extrabiblical traditions. What Luther protested was not Roman Catholic tradition as such but the *departure* from received tradition. Both Luther and Calvin were very happy to appeal to figures such as Augustine and Irenaeus, not because they had some independent authority or pipeline to revelation, but because "they had so faithfully and fully expounded the real intention of the Bible writers."[39]

I mention this to set up the contrast with what Alister McGrath cheekily calls "Tradition 0": the idea that people can interpret the Bible without benefit of tradition.[40] What is at stake in distinguishing Traditions 0, I, and II is the meaning of *sola scriptura*. Is Scripture the norm that norms other norms, in which case we can speak of a pattern of authority, or is it the sole norm, in which case we can forget about patterns and simply affirm a single principle of authority: *"solo" scriptura*?[41]

The fundamental problem with *solo scriptura* is that "one Christian measures the scriptural interpretations of other Christians against the standard of

Primer on Scripture, the Magisterium, and the Sense of the Faithful (Collegeville, MN: Liturgical Press, 2003).

36. Vatican II, *Dei Verbum* §10 (emphasis added). We should note, however, Vatican II's *communio* ecclesiology and the conviction that the Roman magisterium works best in consultation with "the sense of the faithful" (see Gaillardetz, *By What Authority?*, 107–20, 139).

37. See also Robert A. Sungenis, *Not by Scripture Alone: A Catholic Critique of the Protestant Doctrine of Sola Scriptura* (Santa Barbara, CA: Queenship Publishing, 1997).

38. Heiko A. Oberman, *The Dawn of the Reformation: Essays in Late Medieval and Early Modern Thought* (Grand Rapids: Eerdmans, 1992), 280.

39. J. N. D. Kelly, *Early Christian Doctrines*, rev. ed. (San Francisco: HarperCollins, 1978), 49.

40. Alister McGrath, *Reformation Thought: An Introduction*, 2nd ed. (Oxford: Blackwell, 1993), 144–45.

41. Compare the similar expression *nuda scriptura*, which refers to Scripture stripped of its ecclesial context (and hence bare-naked or "nude").

his own scriptural interpretation."[42] It may seem as though one is espousing a high view of Scripture, but in fact *solo scriptura* is not biblical: "Scripture itself indicates that the Scriptures are the possession of the Church and that the interpretation of the Scripture belongs to the Church as a whole, as a community."[43] Hermeneutically, *solo scriptura* leads to an impasse: one cannot arbitrate the conflict of interpretations simply by offering one more individual's opinion about what the Bible means. The church ought not to give as much weight to every Tom, Dick, and Harry's opinion as it gives to Nicaea's doctrine of the Trinity.[44] *Solo scriptura* is something altogether different from *sola scriptura*: the latter affirms "that our final authority is Scripture alone, but not a Scripture that is alone."[45]

The Communities of Interpreters (Tradition III?)

Yet another way of construing the relation between Scripture and tradition puts the emphasis back on tradition, understood now not as an official teaching authority but simply as the lived culture of the church, the community of Scripture's interpreters. On this view, what rules Christian language and thinking is the *use* of Scripture in and by the believing community. Christians learn to speak Christian by participating in ecclesial forms of life. Hans-Georg Gadamer is right, claims Merold Westphal: "Tradition exercises authority in/over our thinking, our construals, and our seeings-as. . . . As a matter of observable fact, tradition shapes our interpretations and the resulting understandings."[46]

Hilary of Poitiers made a similar point centuries earlier: "Those who are situated outside the church are not able to acquire any understanding of the divine discourse."[47] *Extra ecclesiam, nulla intellectus*, one might say ("Outside the church, there is no comprehension"). This position views Philip as a stand-in for the way the church reads Scripture. For example, Philip knows who the prophet Isaiah is speaking about when Isaiah writes, "Like a sheep he was led to the slaughter" (cited in Acts 8:32), because he has learned to read

---

42. Keith A. Mathison, *The Shape of Sola Scriptura* (Moscow, ID: Canon Press, 2001), 240.
43. Ibid., 245.
44. Ibid., 249.
45. Ibid., 259.
46. Westphal, *Whose Community?*, 70.
47. Cited in David S. Yeago, "The Bible," in *Knowing the Triune God: The Work of the Spirit in the Practices of the Church*, ed. James J. Buckley and David S. Yeago (Grand Rapids: Eerdmans, 2001), 49.

typologically. The Bible functions authoritatively for insiders who know how to connect its dots. It may be that this postliberal view constitutes a new take on tradition—call it Tradition III.[48] In taking contemporary ecclesial usage of Scripture as its grammar, Tradition III effectively accords interpretive authority to the present-day church community. What the Bible means becomes a function of its contemporary use/interpretation in the church.

Stanley Hauerwas identifies *sola scriptura* as the "sin of the Reformation" because it is the doctrine that opened up what we have described as the Pandora's box of Protestantism, namely, the unchecked subjectivism that follows from the assumption "that the text of the Scripture makes sense separate from the Church that gives it sense."[49] By privileging individual interpreters who can read the Bible for themselves, both "fundamentalists and biblical critics make the Church incidental."[50] Interestingly, Hauerwas makes these comments in a chapter entitled "Stanley Fish, the Pope, and the Bible." Stanley Fish is the literary theorist who argues that textual meaning is a product of a community's interpretive strategies: on his account, readers do not respond to meaning but *construct* it. The *authority* of interpretive communities is, for Fish, a function of their *authorship*.

Elsewhere I have dealt (at length) with the broader issues of such hermeneutical antirealism.[51] Here I want simply to point out that if meaning is use, and if the use that counts (authorizes) is the community's, then the canon has no intrinsic meaning or authority of its own. In what follows I will argue that *sola scriptura* serves the church precisely by preserving intact the *distinction between text and interpretation*, and thus the possibility that the prevailing cultural practices and linguistic habits may be challenged and corrected by Scripture.[52] In the words of Anthony Lane: "*Sola Scriptura* is the statement that the church can err."[53]

---

48. Oberman makes an alternative suggestion: he finds an emerging Tradition III being developed by twentieth-century Roman Catholics who locate doctrinal authority neither in Scripture nor in tradition but in the teaching office of the church (*Dawn of the Reformation*, 289–90).

49. Stanley Hauerwas, *Unleashing the Scripture: Freeing the Bible from Captivity to America* (Nashville: Abingdon, 1993), 155.

50. Ibid., 26.

51. See Kevin J. Vanhoozer, *Is There a Meaning in This Text? The Bible, the Reader, and the Morality of Literary Knowledge* (Grand Rapids: Zondervan, 1998); Vanhoozer, *Drama of Doctrine*, 167–85.

52. So Gerhard Ebeling, *The Word of God and Tradition: Historical Studies Interpreting the Divisions of Christianity*, trans. S. H. Hooke (Philadelphia: Fortress, 1968), 136.

53. Anthony N. S. Lane, "*Sola Scriptura*? Making Sense of a Post-Reformation Slogan," in *A Pathway into the Holy Scripture*, ed. Philip E. Satterthwaite and David F. Wright (Grand Rapids: Eerdmans, 1994), 324.

The Pattern of Authority

"Scripture interprets Scripture." Yes. But how, where, under what conditions, and to whom? The short answer to all of the above is: in, through, and under the economy of grace. "To be an authority is to be connected within the complex web of interrelationships that God has given so that humans may be free."[54] Everything depends on the divine initiative: *Scripture comes into its own when read by God's people in God's way for God's purpose.* "Scripture interprets Scripture" means that the Bible as given by God is sufficient for the purpose for which God gave it. That purpose, I have suggested, is to be the instrument by which God rules his people, administers his covenant, and shapes the people into a holy nation. Authority has to do with authorizing interpretations that are conducive to human flourishing. Recall the orchestra conductor who decides (authorizes) how to perform a symphony. Many composers of symphonies, such as Johannes Brahms, included not only the notes to be played but also various markings that indicate how to play them: accents, dynamics, tempos, and so on. Even so, Brahms's scores are not entirely self-interpreting.

Scripture is like a musical score in that its interpretation too is a kind of performance. When readers respond—to obey a command, heed a warning, believe a claim, trust a promise, and so forth—they have to do something. Even truth is performed: we must "speak the truth in love" (Eph. 4:15) and "obey the truth" (Rom. 2:8; Gal. 5:7). Indeed, Jesus defines the wise person as one who "hears my words *and does them*" (Luke 6:47). Let us therefore define interpretive authority as the right to authorize what should be said and done on the basis of Scripture. The question before us concerns the locus of interpretive authority. Does Scripture conduct its own symphony, or does *sola scriptura* allow for a certain human conductivity as well?

Exegesis, Biblical Theology, and Systematic Theology: A Threefold Interpretive Cord

EXEGESIS AND PHILOLOGY: BEYOND GENERAL HERMENEUTICS?

Back to Philip. What kind of conductor of understanding is he? Recall that, upon being asked whether he understood what he was reading, the Ethiopian eunuch replied, "How can I, unless someone guides me?" (Acts 8:31). The

54. Austin, *Up with Authority*, 38.

Greek verb for "guide" is a compound made up of two terms: *hodos* (road, way) and *agō* (to lead); it is also used in John 16:13: "When the Spirit of truth comes, he will guide you into all truth." Its first cousin, *exagō* (to lead forth) is the origin of our term "exegesis." In guiding the reading, Philip is leading forth the text's meaning. Is Philip a philologist?

Naïve biblicists who hold to *solo scriptura* tend to view exegesis as a scientific procedure that lets the text have its say. They therefore lead the meaning out of the text by following the way the words objectively go. Does *sola scriptura* require the exegete to come to the text with a blank theological slate: Scripture alone, no systematics? If you think that it does, you probably have a low view of theology, perhaps because you fear that it imposes its doctrinal concerns upon the text. I am familiar with, even sympathetic to, this concern. We all can think of examples of theologians who come to the text with a system of conceptual categories already in place and then proceed to bend the text to their wills, forcing it into some procrustean philosophical bed, of which there are many in the showroom, ranging from older models like Platonism to newer, memory-foam models like panentheism.

I condone no approach to interpretation that forces the Bible to conform to a prefabricated ideological mold. On the other hand, I don't think that *sola scriptura* is a general hermeneutical principle (e.g., the principle of interpreting the parts in light of the whole and vice versa). The Ethiopian eunuch needed more than that. Philip provided the crucial clue: "And beginning with this Scripture [Isaiah] he told him the good news about Jesus" (Acts 8:35). That was precisely the Ethiopian eunuch's problem: he could understand the words and follow their grammar, but he could not say what the text was about. He knew the sense, but not the referent.

Does *Sola Scriptura* Favor Biblical Theology over Systematic Theology?

Here I need to make an excursus, as brief as it is brave, about the relationship of biblical and systematic theology: Does *sola scriptura* favor biblical theology over systematic theology? Stated differently: Is biblical theology *more biblical*—closer to the Bible—than systematic theology? A colleague of mine thinks so. He says, "Systematic theology attempts to organize what the Bible says according to some system . . . to impose a structure not transparently

given in Scripture itself."[55] In contrast, biblical theology "works inductively
. . . to uncover and articulate the unity of *all* the biblical texts taken together,
resorting primarily to the categories of those texts themselves."[56] On my colleague's view, systematic theology thinks in terms of the logical interrelationships of extrabiblical concepts (hiss!), while biblical theology follows the axis
of redemptive history (huzzah!).

I view things rather differently, such that *sola scriptura* authorizes biblical
and systematic theology alike—and without playing favorites. Of course, I
understand the concern that systematic theologians not engage in the wrong
kind of import/export business—as, for example, when Bultmann imports
Heidegger's existentialist philosophy to Pauline theology. But this is not the
place for a full-scale defense of systematics. Here I want merely to explain
its compatibility with *sola scriptura* and its place in the pattern of authority.

Part of the problem derives from Krister Stendahl's distinction between
"what it meant" and "what it means."[57] Given this contrast, it seems obvious
that biblical theology—the description of the biblical authors' thought world
in their own terms (what it meant to the original readers)—is closer to the
Bible than attempts to contextualize it in today's terms. But what if the real
contrast between the two disciplines is not "meant versus means" but "sense
versus reference"? Biblical theology tracks various themes throughout the
Bible, according to the unfolding of God's plan, paying special attention to
what each author says about them. "What each author says" corresponds to
the text's *sense*; but we also have to ask what the text is about, and "about-
ness" has to do with *reference*. Systematic theology comes into its own when
it thinks through the implications of what the biblical authors talk *about*.

There is a second reason to relate systematic theology to *sola scriptura*.
Systematic theology is simply the requirement to think biblical things through,
and to make sure that what one thinks about different biblical themes coheres. I have recently drawn on theater studies rather than philosophy for
the categories with which to organize the theology of the Bible, and I've
done so precisely to do justice to the nature of Christianity, whose essence
is not a theoretical system but a drama featuring the acts of the Triune God

55. D. A. Carson, "Systematic Theology and Biblical Theology," in *New Dictionary of
Biblical Theology*, ed. T. Desmond Alexander and Brian S. Rosner (Downers Grove, IL: Inter-
Varsity, 2000), 101.

56. Ibid., 100.

57. Krister Stendahl, "Biblical Theology, Contemporary," in *Interpreter's Dictionary of the
Bible*, ed. G. A. Buttrick (Nashville: Abingdon, 1962), 1:418–32.

(including speech acts) on the stage of redemptive history. We may describe biblical theology as the articulation of the plot of the drama of redemption (the biblical story line) and systematic theology as large-scale plot analysis that asks the who, what, and why questions characteristic of dramaturgy.[58] So biblical theology narrates the drama of redemption (the economic Trinity), and systematic theology makes explicit its underlying presuppositions, implications, and significance.

A third reason for rethinking the relationship of biblical and systematic theology trades on the distinction between concepts and judgments. *Biblical theology describes what the biblical authors are saying in terms of their original historical contexts in their own particular terms and concepts; systematic theology searches out the underlying patterns of biblical-canonical judgments and suggests ways of embodying these same judgments in our own particular cultural contexts, with our own particular terms and concepts.* The key insight here is that "the same judgment can be rendered in a variety of conceptual terms."[59] For example, Nicaea's concept "of the same substance" (*homoousios*) expresses the same judgment about the relationship of Father and Son as Paul's "equality with God" (*isa theō*) in Philippians 2:6. There are therefore different senses of what it means to be "biblical": at one extreme is the view that in order to think biblically, you have to think in the Bible's own Hebrew and Greek terms. At the other extreme is the idea that you are biblical if you refer to the same broad ideas (e.g., love). I am suggesting that systematic theology is distinctly biblical when it preserves the same underlying prophetic and apostolic judgments in new terms and concepts.[60] This is

58. For a comparison of theology to dramaturgy, see Vanhoozer, *Drama of Doctrine*, part 3. Note Richard Gaffin's observation: "Systematic theology . . . discusses the actors and their interactions that constitute the 'plot.' In this way the topical concern of systematic theology with what the Bible in its unity and as a whole teaches is maintained but in a way that keeps it focused on the unfolding of covenant history to its consummation in Christ (the concern of biblical theology)" (from an email dated February 1, 2000, as cited at http://www.upper-register .com/papers/bt_st.html). See also Gaffin, "The Vitality of the Reformed Tradition," in *The Vitality of Reformed Theology: Proceedings of the International Theological Congress, June 20–24th 1994, Noordwijkerhout, the Netherlands,* ed. J. M. Batteau, J. W. Maris, and K. Veling (Kampen: Kok, 1994), 29.

59. David S. Yeago, "The New Testament and the Nicene Dogma: A Contribution to the Recovery of Theological Exegesis," in *The Theological Interpretation of Scripture: Classic and Contemporary Readings,* ed. Stephen Fowl (Oxford: Blackwell, 1997), 93.

60. See further Kevin J. Vanhoozer, "Is the Theology of the New Testament One or Many? Between (the Rock of) Systematic Theology and (the Hard Place of) Historical Occasionalism," in *Reconsidering the Relationship between Biblical and Systematic Theology in the New Testament: Essays by Theologians and New Testament Scholars,* ed. Benjamin Reynolds, Brian

how the word of God "increases" and multiplies, as it gets translated into new cultural contexts (cf. Acts 12:24). Here endeth the systematics lesson.

SOLA SCRIPTURA, CANONICAL CONSCIOUSNESS, AND THE ANALOGY OF FAITH

David Starling's book *Hermeneutics as Apprenticeship* explores a suggestion that I made about readers of Scripture needing to become apprentices to the various "canonical practices" in Scripture, including the practice of reading Scripture the way Jesus reads Scripture and, in general, the way the New Testament uses the Old Testament.[61] We interpreters are apprentices who learn to read Scripture as Scripture by sitting at the feet of the biblical authors. I am choosing my words carefully. *Sola scriptura* is not simply a principle but a *practice*: the practice of using Scripture to interpret Scripture.[62]

To be apprenticed to Scripture is to begin to see Christ, the *res*, as the key insight into what Scripture is about. It is to learn to invoke the so-called analogy of faith (cf. Rom. 12:6), which means, first, using clearer passages to interpret those that are less clear. Henri Blocher suggests that most Protestants adopt a "formal" version of this analogy that takes coherence with the whole of Scripture, rather than any single theme, as the supreme norm by which all interpretations must be tested: "Like every other rule, it may be misapplied, but, within its frame, constitutional provision is made for correction by an objective standard."[63]

Sola scriptura is shorthand for "Scripture interprets Scripture"—and for one's apprenticeship to this canonical practice. Canon is the crucial concept, for it refers to the means by which God rules his people. Consider: canon involves authority (*kanōn* = "measuring rod" or "ruler"), interpretation (e.g., the relationship between whole and parts—everything from the New Testament use of the Old Testament to intertextuality), and community (i.e., those interpreters for whom just these books are authoritative Scripture). All three elements—authority, interpretation, community—come together in Galatians 6 when Paul, after invoking the order of the new creation established

---

Lugioyo, and Kevin Vanhoozer, Wissenschaftliche Untersuchungen zum Neuen Testament 2.369 (Tübingen: Mohr Siebeck, 2014), 17–38.

61. David Starling, *Hermeneutics as Apprenticeship: How the Bible Shapes Our Interpretive Habits and Practices* (Grand Rapids: Baker Academic, 2016).

62. See further Vanhoozer, *Drama of Doctrine*, 231–37.

63. Henri Blocher, "The 'Analogy of Faith' in the Study of Scripture," *Scottish Bulletin of Evangelical Theology* 5 (1987): 28.

by the cross of Christ, refers to "all who walk by this rule" (Gal. 6:16): "all who," the community; "walk by," the practice of interpretation; "this rule," the canonical Scriptures. This one verse more or less defines the task of systematic theology: to set forth in speech "what is in Christ" as attested in the canon in order to direct the people of God to conform their lives to this new reality and so participate fittingly (i.e., walk) in the drama of redemption attested in the Scriptures.

Meanwhile, Philip is still sitting in the chariot. Who (or what) do we say that he is? Martin Chemnitz says that Philip represents the ministry of the Word that leads to understanding.[64] Philip personifies the work of biblical and systematic theology, connecting the dots of redemptive history, explaining how they converge on Christ, and thus exemplifying good apostolic judgment. Philip personifies canon consciousness and exemplifies "ruled reading" of Scripture when, in imitation of his master, Philip starts with Isaiah and proclaims to the Ethiopian eunuch "the good news about Jesus" (Acts 8:35).[65] Philip enacts the rule for right reading, identifying Jesus as the ultimate reference of the Scriptures, and he does so as an apprentice to his master: "And beginning with Moses and all the Prophets, he [Jesus] interpreted to them [the disciples on the road to Emmaus] in all the Scriptures the things concerning himself" (Luke 24:27).

This is also the purpose of the ancient Rule of Faith (regula fidei): to encourage canon-conscious and Christ-centered reading. Like Philip, the Rule of Faith summarizes the basic biblical story line and shows how the story is fulfilled in the death and resurrection of Jesus. Irenaeus believed the regula fidei to be necessary for the correct interpretation of Scripture (the "key" that allows us to put the very pieces of the mosaic together in the right way to form the picture of a king rather than a dog), but only because it states succinctly and summarizes what Scripture is about.[66]

---

64. Chemnitz, Examination of the Council of Trent, trans. Fred Kramer (St. Louis: Concordia, 1971), 216.

65. "Canon consciousness" refers to the idea that "just these books" are authoritative for the church and to the awareness that the canonical shape of the whole of Scripture, with Jesus at the center, is intended as an interpretive help. Chad Spellman remarks, "The hermeneutical payoff of this governing function is that the canon helps guide contemporary readers through the biblical material by limiting and generating textual connections, and also helps identify the intended audience of the Christian Bible as a whole" (Toward a Canon-Conscious Reading of the Bible: Exploring the History and Hermeneutics of the Canon [Sheffield: Sheffield Phoenix Press, 2014], 217).

66. Irenaeus, Against Heresies 1.8, 10.

Sola scriptura is not a prohibition against using interpretive keys, be they dominical, apostolic, or patristic, as long as the key opens the mystery at the heart of the canon. *Sola scriptura* no more rules out systematic theology than it does Philip's ministry of canonical understanding. For theology is the task of making judgments that minister understanding, and what authorizes theology's judgments is Scripture itself. Further, theology makes explicit the judgments that are implicit in Scripture. Of course, "theology" is an abstraction: the real work—getting understanding—is done by real people in real-life situations. It is to their work, and to the task of practicing *sola scriptura*—making biblical judgments—that we now turn.

Councils: Catholicity, Part 1

Critics of *sola scriptura* who regard it simply as a principle of general hermeneutics (read the parts in light of the whole) accuse the Reformers of chasing the Holy Spirit out of the life of the church and into the confines of a book, with which individual interpreters then have their way. The basic contention of the present chapter is that *sola scriptura* belongs with the other *solas*, which is another way of saying that it belongs in the triune economy of grace. The Father works his sovereign, merciful, wise will to reign over his people in Christ through the Spirit *by means of* the Bible *in* the church: "The Spirit who enables and sustains our reading of Holy Scripture also provides a community to aid us in our reading."[67]

Mere Protestant Christianity holds to the unabbreviated pattern of authority in which both Word and Spirit have a place. And, just as the canon intends a community of readers, so the Spirit creates one. It is significant that Calvin did not conclude his *Institutes* with book III ("The Way We Receive the Grace of Christ") but went on to write book IV, the longest: "The External Means or Aims by Which God Invites Us into the Society of Christ and Holds Us Therein." The church is the "society of Christ" and "communion of saints," and it is arguably for this communion that God communicated to us in Scripture. The church therefore has a necessary role to play in the economy of grace—and in the pattern of interpretive authority.

If *sola scriptura* belongs in an economy in which both the Holy Spirit and the church are necessary ingredients, then individual interpreters cannot use

---

67. Scott R. Swain, *Trinity, Revelation, and Reading: A Theological Introduction to the Bible and Its Interpretation* (London: T&T Clark, 2011), 100.

Scripture as a blunt instrument with which to bludgeon rival expositors. While it may seem counterintuitive to those in the habit of proceeding from *sola scriptura* directly to "no" (as in "no creed but the Bible"), the reality is more complex. *Sola scriptura* functions properly only in the context of the whole church. What God has joined together—canonicity and catholicity—let no one (especially theologians) put asunder. Catholicity (Gk. *kata* [with respect to] + *holos* [whole]) pertains to the church universal, but everything depends on how we construe wholeness. The Reformers reacted against the narrowing of catholicity to the institution centered at Rome (i.e., *Roman* Catholicism). The Reformers would no doubt be shocked to learn that some in the twenty-first century have gone to the other extreme, broadening catholicity to refer to the whole cosmos, as if it signaled cosmological rather than ecclesiological wholeness.[68] On this view, the Roman Catholic Church is a particularly intense instance or sacrament of what is universally the case: in the Roman Catholic Church we see the invisible wholeness of the entire cosmos made visible in institutional form.

Mere Protestants are catholic Christians too, though they conceive catholicity differently. In brief: the wholeness that counts is primarily a function of the Spirit-enabled hearing of the gospel in faith (illumination), and only secondarily of stable structures (institutions). Even more succinctly: canonicity generates and governs catholicity. The whole in question refers to the communion of those who hear and respond in faith and obedience to their Master's voice speaking in the Scriptures.

THE JERUSALEM COUNCIL (ACTS 15)

The Jerusalem Council in Acts 15 is a paradigmatic case of what it means to practice *sola scriptura*.[69] F. F. Bruce sees this council as "an event to which Luke attaches the highest importance; it is as epoch-making, in his eyes, as the conversion of Paul."[70] The issue at stake: Do gentiles have to become like Jews in order to become Christians, and, in particular, is circumcision necessary for salvation? Some from Judea answered yes, and that is what

68. See Ilia Delio, *Making All Things New: Catholicity, Cosmology, Consciousness* (Maryknoll, NY: Orbis, 2015).

69. Darrell Bock calls the meeting a "consultation" rather than an ecclesial council (*Acts*, Baker Exegetical Commentary on the New Testament [Grand Rapids: Baker Academic, 2007], 486).

70. F. F. Bruce, *The Book of the Acts*, rev. ed., New International Commentary on the New Testament (Grand Rapids: Eerdmans, 1988), 282.

they were teaching believers at Antioch, much to Paul's consternation (Acts 15:1–2). Such a requirement would strike at the fundamental issue of the gospel—whether salvation is by grace *alone*—which is why it provoked "no small dissension and debate" (Acts 15:2) and, like many doctrinal topics, threatened to divide the body. When Paul goes to Jerusalem, he encounters similar opposition, with some insisting that it was "necessary" (Gk. *dei*) for gentiles to be circumcised.

The Jerusalem Council was a gathering of apostles and elders for the express purpose of investigating this matter (Acts 15:6). After considerable debate, Peter reminds them how God had blessed Cornelius and his gentile family with the gift of the Holy Spirit—having circumcised not his flesh but his heart—after which James makes a decisive intervention, citing verses from Amos about God's intention to include the gentiles in the Davidic restoration (Acts 15:15–18). James concludes, "Therefore my judgment is . . ." (Acts 15:19). Is James here exercising the much-maligned "right of private judgment"? F. F. Bruce softens James's tone with his translation "this is my vote," suggesting that James acts more or less like a chairman formulating a motion that he puts to the whole assembly.[71]

The motion passes! Luke describes the consensus, saying, "It seemed good to the apostles and the elders, with the whole church" (Acts 15:22), and again, "It has seemed good to us, having come to one accord" (15:25). Something more than democracy is going on here, for they add this explanation to the letter that they're sending to gentile believers in other churches: "It has seemed good to the Holy Spirit and to us" (15:28). We can infer that this unanimity was a sign of the Spirit's presence and activity in guiding the community to interpret the acts of God in light of the Scriptures in a way that was consistent with the truth of the gospel.[72] F. F. Bruce translates the opening of 15:28 ("It has been resolved by the Holy Spirit and ourselves") to underline the church's role "as the vehicle of the Spirit."[73] The "it has been resolved" phrase connotes authority and "was a form widely used in the wording of imperial and other government decrees."[74] The mention of the Spirit before the church consensus indicates the ultimate locus of the authorization.

---

71. F. F. Bruce, *The Acts of the Apostles: The Greek Text with Introduction and Commentary* (Grand Rapids: Eerdmans, 1951), 299.

72. So David G. Peterson, *The Acts of the Apostles*, Pillar New Testament Commentary (Grand Rapids: Eerdmans, 2009), 439.

73. Bruce, *Acts of the Apostles*, 298.

74. Ibid., 299.

The Jerusalem Council yields a precious insight into the practice of *sola scriptura* in the early church. The council was called so that the church, guided by the Spirit, could rightly judge what God was saying in the Scriptures about an important issue threatening to divide the fellowship. The council displayed canonical consciousness in producing a distinct theological judgment that indicated the gospel way forward. Moreover, the council was careful to respect the independence of the *ecclesia* of Antioch, "yet not in such a way as to encourage disregard either of the great mother Ecclesia, or of the Lord's own Apostles, or of the unity of the whole Christian body."[75] *What authorized the theological judgment of the council was the whole church agreeing on the import of the Word in the guiding power of the Spirit.*

Jaroslav Pelikan notes that Acts 15 has served throughout church history "as a model for decision-making in the church and as a charter both for authority *at* church councils and for the authority *of* church councils."[76] He points out that the words "It has seemed good to the Holy Spirit and to us" were quoted by later church councils, including some that were Protestant.[77] Historically, councils proved necessary when there were matters of "no small dissension and debate" (Acts 15:2) that, like the question of gentile circumcision, threatened both the integrity of the gospel and the unity of the church.[78]

Conciliarism and the Pattern of Authority

"It seemed good to the Holy Spirit and to us." Is it ever appropriate for church councils after the council at Jerusalem to use this formula, particularly if it prefaces authoritative dogmas? The conciliar movement got under way in the medieval period as a way to deal with rogue popes and, in particular, to deal with the Great Schism of 1378, when the papacy split into two (and then three). Councils seemed to be the only way to deal with rival papal claims. Indeed, throughout the later medieval period many people pinned their hopes on a general council that would both unite and reform the Roman Catholic

75. Fenton J. A. Hort, *The Christian Ecclesia: A Course of Lectures on the Early History and Early Conceptions of the Ecclesia* (London: Macmillan, 1914), 82.

76. Jaroslav Pelikan, *Acts*, Brazos Theological Commentary on the Bible (Grand Rapids: Brazos, 2005), 175.

77. Ibid.

78. Pelikan mentions the seven ecumenical councils as examples (ibid., 176).

Church, and for this reason we can say that the fifteenth-century councils were among the forerunners of the Reformation.[79]

According to the Anglican theologian Paul Avis, "The Reformation can be seen as an explosion of pent-up conciliar, reforming energy . . . part of the legacy of the Conciliar Movement."[80] Whereas Luther hoped that a council would scale back papal authority, later Protestants like Calvin, Melanchthon, and Cranmer wanted to convoke a Protestant council to iron out their differences: "The Reformation should be seen as at one and the same time a reaction to the failure of the Conciliar Movement and a perpetuation of conciliar ideals by other means."[81]

John McNeill argues that conciliarism is the "constitutional principle" of what he calls "unitive Protestantism," a clear anticipation of my "mere Protestant Christianity."[82] Even in the late Middle Ages there were conciliarists who believed that authority was not monarchical but constitutional: "In the former, authority rests with a ruler [the pope] who is not responsible to the ruled. In the latter, it is the ruled who also rule, though ordinarily through delegated and responsible bodies."[83] The Council of Constance (1415) claimed to "hold authority directly from Christ" and accordingly asserted its superiority over papal authority. Significantly, the conciliar movement accepted both the premise and the promise of catholicity but wanted to expand it beyond its Roman confines: "Conciliar thought advocated a form of distributed authority in which fullness of authority was located in the whole body of the Church and came to focus and expression in councils."[84]

Both Luther and Calvin had much to say about church councils. Luther cared more about preserving the freedom and integrity of the gospel than he did about ecclesial structures. Yet, in a 1518 appeal to a general council for vindication, he wrote, "A sacred council lawfully assembled in the Holy Spirit, representing the Holy Catholic Church, is superior to the pope in matters

79. In Paul Avis's pithy words: "Conciliarism attempted to call in the resources of the whole Church, dispersed throughout the nations and the universities, in order to redress the failings of the centre" (*Beyond the Reformation? Authority, Primacy and Unity in the Conciliar Tradition* [London: T&T Clark, 2006], xvii–xviii).

80. Ibid., xix, 106.

81. Ibid., 108.

82. McNeill, *Unitive Protestantism*, 89.

83. Ibid.

84. Avis, *Beyond the Reformation?*, 22.

that concern the faith."[85] McNeill points out that the "Protest" of the Diet of Speyer, so often trotted out as clear evidence of the Reformers' putting all their dogmatic eggs in the basket of individual conscience, is instead "the reiteration by the Lutheran princes and cities of the conciliar principle inculcated by Luther himself."[86]

Luther's treatise "On the Councils and the Church" (1539), written on the eve of the Council of Trent, acknowledges that councils, though useful, could also err. He thinks that councils should represent the whole church, be called for one primary purpose, and speak with representative, though still provisional, authority only when they address that central issue: "The truth of a council's decisions is a function of its faithfulness to Scripture, to the gospel, and its humble dependence on the guidance of the Holy Spirit."[87] Pelikan summarizes Luther's position: "As a Protestant, he subjected the authority of church councils to the authority of the word of God; as a Catholic he interpreted the word of God in conformity with the dogmas of the councils and in this sense made the councils normative. . . . Catholic substance and Protestant principle belong together."[88]

Calvin, writing after the Council of Trent, is much less conciliatory to the papacy, but it does not follow that he was less catholic.[89] Calvin opens his section on "Councils and Their Authority" by acknowledging that he will be severe, but he says, "I venerate [the ancient councils] from my heart, and desire that they be honored by all."[90] His problem with councils is, first, that many (such as Trent) are not truly representative of the whole church. Second, even when they are representative of the whole church, they remain fallible because their pastors (bishops) are fallible.

Calvin examines particular conciliar decisions, insisting that he does not wish to rescind all their acts or deny their authority. He is particularly sensitive to the charge that he is setting himself up as a council of one "so that every man has the right to accept or reject what the councils decide."[91] On

85. Martin Luther, "Appeal of Brother Martin Luther to a Council," in Luther, WA 2:36–40. See further McNeill, *Unitive Protestantism*, 96–109.

86. McNeill, *Unitive Protestantism*, 106.

87. Avis, *Beyond the Reformation?*, 118.

88. Jaroslav Pelikan, *Obedient Rebels: Catholic Substance and Protestant Principle in Luther's Reformation* (London: SCM, 1964), 76.

89. According to McNeill, "Protestantism continued the tradition of conciliar, as opposed to monarchical, catholicism" (*Unitive Protestantism*, 89).

90. Calvin, *Institutes* IV.9.1.

91. Calvin, *Institutes* IV.9.8.

the contrary, when a conciliar decision is considered, we do well to ask who was present, whether they gathered in Christ's name (Matt. 18:20), what the issue was, and whether they contain nothing contrary to the Word of God. Calvin thinks that we should accept the "provisional judgments" of Nicaea and Chalcedon insofar as they contain nothing but the genuine exposition of Scripture.[92]

Calvin then states what he thinks is the positive purpose of councils: not to invent new doctrine but to address interpretive disputes. The best remedy for doctrinal disagreements is for a general council to be convened. Calvin notes that a decision that pastors at a council agree on "will have much more weight than if . . . a few private individuals should compose it."[93] Here he appeals to the Pauline principle "Let two or three prophets speak, and let the others weigh what is said" (1 Cor. 14:29), on the grounds that if this is the procedure for one church, how much more important in more serious cases for the several churches to take "common cognizance among themselves."[94] Calvin's final position is perhaps best summed up in his reply to Cardinal Sadolet's accusation that Protestants encourage every individual to interpret for himself: "For, although . . . Fathers and Councils are of authority only in so far as they agree with the rule of the Word, we still give to Councils and Fathers such ranks and honor as it is proper for them under Christ to hold."[95]

Church councils are called at particular times and places where decisions about something vital to the story of redemption have to be made in order to preserve the integrity of the gospel and the unity of the church (e.g., the charge that the Son is the highest created being was refuted by the *homoousios* of the Council of Nicaea). They reflect the conviction that authority is vested in the whole church, not simply a monarchy or hierarchy. "Catholicity" means the whole congregation of the faithful. Conciliarism is more or less the mere Protestant principle of government in ordinary and extraordinary times alike. Synods and general assemblies follow conciliarism's representative form of government, and at the level of the local church we know conciliarism as congregationalism.[96] In Avis's words: "The central conviction of conciliarism—its

92. Calvin, *Institutes* IV.9.8.

93. Calvin, *Institutes* IV.9.13.

94. Calvin, *Institutes* IV.9.13.

95. John Calvin, *Calvin: Theological Treatises*, trans. J. K. S. Reid, Library of Christian Classics 22 (Philadelphia: Westminster, 1954), 255 ("Reply to Sadolet").

96. McNeill cites a 1523 treatise of Luther's entitled "That a Christian Assembly or Congregation Has the Right to Judge All Doctrines, to Call, Install and Dismiss Teachers: Proof

pivotal ecclesiological axiom—is the belief that responsibility for the well-being (the doctrine, worship, and mission) of the Church rests with the whole Church."[97]

Here we may recall what I said in the previous chapter about authorities being authorized to decide things. There is a certain parallel between church councils and orchestra conductors. In both cases decisions need to be made about how to perform the script or score, respectively. The text is supremely authoritative, but conductors and church councils alike have to make decisions as to how best to interpret it if the society in question—orchestra or church—is to act in harmony. A church council is not an individual, as is a conductor, but rather a corporate personality. This better reflects the Reformers' belief that the welfare of the whole church resides in the whole church. The Council of Nicaea displayed canon consciousness when it made its theological judgment affirming the Son as the same substance as the Father. *The Council of Nicaea made explicit what Christians are authorized to say on the basis of the prophets and apostles.* We ought therefore to conclude (to stick with the analogy of the conductor) that the Nicene Creed was a great performance, a theological judgment that rightly explicated the implicit logic of the biblical account of the person and work of Jesus Christ, with a view to refuting the Arian heresy. And, though the conceptual formula of Nicaea had primary reference to a specific problem in the church's fourth-century context and was expressed in Greek concepts, the *judgment* underlying that formula identifying the Son as very God of very God has perennial significance for Christians in all times and places who acknowledge it as thoroughly biblical.

Tradition: Catholicity, Part 2

Sola scriptura is the practice of attending to the Spirit speaking in the Scriptures and to saints, equally attentive, who do the same. There is only one church of Jesus Christ, but it is extended through space and time. The Reformers' main objection to Roman Catholicism was not its catholicity but its centeredness on Rome. The Reformers believed that they were more in line than Rome when it came to tradition, for they (the Reformers) believed what the early church believed about tradition, namely, that it was the church's

---

and Reason from the Scriptures" and comments that this is "conciliarism in its elemental, congregational form" (*Unitive Protestantism*, 121–22).

97. Avis, *Beyond the Reformation?*, 184.

consensus teaching on Scripture's fundamental story line. Indeed, the one thing on which patristic and medieval theologians were agreed was the notion that doctrine must be grounded in Scripture. Hence, those who affirm *sola scriptura* are more in line with the catholic tradition than those who deny it. Rome is downright sectarian in its insistence that there were some truths or customs handed on orally to the apostles alongside Scripture.

Christians today need to listen to all their predecessors who attended to the Spirit speaking in the Scriptures in order to make theological judgments about issues in their day that threatened the integrity of the gospel and the unity of the church (unity in Christ is an implication of the gospel too). Calvin does not violate *sola scriptura* when he encourages individual interpreters to submit their judgments about Scripture's meaning "to the judgment of the Church."[98] Of course, when Calvin says "church," he means the whole fellowship of the saints, not the Roman hierarchy. "Catholicity" for Calvin means the sum total of those local, visible churches where God's Word is rightly preached and the sacraments are rightly administered. This listening in the fellowship of the Spirit to the authorship of the Spirit has a cumulative effect. As more people receive and hand on Christ, the understanding of the whole church grows: "Through Holy Scripture, the church's foundational authority, the Lord who possesses all authority *authorizes the church to build* on that foundation."[99] As God gave Adam and Eve a creation mandate, so Christians have an ecclesial mandate: build my church; feed my sheep.

"Tradition" refers to the passing on from one generation to the next of a set of beliefs and a way of life. It is a thoroughly biblical notion. Here is Paul's exhortation to the Thessalonians: "So then, brothers, stand firm and hold to the traditions that you were taught by us, either by our spoken word or by our letter" (2 Thess. 2:15). It is a grievous mistake to think that *sola scriptura* entails *nulla traditio* (no tradition or Tradition 0). The biblical authors and Reformers rightly show disregard for merely human traditions, since these lack divine authorization. The tradition that interests me in the present context is the one that is a part of the economies of grace and faith—that is, the postapostolic conversation about the meaning and implications of apostolic discourse, a conversation that the Spirit uses to guide the whole ("catholic")

---

98. John Calvin, *Canons and Decrees of the Council of Trent, with the Antidote* (1547), in *Selected Works of John Calvin: Tracts and Letters*, vol. 3, *Tracts, Part 3* (Grand Rapids: Baker, 1983).

99. Allen and Swain, *Reformed Catholicity*, 43.

church into all truth. Tradition too is an element in the economy of grace that, like the church, exists to nurture the society of Jesus.

Spirit and Tradition

When Luther was accused of interpreting the Bible according to his own private spirit (*proprio spiritu*), and thus of wanting his spirit to lord it over the meaning of Scripture, he replied, "I do not want to be boasted of as more learned than all, but Scripture alone to rule: nor for it to be interpreted by my spirit or by any human spirit, but understood through itself and by its own spirit [*per . . . suo spiritu intelligi*]."[100] Scripture interprets Scripture through itself *and* by its own spirit. If we are to get beyond general hermeneutics, we must acknowledge the Spirit's role in the historical process of the community's struggle to understand and reach consensus on the meaning of Scripture.

Let's return to Philip and Acts 8 one more time. The Acts of the Apostles could well have been called the Acts of the Spirit: the Spirit is clearly directing the action, prompting the apostles what to say, when to say it, and to whom. The Spirit is the ultimate interpreter of the word that he authored, Philip his chosen means. If the church has a role to play in the pattern of interpretive authority, it is not simply because it is one more interpretive community, as Stanley Fish thinks, but because it has been appointed to participate in the triune economy of communication. Tradition—the messy human historical process of seeking understanding—is an external means, like the church itself, which the Spirit, "the Supreme Magisterium of God,"[101] uses to minister Christ.

Herman Bavinck views tradition as "the method by which the Holy Spirit causes the truth of Scripture to pass into the consciousness and life of the church."[102] Moreover, as Michael Allen and Scott Swain observe, "everything that the Spirit does *in* us to illumine Holy Scripture, he does *by* us, by the instrumentality of created reason in its social and historical expression."[103] Tradition too is a divinely designed and designated route for attaining to Christian maturity, for obtaining "the measure of the stature of the fullness of Christ" (Eph. 4:13). Tradition's products—the Rule of Faith, creeds, and

100. Luther, *WA* 7:98.4–6.
101. Charles Colson and Richard John Neuhaus, introduction to *Your Word Is Truth: A Project of Evangelicals and Catholics Together*, ed. Charles Colson and Richard John Neuhaus (Grand Rapids: Eerdmans, 2002), 7.
102. Bavinck, *Reformed Dogmatics*, 1:494.
103. Allen and Swain, *Reformed Catholicity*, 37.

confessions—may be viewed as sanctified instruments in the economy of grace, "true and proper effects of [the Spirit's] pedagogical grace."[104]

Please note: tradition has no independent authority. Tradition is but the moon to Scripture's sun: what light tradition casts, and what authority it has, is secondary and derivative—ministerial—though it is nonetheless real light. The Spirit has been guiding the church into all truth for centuries. The proper context of theological work is not simply the immediate present (or, we could add, our particular place) but rather "the long past" of the Spirit's work: hence "'tradition'—the intellectual and spiritual culture of the communion of saints—is indispensable to the operation of theological reason."[105]

TESTIMONY AND TRADITION

One way of capturing the derivative authority of tradition is to view it as a species of testimony, or "astonished indication."[106] Tradition is not the Word of God; it is testimony to that Word. Putting it this way helps us to see that tradition bears the authority of a witness rather than of a judge.

Viewing tradition rightly involves seeing it in the context of what we might call the triune "economy of testimony." (By now you're probably thinking that I should have been an economist!) If we are to understand the relation of tradition to Scripture, we need to understand the place of human testimony in the drama of redemptive history. Giving testimony in ancient Israel was a judicial affair, for which at least two or three witnesses were needed (Deut. 17:6; 19:15). This is the background for Jesus's statement: "If I alone bear witness about myself, my testimony is not true" (John 5:31). The entirety of the Fourth Gospel is structured to show that not only Jesus's words and deeds testify to who he is, but that the Father and the Spirit do so as well (John 5:37; 8:18; 15:26). Jesus is explicit about the Spirit's testimony: "He will not speak on his own authority, but whatever he hears he will speak" (John 16:13). It is this Spirit-witness that Jesus gives his disciples: "But when the Helper comes, whom I will send to you from the Father, the Spirit of truth, who proceeds from the Father, he will bear witness about me. And you also will bear witness" (John 15:26–27). Hence the testimony that begins with God the Father

104. Ibid., 45.
105. Webster, "*Ressourcement* Theology," 493.
106. John Webster, "The Visible Attests the Invisible," in *The Community of the Word: Toward an Evangelical Ecclesiology*, ed. Mark Husbands and Daniel J. Treier (Downers Grove, IL: InterVarsity, 2005), 106.

and proceeds to the Spirit also proceeds to the disciples. The Spirit will bear witness to the disciples and through the disciples (to us).

The substance of tradition—what gets handed on and passed down—is essentially testimony. The content of the four Gospels is apostolic testimony to the identity, teaching, life, death, and resurrection of Jesus Christ. Paul's Epistles are testimony too, but primarily to what God was doing in Christ and its universal significance. The Rule of Faith and creedal statements are forms of postapostolic testimony that summarize salvation history and earlier apostolic testimony.

Victor Austin likens an individual church member's confession of faith to an aria in Bach's *St. Matthew Passion*. An aria does not advance the story line (recitatives do that), nor does it represent the church as a whole (choruses do that). Rather, the aria—singing *sola*—is the individual's acknowledgment, in the context of the believing community, that she also personally appropriates to herself Christ's death and resurrection.[107] Church authority comes alive "only when one stands to profess."[108] The exercise in question is an exercise of what we might call *testimonial authority*: "Authority is actualized in the church when Christ is confessed."[109]

As we saw in the previous chapter, it is as rational to trust testimony as it is to trust our own memory and perceptions. Epistemic dependence is part and parcel of what it means to know as humans.[110] Whether it is learning medicine, how to play the piano, or how to follow Christ, an individual has reason "to believe what the authority tells her because that is a necessary condition for learning the practice."[111] Supreme authority belongs to Christ and his commissioned witnesses, the apostles, but church tradition has testimonial authority too insofar as it bears faithful witness to the truth of Scripture. Tradition bears corporate witness to the truth of Scripture in much the same way that an individual does, though we need to distinguish second-person singular from second-person plural testimonial authority. If we are epistemically conscientious and spiritually honest, we have to admit that other Spirit-guided believers are seeking to bear faithful witness to Scripture as much as we are: "The authority of my community is justified for me by my conscientious

107. Austin, *Up with Authority*, 96.

108. Ibid., 98.

109. Ibid., 100.

110. Benjamin McMyler, *Testimony, Trust, and Authority* (New York: Oxford University Press, 2011), 4; cf. 170.

111. Zagzebski, *Epistemic Authority*, 149.

judgment that I am more likely to believe the truth and avoid falsehood if I believe what We believe than if I try to figure out what to believe in a way that is independent of Us."[112] Still, the authority of tradition is provisional: it is possible that an individual could reasonably withdraw the judgment that one is more likely to arrive at the truth by believing the community's testimony, if the community gives evidence of no longer being a reliable witness. This was Luther's judgment on the papacy of his day.

When tradition serves as an external aid to biblical interpretation, mere Protestant Christians accord it the authority of *corporate testimony*.[113] Recall Alvin Plantinga's account of warranted belief, according to which people are entitled to believe something if it is produced by their cognitive faculties, when they are functioning properly in the environment for which they were designed.[114] Cognitive faculties that meet these conditions enjoy epistemic authority, and we are authorized to believe on their say-so. I submit that we transpose what Plantinga says about cognitive faculties to corporate testimony.

Consider: like memory, tradition too is a reliable belief-producing mechanism when corporate witnesses are testifying properly in the church, the environment that is not only designed but also sustained by the Holy Spirit precisely for the purpose of guiding believers into the truth of Scripture's own testimony to Jesus Christ. Putting it this way highlights what is distinctive about the corporate testimony (i.e., corporate memory) that is the warp and woof of Christian tradition: it is an external means that the Spirit uses as part of the broader triune economy of testimony. It is part of the divine design plan—the triune economy—for transmitting Christian faith. In deferring to the testimonial authority of tradition, we are trusting not generic "others" but Christian "brothers and sisters," people who, like us, orient themselves to hearing and doing the Word of God.

SOLA SCRIPTURA AND TRADITION

The purpose of tradition is to shape and authorize individuals to add their own voices to the economy of testimony. This authority flows from the Father to the Son, and from the Son through the Spirit to individuals. To confess Christ on the basis of the Scriptures is to give expression to what has been

112. Ibid., 155.
113. I am thinking here of "'weak' Tradition I" (i.e., the ancillary view).
114. Plantinga, *Knowledge and Christian Belief*, 28.

internalized: the testimonial authority of tradition. "It seemed good to the Holy Spirit and to us." The authority of the individual's confession—the goodness of its theological judgment—is the goodness of listening to what one has been told.

To be a person of good theological judgment is to be a good listener—above all, to the voice of God speaking in the Scriptures, the writings of Christ's commissioned witnesses: "Those who listen to the Word hear and are guided by the Holy Spirit to make the judgment of God their own judgment, and thereby to judge for themselves."[115] But we also learn good theological judgment by listening to those who have been taken up as instruments of the Spirit in the economy of testimony, especially that "great cloud" of postapostolic witnesses (cf. Heb. 12:1), whose corporate testimony is the substance of tradition. Tradition is the result of sustained listening to Scripture and sustained thinking about its meaning, truth, and significance. The Reformers agreed that many of the church fathers were reliable interpreters, and they did not hesitate to appeal to the fathers in polemical contexts to authorize their own readings, especially when arguing with other Protestants. Both Lutherans and Calvinists wanted to claim Augustine as their own, for example.[116]

Michael Allen and Scott Swain have recently argued that the catholic church is the proper context for interpreting Scripture and doing theology, and they claim to have retrieved this idea from the Protestant Reformers themselves. They define "tradition" as "the church's stance of abiding in and with apostolic teaching through time,"[117] "the temporally extended, socially mediated activity of renewed reason."[118] It all ultimately goes back to the idea that the church is not only a consequence of the gospel but also a means for helping people to grow into the reality that the gospel proclaims. The church is part of the economy of the gospel, the plan by which God purposes to form a holy nation, and all the processes and products of church tradition are external means of expanding the domain of the Word of God. These processes and products are authoritative to the extent that they faithfully testify to the truth of Scripture; and they do that when they are functioning as divinely intended in the environment for which they were designed to function: the church.

---

115. Austin, *Up with Authority*, 120–21.

116. See further Chung-Kim, *Inventing Authority*. Chung-Kim may go too far, however, in claiming that the fathers became "authenticators of the Protestant tradition" (143), unless she means "secondary authenticators."

117. Allen and Swain, *Reformed Catholicity*, 34.

118. Ibid., 36.

The church exists in time and has a history. This history belongs to the economy of testimony superintended by the Holy Spirit. The early Protestant confessions recognized this and, like Luther and Calvin, honored the witness of the catholic past. Here is the First Helvetic Confession (1536): "Where the holy fathers and early teachers, who have explained and expounded the Scripture, have not departed from this rule, we want to recognize and consider them not only as expositors of Scripture, but as elect instruments through whom God has spoken and operated." Michael Horton says something similar: "We have creeds, confessions, and catechisms not because we want to arrogantly assert ourselves above Scripture . . . but for precisely the opposite reason: We are convinced that such self-assertion is actually easiest for us when we presume to be going to Scripture alone and directly, without any presuppositions."[119]

In sum, tradition is the effective history of the biblical word, effective because in the pattern of triune authority the Spirit is the efficacy of the Word, the persuasive guide that opens minds and hearts to see Scripture's light. Not everything in church history is tradition, however. As we have seen, *sola scriptura* is the reminder that the church can err. What particularly possess testimonial authority are those Spirited occasions when individuals and councils had to make discerning theological judgments in order to preserve the integrity of the gospel and the unity of the church.[120]

Sola Scriptura for Bible, Church, and Interpretive Authority

We began this chapter by examining the charge that *sola scriptura* paved the way for doctrinal chaos, where every individual Protestant read Scripture in the way that was right in his or her own eyes. I now conclude with four more theses, one on the pattern of interpretive authority, the other three on the relationship between Scripture (canonicity) and tradition (catholicity).

9. The mere Protestant pattern of interpretive authority begins with the Triune God in communicative action, accords first place to Scripture interpreting Scripture (the canonic principle), but also acknowledges the appointed role of church tradition (the catholic principle) in the economy of testimony.

119. Michael Horton, "The *Sola*'s of the Reformation," in *Here We Stand! A Call from Confessing Evangelicals for a Modern Reformation*, ed. James Montgomery Boice and Benjamin E. Sasse (Phillipsburg, NJ: P&R, 1996), 107.
120. See Ramm, *Pattern of Religious Authority*, 57.

Sola scriptura means that Scripture alone is the supreme normative standard of Christian faith and life. This means that Scripture is also the norm and criterion for Jesus Christ: we have no other authorized and infallible testimony to Christ aside from the Scriptures. Scripture is thus the *norma normans* (norming norm), what we might also term the "unnormed norm." Tradition is a *norma normata* (normed norm). The normed norm of tradition has derivative or relative authority—what some have understood as ministerial (as opposed to magisterial) authority, and what I have here been calling *testimonial* as opposed to *judicial* authority. So: Scripture *alone* is the supreme authority, but God in his grace decided that it is not good for Scripture to be alone.[121] He thus authorized tradition, and Scripture when it saw it said, "This at last is norm of my norm and light of my light; she shall be called postapostolic testimony, because she was taken out of apostolic testimony." This is essentially Anthony Lane's "ancillary view," or what I prefer to call "weak" Tradition I.

Sola scriptura is not alone in the pattern of interpretive authority; the other *solas* have roles to play as well. *Sola gratia* reminds us that there is an economy of light: God is light, Christ is the light of the world, and the Spirit is the one who opens eyes and ears to the light of Christ that shines forth from the lamp of Scripture. For Bernard Ramm, the pattern of authority begins with Christ, who is the supreme content of the Scriptures and the supreme object of the witness of the Spirit, and then moves to the Scriptures, which the Spirit inspires and uses as his instrument in effecting illumination.[122] But Ramm rightly goes further, insisting that if Christ has given the Spirit to teach the church, "*then every generation of Christian theologians must be prepared to take seriously the history of theology. . . .* To uproot theology from the past is not part of the essence of Protestantism."[123] This too is catholicity: a respect for the unabbreviated, unadulterated hearing of God's Word across centuries and cultures. Not everything in the history of theology is worth preserving, but what we must not neglect are the efforts of those who have gone before us to listen to, and hear, every word that has come out of the mouth of God and was written in Scripture. Protestants forbid any interpretation from enjoying the same authority as Scripture itself, yet mere Protestant Christians

---

121. As Mathison says, "Our final authority is Scripture alone, but not a Scripture that is alone" (*Shape of Sola Scriptura*, 259).

122. Ramm, *Pattern of Religious Authority*, 36–37.

123. Ibid., 57 (emphasis original).

acknowledge the Spirit's use of fallible teachers, councils, and tradition to lead the church into all truth.

> 10. *Sola scriptura* is not a recipe for sectarianism, much less an excuse for schism, but rather a call to listen for the Holy Spirit speaking in the history of Scripture's interpretation in the church.

Sectarianism is "the denial of the presence of the Holy Spirit in the community of believers"[124] and, as such, a denial of mere Protestant Christianity. Sectarianism partakes of an individualist mind-set and ethos but applies them to the level of one's community. The danger, in other words, is that of interpretive egoism. I have been at pains to indicate the biblical warrants for paying attention to external aids that can help us better understand Scripture. This was the moral of Philip's ministry to the Ethiopian eunuch. Tradition, like Philip, is the "creaturely social co-efficient"[125] of the Spirit's interpretive activity, an external means of hermeneutical grace. As such, it is deserving of *prima facie* (at first glance; provisional), not *ultima facie* (as a final consideration) respect and obedience.[126]

> 11. *Sola scriptura* entails not a naïve but a critical biblicism.

Naïve biblicism confuses *sola scriptura* with *solo scriptura*. So do many of its critics. While the Bible is the primal and final authority for making theological judgments, strictly speaking it is not alone. "Critical biblicism" affirms the supreme (magisterial) authority, determinate meaning, and unified truth of Scripture (= biblicism) while acknowledging the secondary (ministerial) authority, plurality, and fallibility of human interpretations (= critical). The critical biblicist appeals to biblical authority in the manner of a critical realist. Scripture interprets itself, but there is no guarantee that one's grasp of what Scripture says coincides with Scripture itself. *Sola scriptura* means that *Scripture alone is the supreme norm*, not that Scripture is alone (i.e., the sole norm). Naïve biblicism errs in short-circuiting the economy of testimony—that is, the pattern of theological authority by which the Spirit leads the church into the full measure of Scripture's meaning by utilizing previous readings.

---

124. Ibid., 58.

125. John Webster, "'In the Society of God': Some Principles of Ecclesiology," in *God without Measure: Working Papers in Christian Theology*, vol. 1, *God and the Works of God* (London: Bloomsbury T&T Clark, 2016), 177–94.

126. The distinction comes from Nicholas Wolterstorff, *The Mighty and the Almighty: An Essay in Political Theology* (Cambridge: Cambridge University Press, 2012), 61.

Readers—Ethiopian or not—often need the external aid of apostolic tradition and catholic councils.

12. A mere Protestant practice of *sola scriptura* constitutes a catholic biblicism.

Mere Protestant interpreters do well to consult and be guided by the theological judgments of earlier generations of Christians and of Christian communities in other parts of the world: Protestants who affirm *sola scriptura* ought also to affirm *prima facie* the catholic tradition as *a Spirit-guided embodiment of right biblical understanding.* John McNeill states that "the Reformers aimed at a reformed catholicity, a catholicity freed from papal domination and medieval obscurantism."[127] The norm of Christian wisdom remains the Word of God (biblicism), yet the corporate confessions of the church—the sum total of its creedal, conciliar, and confessional theological judgments (catholicity)—have testimonial authority as to Scripture's meaning. Hence, counterintuitive though it may be, "Catholicity is the *only* option for a Protestantism that takes *sola scriptura* seriously."[128]

At the same time, we must remember that "unless the LORD builds the house, those who build it labor in vain" (Ps. 127:1). There are many houses on Evangel Way: a few are well established (up to canonical code); some have remodeled on the strength of testimonial authority (catholic tradition); others have constructed additions without waiting for the proper building permits, thus falling foul of canonicity and catholicity alike. Those who live in the latter do well to remember that God's Word is not only a two-edged sword but also a sledgehammer that strips away false fronts and knocks down non-load-bearing dividing walls. At the limit, those who live in houses built on foundations other than the apostles and prophets (Eph. 2:20) will eventually find posted on their doorposts the notice "This property is condemned."

---

127. McNeill, *Unitive Protestantism*, 86.
128. Peter J. Leithart, "Sola Scriptura, Una Ecclesia," *First Things*, May 1, 2014, http://www
.firstthings.com/blogs/leithart/2014/05/sola-scriptura-una-ecclesia.

4

In Christ Alone

The Royal Priesthood of All Believers

Wherever Christ is, there is the catholic church.

—Ignatius[1]

Number 62 of Luther's Ninety-Five Theses reads: "The true treasure of the church is the most holy gospel of the glory and grace of God."[2] Yet those who cherish the gospel must also cherish the church, for the church is an implication of the gospel, a figure of its *telos*, giving body to the lordship of Christ. The church is wherever two or three are gathered by God in Christ through the Spirit and the hearing of God's Word.

Solus Christus affirms Jesus Christ as the only mediator between God and humanity; it does not mean "Christ alone, independent of the church." Following Cyprian, Calvin refers to the visible church as the "mother" of all believers. Though Christ becomes ours through faith, "we need outward helps to beget and increase faith within us."[3] The risen Christ has accommodated

1. Ignatius, *Letter to the Smyrnaeans* 8:2, dated around AD 110, the earliest recorded reference to the phrase "catholic church." Quotation from *Early Christian Fathers*, trans. Cyril C. Richardson (New York: Macmillan, 1970), 115.
2. Luther, *Basic Theological Writings*, 27.
3. Calvin, *Institutes* IV.1.1 (cf. IV.1.4). Cf. Cyprian, Treatise 1.6, "On the Unity of the Church."

himself to our weakness in the economy of redemption and has given us the church, a tangible fellowship of his Spirit. The burden of this chapter is to show that mere Protestant Christianity ought to treasure the church *because* it treasures the gospel. Christ authorizes a royal priesthood of believers not only to proclaim the gospel but also to put hands and feet on it. I therefore propose to treat *solus Christus* in connection with *corpus Christi*: the body of believers in the midst of which the risen Christ exercises his rule on earth as it is in heaven. The royal priesthood of all believers is a high point of this book, in particular because it is ground zero of Christianity's "dangerous idea" and patient zero of Protestantism's "dangerous disease."[4]

The present chapter gestures toward a mere Protestant ecclesiology, by which I mean an ecclesiology rooted in the singular gospel that nevertheless affirms the church's unity-in-diversity. The church is called "catholic" or "universal," says Calvin, "because there could not be two or three churches unless Christ be torn asunder [cf. 1 Cor. 1:13]—which cannot happen!"[5] There is one body, but many members (Rom. 12:4–5; 1 Cor. 10:17; 12:12–13; Eph. 4:4). Catholicity was a major concern of the Reformation: "Medieval Christendom had surrendered the notion of catholicity to a limited and distorted understanding of the Christian faith. And the Reformers, in trying to recapture the wholeness and universality of the faith, were simply trying to be true 'catholics.'"[6] Calvin proposed assembling a universal council that would put an end to Protestant divisions over the Lord's Supper, and, though that never came about, the churches that he founded successfully formed bonds across national borders.[7] The *solas* center and preserve the church's unity (its mereness), thus helping to mitigate the centrifugal forces that lead to its all-too-conspicuous diversity (its fissiparousness).

Solus Christus: What the Reformers Meant

In the context of the Reformation, *solus Christus* (Christ alone), like *sola gratia* and *sola fide*, expressed the Protestant conviction that "there is no other

---

4. Brian Gerrish ranks the priesthood of all believers as one of the three main points of Reformation theology, along with biblical authority and justification by faith ("Priesthood and Ministry in the Theology of Luther," *Church History* 34, no. 4 [1965]: 404).

5. Calvin, *Institutes* IV.1.2.

6. Brown, *Spirit of Protestantism*, 19.

7. See further McNeill, *Unitive Protestantism*, 178–220, esp. 218. Thomas Cranmer, similarly, wanted to convene a general council of Protestantism that would unite the various estranged parties (252).

name under heaven given among men by which we must be saved" (Acts 4:12) and that there is only "one mediator between God and men, the man Christ Jesus" (1 Tim. 2:5). In Jesus's words, "No one comes to the Father except through me" (John 14:6).[8] At first blush, this seems to exclude the necessity of the church, and the priestly class. Upon closer inspection, however, we will see that *solus Christus* does not negate the priestly office but relocates and redefines it. Insofar as it lifts up Christ and his kingdom, *solus Christus*, together with the other *solas*, implies the royal priesthood of all believers, the public domain where God's will is done on earth as it is in heaven.

What Is in Christ

Solus Christus is an excellent summary of theology's first principle, and first love. The gospel is essentially the announcement—the setting forth in speech—of *what is in Jesus Christ*. Nothing that I say here is intended in any way to detract or distract from the gospel of Jesus Christ. Indeed, I have recently taken to defining "Christian theology" as the conceptual indication of what is in Christ. In philosophy, metaphysics is the study of ultimate reality: *what is*. Theology focuses on ultimate reality too but defines it in terms of *what is in Christ*.

What is in Christ is a capacious notion: in Christ there is not only perfect humanity (Heb. 4:15) but also "the whole fullness of deity" dwelling bodily (Col. 2:9). In Christ there are trinitarian relationships: the filial piety of the Son for the Father and the unbreakable love of the Father for the Son in the Spirit. In Christ there is "the last Adam" (1 Cor. 15:45), who recapitulates and puts right the botched history of the first. In Christ there is the obedient Son that Israel never managed to be. In Christ there is salvation and "every spiritual blessing" (Eph. 1:3). Theology is the joyful science of describing the astounding reality that "in Christ God was reconciling the world to himself" (2 Cor. 5:19).

The Three Offices of Christ

What is in Christ thus refers to Jesus's work as inaugurator and mediator of a new covenant. Scripture provides insight into the nature of Jesus's saving work by

---

8. Goldsworthy focuses on "Christ alone" as providing the interpretive key to Scripture and the whole universe (*Gospel-Centered Hermeneutics*, 47–48). While not denying that *solus Christus* pertains to the hermeneutical priority of the gospel, here I want to focus on its implicit connection to ecclesiology.

relating it to the offices that structured ancient Israelite society: prophet, priest, and king. The title "Christ" (Greek for "messiah" or "anointed one") signals Jesus's mediatorial role, for those appointed to an office were also anointed.

Calvin used Christ's threefold office (the *munus triplex*) to explain the Son's mission.[9] What in the Old Testament were distinct offices become aspects for understanding the unity and completeness of Christ's mediatorial work. *Solus Christus* means that we need no further prophets to deliver new revelation, no more priests to make propitiation and mediate salvation (Heb. 2:16–17; 4:14–16; 7:25–26), and no other king to rule the church.[10] For Calvin, there is prophecy in the church, but "prophecy" refers to biblical interpretation—not simply the "bare" interpretation but "the knowledge of making it apply to the needs of the hour."[11] In particular, no priest ever again needs to enter the holy of holies with a blood sacrifice to make atonement for sins (Heb. 9:12–14, 25–28; 10:11–14). Christ's work *alone* saves; Christ's person *alone* mediates salvation: *solus Christus*. God's people nevertheless compose a "kingdom of priests" (Exod. 19:6; cf. 1 Pet. 2:9), a crucial point to which we will return later.

Union with Christ

What is in Christ is ours by grace through faith. This is the good news. To receive the gospel in faith is to participate in the new creation in Christ. To be "in Christ" is to be restored to one's true humanity and to a right relationship with God, and thus to the possibility of being able rightly to image God. Union with Christ is therefore of all words the best that can be heard. *What is in Christ* is nothing less than the love, light, and life of God, and to have Christ means having a share in *that*: communion with God. To be "in Christ" means that one is elect, adopted, justified, and sanctified. It means sharing in all the benefits of Jesus's sonship, in particular the incomparable privilege of calling God "Father."

Communion with God is the supreme covenant blessing (Exod. 6:7; 2 Cor. 6:18). But there is more: union with Christ means union with others who are

9. See the discussion in Calvin, *Institutes* II.15.1–6.
10. For a discussion of Christ's saving work structured according to his threefold office, see Robert Letham, *The Work of Christ* (Downers Grove, IL: InterVarsity, 1993).
11. Calvin, commentary on 1 Cor. 14, in *Opera Quae Supersunt Omnia* 49:519, cited in Erik Alexander de Boer, *The Genevan School of the Prophets: The Congrégations of the Company of Pastors and Their Influence in 16th Century Europe* (Geneva: Librairie Droz, 2012), 27.

in him too. To be in Christ is to be incorporated into a body (Eph. 2:21). *What is in Christ* is not just a set of isolated individuals but a new humanity—a company of communicants, a communion of saints. In short, as the Lord's Supper makes clear, *what is in Christ* includes the church: "Because there is one bread, we who are many are one body, for we all partake of the one bread" (1 Cor. 10:17; cf. John 6:35, 48).

Christology and Ecclesiology: Other Views

Calvin calls the church the "society of Christ,"[12] and this may be enough to justify my treating ecclesiology under *solus Christus*. There is no one agreed-upon Protestant doctrine of the church, but mere Protestants agree that (1) the church is a creature of the gospel; (2) the church is Christ's; (3) the church is a gathering where God's Word is proclaimed in word and sacrament; and (4) such gatherings are apostolic. We can distinguish mere Protestant ecclesiology from three other ways of relating Christ and church.

Totus Christus *(Roman Catholic Ecclesiology)*

Totus Christus is Latin for "the whole Christ," the Roman Catholic teaching that "Christ" includes both head and body.[13] In Augustine's words: "For Christ is not in the head *or* in the body, but Christ is wholly [*Christus totus*] in the head *and* in the body."[14] Aquinas says something similar: "Head and members form as it were one and the same mystical person."[15] Carried to its logical conclusion, *totus Christus* implies that the visible church (i.e., all those in communion with the Roman Catholic Church) is a continuation of Christ's incarnation.[16] Indeed,

---

12. Calvin, *Institutes* IV.1.3.

13. It is beyond the scope of the present work to include Eastern Orthodoxy, though I acknowledge the incompleteness of my account without it. The burden of this book is to set forth a vision for mere Protestant Christianity.

14. Augustine, *Tractates on the Gospel of John* 28.1. Quotation from *Tractates on the Gospel of John 28–54*, trans. John W. Retig, Fathers of the Church (Washington, DC: Catholic University of America Press, 1993), 3.

15. Aquinas, *Summa Theologiae* III, q. 48, a. 2, *ad* 1.

16. Calvin, in his commentary on Col. 1:24 ("In my flesh I am filling up what is lacking in Christ's afflictions for the sake of his body, that is, the church"), is relevant here. Calvin complains that Roman Catholics use this verse to justify the system of indulgences, namely, the remission of sins on the basis of the blood of martyrs that "along with the blood of Christ, serve as an expiation" (*Commentaries on Philippians, Colossians, and Thessalonians* [Edinburgh: Calvin Translation Society, 1851], 165).

Augustine refers not only to Christ's divine and human natures but also to his "ecclesial" nature.[17] The problem with this view is its tendency to assimilate Christology into ecclesiology, thus threatening the integrity of *solus Christus* (i.e., Jesus's unique and exclusive saving agency).[18] Not only was the unity of the church institutional, but also, beginning with Cyprian, "this unity is not grounded in the collective priesthood of the church, but in a set aside clergy who are now considered the priesthood."[19]

Mere Protestants beg to differ: the church is not a continuation of the incarnation. In the first place, the church is not constitutive of the Son's identity as are the Father and the Spirit; its relation to the Son is not substantival but covenantal, a matter of fellowship, not ontology.[20] Second, Jesus was impeccable; the church is fallible. Third, Jesus's sacrificial offering was absolutely definitive and unique; there is nothing further the church can do to secure grace ("It is finished," John 19:30). Fourth, the ascension means that Christ, in one sense, is not here (which is why the church is a fellowship of the Holy Spirit): "The church is risen *with* Christ, but it is not risen *as* Christ."[21]

Protestants and Roman Catholics may both be disciples on the way to Emmaus, but ecclesiology represents a fork in the road: "The danger inherent in Roman Catholicism is that it will equate the treasure and the earthen vessels, and that it will therefore assert that the vessels are no longer earthen."[22] The Roman Catholic Church errs in understanding itself as the only true church and in limiting catholicity only to those ecclesial roads that radiate from Rome. Christ is no tame lion: he cannot be domiciled in and domesticated by any single church or denomination. On the contrary: "Christ's perfection

---

17. Augustine clarified that it was not that Christ would be incomplete without the church but that he did not *wish* to be complete without the church (*Sermons* 341.1.1).

18. Michael Horton notes the affinities of *totus Christus* with the *communio* ecclesiology favored by many at Vatican II, which, for all its use of biblical imagery, emphasizes the institutional and hierarchical Roman Catholic Church in sacramental terms, an extension of Christ's person and work. Horton also sees the *totus Christus* model in Radical Orthodoxy, Eastern Orthodoxy, and a number of recent Protestant ecclesiologies, like that of Robert Jenson, that tend to prioritize ecclesiology over soteriology (Horton, *People and Place: A Covenant Ecclesiology* [Louisville: Westminster John Knox, 2008], 155–68).

19. Tom Greggs, "The Priesthood of No Believer: On the Priesthood of Christ and His Church," *International Journal of Systematic Theology* 17, no. 4 (2015): 385.

20. See further John Webster, "The Church and the Perfection of God," in Husbands and Treier, *Community of the Word*, 75–95.

21. Ibid., 94 (emphasis added).

22. Brown, *Spirit of Protestantism*, 48.

is not integrative or inclusive, but complete in itself, and only so extended to the saints in the work of the Spirit."[23]

The Christless Congregation (Secular Church)

Not every community gathers to hear the gospel. One noteworthy trend is the rise of so-called godless congregations. The creed of the Humanist Community at Harvard University is "I believe in community." This community, and others like it, holds Sunday morning meetings geared toward that part of the population that responds to surveys regarding religious affiliation by choosing "none." They outwardly resemble Christian churches (hence the term "godless congregation"), but they are trying to do community, and achieve communion, without Christ.

Such communities force the church to think more carefully about its own distinct nature, identity, and mission. What makes the church a distinct and unique theater of reconciliation? Ought we to think of these godless congregations as "anonymous churches" that inadvertently participate in the practices, and politics, of Jesus? The basis for the reconciling practices that constitute the Christian community is the cross of Christ. One important difference between the church and godless congregations is that the church is not trying to accomplish reconciliation but rather is attempting to bear witness to what God has already achieved. As Dietrich Bonhoeffer says in *Life Together*, "Christian community is not an ideal we have to realize, but rather a reality created by God in Christ in which we may participate."[24]

The Congregationless Christ (Dispensable Church)

How important is church, really? Many Bible-believing Christians stress the immediacy of their access to Christ through faith. Does not *solus Christus* mean that all a person needs to be a good Christian is "Christ *alone*"?[25]

23. Webster, "Church and the Perfection of God," 95. See also the discussion in Allison, *Roman Catholic Theology*, 56–67.

24. Dietrich Bonhoeffer, *Life Together; Prayerbook of the Bible*, ed. Geffrey B. Kelly, trans. Daniel W. Bloesch and James H. Burtness, Dietrich Bonhoeffer Works 5 (Minneapolis: Fortress, 1996), 38.

25. Lesslie Newbigin identifies the "virtual disappearance of the idea of the Church as a visible unity" as the "second distortion" of Protestant ecclesiology, the first being an overintellectualizing of the content of "faith" (*The Household of God: Lectures on the Nature of the Church* [New York: Friendship Press, 1953], 53–58).

While the Reformers may have displayed a certain anticlericalism, some of their Protestant descendants manifest an antiecclesial prejudice.[26] One observer of the North American scene sees a parallel between the "nones" (i.e., those who have no religious affiliation) and the "nons" (i.e., Christians and Christian churches who refuse to identify with any particular tradition or denomination).[27]

The gospel is good news for men and women individually, but to identify the good news with the promise of one's "going to heaven to be with Jesus" is to reduce the greatness of the gospel. In the reduced version of the gospel, the church is either a place from which to recruit new converts or an antechamber in which to share one's excitement while waiting for one's ride to heaven. These are, admittedly, poorly drawn caricatures. Yet the serious point is that, in the framework of the reduced gospel, it is difficult to see why (or whether) the church is necessary: "The danger inherent in sectarian Christianity is that it will assume that the treasure can be possessed apart from earthen vessels, and that therefore the vessels are no longer necessary."[28]

In contrast to this ecclesial thin gruel, mere Protestant Christianity views the church as the theater of evangelical operations. The church is a theater of the gospel, the bodily enactment of the reconciliation accomplished in and through Christ. The gospel is not simply that "God has a wonderful plan for *my* life" but that "God has a wonderful plan for all creation" and has already begun to realize it in Christ.[29] The church too is an event in the drama of redemption: every local gathering of two or three in Christ's name is a *happening*, a living out of the new humanity made possible by the Spirit of Christ. The church is not an accident, a parenthesis, or an appendix in God's plan of salvation but is arguably the climax of the drama of redemption. After all, the central plot in Scripture has to do with God

---

26. Malcolm Yarnell rightly calls attention to the ambiguity of the term "anticlericalism." Being against the abuses of power is one form; wanting to do away with the very office of the clergy is quite another, which Yarnell refers to as "radical anticlericalism" (*Royal Priesthood in the English Reformation* [Oxford: Oxford University Press, 2013], 9–12).

27. See David Buschart, "The Nones and the Nons: Surprising Similarities?," *Patheos*, July 22, 2015, http://www.patheos.com/Topics/Future-of-Faith-in-America/Evangelicalism/The-Nones-and-the-Nons-David-Buschart-07-22-2015.html.

28. Brown, *Spirit of Protestantism*, 48.

29. N. T. Wright has written about this "slimmed-down" version of the gospel at length. See especially his *Simply Good News: Why the Gospel Is News and What Makes It Good* (New York: HarperOne, 2015).

forming a holy nation and bringing into being "a people under his rule in his place."[30]

The Royal Priesthood

Christ is the sole mediator between God and humanity (1 Tim. 2:5). This must be firmly established. We have no need of human priests to intercede on our behalf before God. We have no need of human priests to offer up sacrifices to atone for our sins. But it does not follow that we have no need of the church, or its officers. On the contrary, Christ's work had as its aim the establishment of a church. Mere Protestant Christians know better than to oppose the church to a "personal relationship with Jesus," for the church is the concrete social form that one's personal relationship with Jesus takes.

We see the first indication of the *telos* of redemptive history in an important passage where God explains the purpose for which he brought Israel, the first holy nation, out of Egypt: "Now therefore, if you will indeed obey my voice and keep my covenant, you shall be my treasured possession among all peoples . . . and you shall be to me a kingdom of priests and a holy nation" (Exod. 19:5–6). Peter addresses the church as "elect exiles," with similar language: "But you are a chosen race, a royal priesthood, a holy nation" (1 Pet. 2:9; cf. 2:5). The Reformers adopted the phrase "priesthood of all believers" and waved it in defiance of the Roman Catholic idea that believers needed a priestly caste to mediate grace and interpret Scripture.

In the introduction I referred to the priesthood of all believers as the final principle of mere Protestant Christianity—that is, the end or purpose of salvation history. As Luther said, "God's word cannot be without God's people and, conversely, God's people cannot be without God's word."[31] As it worked out after the Reformation, however, the principle was misunderstood, eventually mutating into an idea that appeared to license interpretive anarchy, namely, that every individual Christian can interpret the Bible for himself or herself. This is the hermeneutical Babel to which the title of this book alludes. To make matters worse, the idea of a "royal" priesthood seems to confer authority on interpreters. Is the royal priesthood of all believers simply a pious way

30. J. G. Millar, "People of God," in *New Dictionary of Biblical Theology*, ed. T. Desmond Alexander and Brian S. Rosner (Downers Grove, IL: InterVarsity, 2000), 684.

31. Martin Luther, *On the Councils and the Church* (1539), in Luther, *Basic Theological Writings*, 547.

of speaking of the interpretive authority of individuals or, alternately, a way of ordaining interpretive communities as authoritative, in which case we can speak of the sacred (Stanley) Fish?

The Royal Priesthood: God's Household

With this question we return to the original scene of the crime, the moment when the Reformation allegedly loosed interpretive anarchy upon the world. Yet the scene looks different now that we have retrieved the *solas*. If we do our math correctly, we discover that the *solas* add up to the priesthood of all believers. God in his grace assembles a community of faith around the word that attests Jesus as the Christ, the one in whom God has decided to unite all things (Eph. 1:3–10). God in his grace has saved sinners through faith and "made us alive together with Christ" (Eph. 2:5). Those who are in Christ are raised up with him and seated in the heavenly places with him (Eph. 2:6), and through him we have access in one Spirit to the Father (Eph. 2:18). Those who are in Christ are "members of the household of God" (Eph. 2:19)—a royal priesthood (1 Pet. 2:9).

The royal priesthood is the sum of the *solas*—and a *summa* of mere Protestant Christianity.[32] It is also the counterintuitive response to the problem of biblical authority after the Babel of conflicting interpretations. Where, then, does the royal priesthood fit in the economy of interpretive authority? The decisive clue is the term "royal." There is indeed an institutional aspect to the church, an ordered distribution of the authority that belongs to Christ alone. The Reformers never meant the distinction between the invisible and visible church to render the latter unimportant. The distinction simply acknowledges the tares among the wheat. David Wells nevertheless has a point: "In practice this distinction has become quite injurious to Christian faith because it has been taken to mean that all we need be serious about is the gospel. The church has become an irrelevance or, at best, a luxury."[33]

Let me now unfold the concept of the royal priesthood of all believers by posing three questions: Who are the church's priests? What do priests do? Why call the priesthood "royal"?

---

32. Cyril Eastwood remarks, "As the Reformers expounded these three truths [*sola scriptura, sola fide, sola gratia*] they found themselves proclaiming the doctrine of the priesthood of all believers" (*The Priesthood of All Believers: An Examination of the Doctrine from the Reformation to the Present Day* [London: Epworth, 1960], 241).

33. David Wells, *The Courage to Be Protestant: Truth-Lovers, Marketers, and Emergents in the Postmodern World* (Grand Rapids: Eerdmans, 2008), 220.

Who Are the Church's Priests?

In the Old Testament, priests were set apart for the service of God (especially in the temple) and to maintain the people's holiness before God, not least by teaching God's people God's law ("They shall teach Jacob your rules and Israel your law," Deut. 33:10). Significantly, the word "priest" is never used in the New Testament to refer to the church's ministers. It is, however, used to describe Christ as "a high priest forever after the order of Melchizedek" (Heb. 6:20; cf. 7:26–27)—that is, a priest-king.[34] Christ alone mediates salvation, yet Peter picks up the language from Exodus 19 and applies it to the church: "But you are a chosen race, a royal priesthood, a holy nation" (1 Pet. 2:9; cf. Rev. 5:10: "You have made them a kingdom and priests to our God"). Calvin helps resolve the apparent discrepancy: only Christ's sacrifice reconciles the world to God, yet *"in him* we are all priests, but to offer praises and thanksgiving, in short, to offer ourselves and ours to God."[35]

The universal priesthood of believers was at the heart of Luther's reform: "It is," Paul Avis says, "nothing less than a paraphrase of the Reformation concept of the Church."[36] As a slogan, however, it is susceptible of misunderstanding. The same people who distort *sola scriptura* into *solo scriptura* also tend to assert the right of private judgment. Some people appeal to the priesthood of every believer to minimize the role of pastors and teachers on the grounds that "every person is his or her own priest"—a magna carta for interpreting the Bible according to the dictates of one's own conscience.[37] Alexander Campbell appealed to the universal priesthood to justify his "no creed but the Bible" stance.[38]

Luther intended the priesthood of all believers as an alternative to the Roman Catholic assumption that the clergy represented a spiritual class of

34. Psalm 110:4 is an important text that establishes a priesthood after the order of Melchizedek. The New Testament authors cite this royal psalm in connection with Jesus over thirty times. Melchizedek is also the first priest to be mentioned in Scripture (Gen. 14:17–18).

35. Calvin, *Institutes* IV.19.28 (emphasis added).

36. Avis, *Church in the Theology of the Reformers*, 95.

37. Some Southern Baptists have linked the priesthood of all believers to the Baptist concept of "soul competency"—that is, "all persons have an inalienable right of direct access to God." However, as Timothy George rightly points out, soul competence is a "natural" capacity the soul has for God, whereas the priesthood of all believers pertains to Christians only ("The Priesthood of All Believers and the Quest for Theological Integrity," *Criswell Theological Review* 3 [1989]: 284–85).

38. See further William R. Baker, ed., *Evangelicalism and the Stone-Campbell Movement* (Downers Grove, IL: InterVarsity, 2002).

people superior to the laity (i.e., sacerdotalism). This was the first wall protecting the papacy to which Luther laid siege in his "Appeal to the Christian Nobility of the German Nation": "All Christians are truly of the spiritual estate . . . for baptism, gospel and faith alone make us spiritual and a Christian people . . . we are all consecrated priests through baptism."[39]

The important point, not to be missed, is the corporate reference and ecclesial context of Luther's idea. Luther never spoke of the priesthood of the *believer*, in the singular, and neither does the New Testament. The Reformers emphasized the priesthood of all believers not as *isolated* but as *gathered* individuals, baptized members of a local body anointed with the Holy Spirit. The phrase is not a charter for rank individualism: "It means the opposite: 'every man is priest *to every other man*.' It does not imply individuality. It necessitates community."[40] Far from upholding the right of private judgment, the priesthood of all believers refers to the freedom and responsibility of every Christian to minister the gospel in word and deed to one's neighbor.

WHAT DO PRIESTS DO?

Taking Christ the high priest as our paradigm, we can say that, as fully human, he represents human beings before God and, as fully divine, he represents God to humanity.[41] Christ's once-for-all sacrifice suffices for the forgiveness of sins; believers function as priests when they *proclaim* Christ's finished work: "The proclamation of the Word, by which the Church lives, belongs to the Church as a whole and to each member individually."[42]

Luther was fond of citing Malachi 2:7 to show that the principal task of Old Testament priests was to teach people the law of God. All believers are priests and, as such, responsible for teaching, sharing, and embodying the Word: "We stand before God," Timothy George observes, "and intercede for one another, we proclaim God's Word to one another."[43] As Paul says, we are

39. Martin Luther, *Luther's Works*, ed. Jaroslav Pelikan et al., 55 vols. (St. Louis: Concordia; Philadelphia: Fortress, 1958–86), 44:127. This theme is particularly pronounced in Luther's four great 1520 treatises. Things looked a bit different a few years later, however, when various Enthusiasts pushed the idea to an extreme, questioning the idea of the ministerial office altogether and threatening to throw the church into disorder.

40. Brown, *Spirit of Protestantism*, 97.

41. See Thomas F. Torrance, *The Mediation of Christ*, 2nd ed. (Colorado Springs: Helmers & Howard, 1992).

42. Gerrish, "Priesthood and Ministry," 410.

43. George, "Priesthood of All Believers," 292.

to address one another "in psalms and hymns and spiritual songs" (Eph. 5:19; cf. Col. 3:16). Similarly, Peter says that the function of the royal priesthood is to "proclaim the excellencies of him who called you out of darkness into his marvelous light" (1 Pet. 2:9). What I wish to highlight here is the distinctly *communicative* nature of the priestly task: "These functions are understood as concrete forms of the Word."[44] For Luther, being priests to one another means sharing Christ by proclaiming his Word, interceding for others, and sacrificing ourselves for others. In short: the most important function of the priest is to communicate the gospel.[45]

This conception of the priesthood of all believers—that all of us are priests for one another, communicants of God's Word—also goes a long way toward explaining the rise to prominence of certain distinctive forms of Protestant communication. The most conspicuous example is vernacular translation: one of Luther's first priestly priorities was to make the Bible available to the laity by translating it into German. Sermons are another example; in Protestant churches the pulpit became the visual focal point. Lastly, commentaries proliferated after the Reformation, providing aids to understanding and exposition, thereby increasing biblical literacy even more.

One more form of Protestant priesthood deserves special mention. In sixteenth-century Geneva, ministers and interested laypeople gathered on a weekly basis to study the Bible. As they explained in a letter to their colleagues at Lausanne: "Through Christ we have established colloquies."[46] These gatherings were called *congrégations*, and they sought to work out what they saw happening in the early church: "When you come together, each one has . . . an interpretation [*hermēneian*]. Let all things be done for building up" (1 Cor. 14:26). Ministers took turns expositing the Bible and bringing it to bear on the present. It was not a sermon but a conference. Here is how one former Italian bishop reported his visit to Geneva in 1550:

> Every week, on Fridays, a conference is held in the largest church in which all their ministers and many of the people participate. Here one of them reads a passage from Scripture and expounds it briefly. Another speaks on the matter

44. Gerrish, "Priesthood and Ministry," 412.

45. For a more comprehensive survey of Luther's position, see Eastwood, *Priesthood of All Believers*, chap. 1.

46. De Boer, *Genevan School of the Prophets*, 38.

what to him is according to the Spirit. A third person gives his opinion, and a fourth adds some things in his capacity to weigh the issue.[47]

The emphasis of these weekly conferences was biblical exposition and doctrinal formulation and, if necessary, the training and correcting of ministers. First Corinthians 14:27–33 suggested a collaborative model of biblical interpretation: "Let two or three prophets speak, and let the others weigh what is said. . . . For you can all prophesy one by one, so that all may learn and be encouraged" (1 Cor. 14:29, 31).[48] These Genevan conferences were doubly ministerial: not only did they allow ministers to hone their expository skills, but they also provided opportunities for a ministry of correction: "A sense of collegiate responsibility for the office of preaching came to expression in the Bible studies in Geneva."[49] Calvin urged other towns to adopt the practice: "This is also the best bond to retain consensus in doctrine."[50] Calvin ended his own expositions by saying, "This is what God has given me on this passage," after which he would invite others to respond, not least by compensating for his shortcomings.[51] This is a striking example of the kind of epistemic conscientiousness, and humility, that we examined in chapter 3.

WHY CALL THE PRIESTHOOD "ROYAL"?

Luther never really does anything with the qualifier "royal," but as I have already indicated, retrieving involves more than merely repeating. Uche Anizor's *Kings and Priests* retrieves the royal priesthood in order to give biblical-theological support to recent efforts in the theological interpretation of Scripture.[52] In particular, he argues that Scripture, not hermeneutics or literary theory, provides the best categories for depicting Scripture's readers, and that the most important categories are priest and king. Priests function

---

47. Pier Paolo Vergerio, letter dated 15 July 1550, cited in de Boer, *Genevan School of the Prophets*, 21. De Boer traces the origins of these *congrégations* or conferences to Zwingli's *Prophezei* in Zurich, where "prophecy" was for all intents and purposes another name for biblical exposition.

48. Note, again, that the Genevans took "prophesying" to mean exposing Scripture with an eye to the present situation.

49. De Boer, *Genevan School of the Prophets*, 33.

50. Calvin, letter to Wolfgang Musculus, cited in de Boer, *Genevan School of the Prophets*, 41–42.

51. De Boer, *Genevan School of the Prophets*, 33.

52. Uche Anizor, *Kings and Priests: Scripture's Theological Account of Its Readers* (Eugene, OR: Pickwick, 2014).

as the paradigm for didactic reading, not only teaching Torah (Lev. 10:11) but also teaching how to apply it—for example, by distinguishing between sacred and profane and judging difficult civil cases (e.g., Deut. 17:8–13).[53] As to the "royal" qualifier, Anizor suggests that the Old Testament kings were to be exemplars of wise and virtuous reading practices: "Chief among the characteristics of the ideal reader were the fear of God, humility, delight in the Word, dependence on YHWH, and the . . . response of obedience."[54] What is valuable in Anizor's account is his analysis of the offices of king and priest in connection to interpretive virtues and the theological interpretation of God's Word written.

Oliver O'Donovan's account of the church in his book *The Desire of the Nations* provides further help in understanding why the priesthood is called "royal."[55] The church is the community that "lives under the authority of him to whom the Ancient of Days has entrusted the Kingdom."[56] The church is a political society, "ruled and authorized by the ascended Christ alone and supremely."[57] "Our citizenship is in heaven" (Phil. 3:20), says the apostle Paul, though we live it out on earth. What constitutional charter the church has pertains to Spirit, not letter: the city of God was incorporated at Pentecost, when the Spirit united the church to the ascended and exalted Christ. In Christ, the church is now "authorized to represent Israel, the people of the Kingdom."[58]

The church is a political community: Augustine called it the *polis* or city of God; Jonathan Leeman calls it an embassy of God's kingdom. The terminology may be different, but the point is the same: the church does not will itself into existence, nor does it exist by permission of the state; rather, it "exists by the express authorization of Jesus."[59] The church has been given a royal charter, and a mandate: to be a living parable of the kingdom of God. Viewed in the perspective of the economy of the gospel, the church is not merely a voluntary association; rather, it is a creature constituted by God's Word: a fellowship of the faithful that the Spirit has incorporated into the risen and

53. See further ibid., chap. 4.

54. Ibid., 81.

55. Oliver O'Donovan, *The Desire of the Nations: Rediscovering the Roots of Political Theology* (Cambridge: Cambridge University Press, 1996).

56. Ibid., 158.

57. Ibid., 159.

58. Ibid., 161.

59. Jonathan Leeman, *Church Membership: How the World Knows Who Represents Jesus* (Wheaton: Crossway, 2012), 21.

ascended Christ. Jesus has instituted the church as a people and place that exhibits his rule on earth as it is in heaven.

Leeman relates the royal priesthood to Adam's vocation to keep watch over and work the garden, the place where God dwelled. Adam was the original holder of the office of priest-king.[60] In the context of the new covenant, however, every believer possesses this same office thanks to his or her union with Christ. The church reigns with Christ and on Christ's behalf: "To submit to Christ is to be authorized by Christ to act in his stead."[61] The priesthood of all believers is thus a royal office: to belong to the church is to be an authorized representative of the kingdom of God.

The church is a creature of the gospel, the Word that gathers the believing assembly; a royal priesthood is that people and place where God's rule takes bodily shape. The local church is therefore "the institution that Jesus created and authorized to pronounce the gospel of the kingdom,"[62] an embassy that speaks and acts as an official representative of Christ and his kingdom. More pointedly: the church is commissioned by Jesus to set forth in speech and life the reality of the gospel—creation reconciled and made new "in Christ." The Christian is thus an officeholder whose "authority resides in the gospel itself."[63] After all, the gospel is a royal proclamation: "Jesus is Lord!"

Pentecost marks the *anointing* (with the Spirit) that typically accompanies the *appointing* of priests and kings. There is therefore an institutional, dare I say political, aspect to Pentecost. The birth of the church is nothing less than a divine commissioning and authorization of an interpretive community, charged with proclaiming and enacting the truth of the gospel.[64] The anointed are the appointed, and the appointed are the anointed. Believers are ex officio members of the royal priesthood—officeholders "in Christ," with all the privileges and responsibilities appertaining thereunto.[65]

---

60. For the material in this paragraph, I am indebted to Jonathan Leeman, *Don't Fire Your Church Members: The Case for Congregationalism* (Nashville: B&H Academic, 2016), chap. 2.

61. Leeman, *Church and the Surprising Offense*, 156.

62. Leeman, *Church Membership*, 64.

63. Avis, *Church in the Theology of the Reformers*, 100.

64. See further Rodney Clapp, *A Peculiar People: The Church as Culture in a Post-Christian Society* (Downers Grove, IL: InterVarsity, 1996), esp. chap. 8, "The Church as Listening Community: The Performance of Scripture" (126–39).

65. Eastwood remarks, "If justification by faith states the believer's relationship to God, the priesthood of faith states the inescapable obligations of that relationship" (*Priesthood of All Believers*, 244).

Pentecost marks not simply the birthday of the church, then, but the divine authorization of an interpretive community, a community with authority—divine appointing and anointing—to proclaim the gospel. Whatever may be the exact meaning of the tongues of fire that settled on the first royal priests (Acts 2:3), it seems clear that the Spirit equips them for the vocation as speech agents—witnesses to Christ and his kingdom.

Mere Protestant Polity: Household Order

The church is what it is by virtue of the relation that its members have to the ascended Christ, independently of church organization. The church is made up of those who are both already and not yet seated with Christ in the heavenlies, where they are blessed with every spiritual blessing. Yes. But to leave the church in heaven is to fall prey to a docetic view, for the church is also a local and historical concrete entity, an earthly embassy of Christ's heavenly kingdom, a visible gathering. The chief difference between the universal church and the local church is that the former is united in faith and the latter in faith *and order*. In other words, the church on earth is "polity-ized."[66] Those who belong to the royal priesthood are "members of the household of God" (Eph. 2:19). This household has a structure. Recall that *oikonomia*, the Greek word from which we get "economy," means "household management." God has a household, and he knows how to manage it (cf. 1 Tim. 3:4–5).

Each house on Evangel Way manages its affairs in a particular manner. Our special concern is not church government per se but the "economy" of interpretive authority: how a household teaches the Scriptures, especially to the young (homeschooling!), and conducts its table talk about Scripture with family members and guests alike. In Victorian England the definitive guide to every aspect of what it took to run a household was undoubtedly *Mrs. Beeton's Book of Household Management* (1861). The first chapter describes the "Mistress" of the house and begins with a quotation from Proverbs 31. Her primary role is to make her husband and children happy, keeping the one from vice and training the others to virtue. Nothing is more important for this task than "a knowledge of household duties; for on these are perpetually

66. I take this term from Jonathan Leeman, introduction to *Baptist Foundations: Church Government for an Anti-Institutional Age*, ed. Mark Dever and Jonathan Leeman (Nashville: B&H Academic, 2015), 3.

dependent the happiness, comfort, and well-being of a family."[67] For present purposes, of course, we would do better to speak of the Master of the house. Not to worry: Mrs. Beeton's second chapter concerns the housekeeper, the "second in command in the house." Of special interest is her insistence that the housekeeper "must consider herself as the immediate representative of her mistress."[68]

THE PROJECT OF CHURCH POLITY

Many of us may be indifferent or even put off by the topic of housekeeping: church polity. However, if the church is indeed a "society of Christ,"[69] as Calvin says, then we must think how to order it. Polity refers to the way of governing and organizing a society; it is a matter of how Christian assemblies live out their citizenship of the gospel on the ground. According to John Webster, "The task of an evangelical dogmatics of church order is to inquire into the entailments of the gospel for the structure of the church as political society."[70] Yet even a cursory glance at the diversity of evangelical Protestant church polity—episcopal, presbyterian, congregational, and so on—makes one doubtful that there can be anything "mere" about it.

I harbor no illusions of here resolving, in short order, centuries-long disputes over the particulars of church government. I nonetheless want to gesture toward what I am calling mere Protestant polity, which begins by acknowledging Jesus Christ as Master of his house. The risen and ascended Christ has not abdicated but has assumed his throne, remaining present and active through his Spirit and through those whom he has called to the vocation of housekeeping. Mere Protestant polity—church order—should reflect mere Protestant Christianity—that is, the truth of *sola gratia, sola fide, sola scriptura,* and, of course, *solus Christus.*[71] Mere Protestant Christianity agrees that the first principle of church polity is acknowledging Jesus's kingly rule by his scepter (the Word) in the power of his Spirit: Jesus Christ is the Master of each house.

67. Isabella Beeton, *Mrs. Beeton's Book of Household Management,* abridged ed. (Oxford: Oxford University Press, 2000), 7.

68. Ibid., 33.

69. Calvin, *Institutes* IV.1.3.

70. Webster, *Word and Church,* 192.

71. Tom Greggs bemoans the Protestant tendency to limit discussions of the priesthood of believers to matters of church leadership and polity rather than reflecting theologically on what it means for the nature of the church ("Priesthood of No Believer"). The present discussion attempts to do both.

THE PURPOSE OF CHURCH POLITY

Polity matters. It is not as important as soteriology, but it still matters that we order our Christian society in a way that preserves the gospel and is conducive to making disciples. It is therefore important that the church have a clear concept of church membership and its responsibilities (i.e., who belongs to the society of Christ and what are they to do?): "Every local church has some polity—some way to constitute itself, maintain criteria for membership, and to make decisions—because its very existence depends in part upon that polity."[72]

Church polity matters, then, because Christians must live out their citizenship of the gospel here on earth, with others who are trying to do the same. To be baptized is to enter into the company of officeholders: "An entire ecclesiology is always reflected in a certain understanding of office, that is, of what officeholders are to do in the church and how they are to become officeholders."[73] Holding office authorizes occupants to do certain things, and polity helps us understand who is authorized to do what.[74] Through union with Christ, believers are incorporated into a covenantal office—royal priesthood—that authorizes them to live as God's new-covenant people: to image God through filial obedience and to be priests to one another.[75] Mere Protestant polity exists to enable disciples to carry out their royal priesthood.

The task of the royal priesthood is not to complete what Jesus has left undone, as if he reneged on his high-priestly and kingly tasks. On the contrary: the church organizes itself in order to attest to, exhibit, and participate in Jesus's finished work, and it does so in preaching, baptism, the Lord's Supper, and its life together. As a member of this royal priesthood, every believer holds the office of martyr, or witness: one who gives authorized testimony to the meaning, truth, and freedom of the gospel—to life in the kingdom of light (cf. Col. 1:13–14).[76]

---

72. Leeman, introduction to Dever and Leeman, *Baptist Foundations*, 2.

73. Miroslav Volf, *After Our Likeness: The Church as the Image of the Trinity* (Grand Rapids: Eerdmans, 1997), 221.

74. Jonathan Leeman comments, "The difference between what people call 'community' and what the Bible calls 'church' comes down to the question of authority" (preface to Dever and Leeman, *Baptist Foundations*, xviii).

75. George, "Priesthood of All Believers," 292.

76. See further Leeman, *Political Church*.

THE PATTERN OF CHURCH POLITY: OFFICES OF MINISTRY

It should now be apparent why I am treating the church under the rubric *solus Christus*. The primary reason is that Jesus Christ has chosen to assert his lordship over the world by commissioning a visible human society to represent him and his rule: "Christ and church cannot be separated, for the church is the body of which Christ is the head."[77] Believers are members of a royal priesthood: they are not only citizens but also officeholders in the new-covenant kingdom. Yet, among these officers there is a special office, a set-apart ministry of word and sacrament. The officers of the church are responsible for administering and monitoring membership in this earthly embassy of Christ's kingdom, and that means "overseeing the unity and authenticity of the testimony of the church."[78]

Mere Protestant polity is less interested in the particulars than in the basic principle of *episkopē*: oversight. Whatever we call them—elders, presbyters, pastors, or bishops—the basic task of overseers is to preserve the integrity of the church's witness to the economy of the gospel as attested in the Scriptures (and tradition): "What orthodoxy is in the realm of reflection, *episcopé* is in the realm of practice and order: an instrument through which the church is recalled to Christianness, to the appropriateness of its action and speech to the truth of the gospel."[79]

For Luther, the priesthood of all believers, important as it is, does not eclipse the God-ordained office of pastors, who minister word and sacrament and administer the keys (see below).[80] Luther finds biblical support for the idea that the office is God-ordained in Titus 1:5–7, where Paul directs Titus to appoint elders in every town and then goes on to call such overseers "God's stewards."[81] Paul uses the term "steward" (*oikonomos*) to describe his own work as a manager of God's household and minister of the gospel (Col. 1:25a). The primary responsibility of such stewards is "to make the word of God fully known" (1:25b).

All believers are to minister the gospel, but a few are called to "the communal office of public teaching . . . which is performed on behalf of all those

77. Carl E. Braaten, "The Problem of Authority in the Church," in *The Catholicity of the Reformation*, ed. Carl E. Braaten and Robert W. Jenson (Grand Rapids: Eerdmans, 1996), 54.

78. Webster, *Word and Church*, 203.

79. Ibid.

80. See further Herman A. Preus, "Luther on the Universal Priesthood and the Office of the Ministry," *Concordia Journal* 5, no. 2 (1979): 55–62.

81. Luther, *Luther's Works*, 36:155.

who are priests, that is, Christians."[82] What sets the steward or pastor apart is the divine call, which the congregation duly recognizes and authorizes: "It is true that all Christians are priests, but not all are pastors. For to be a pastor one must be not only a Christian and a priest but must have an office and a field of work committed to him. This call and command make pastors and preachers."[83] The main difference between a royal priest and a pastor is that the latter performs his or her office (ministering the Word through preaching and teaching) in public (i.e., the local congregation). *"These are not two different ministries. They are two forms of the same ministry."*[84]

Calvin draws on Ephesians 4:10–13 to support his vision of a fivefold ministerial office: the ascended Christ has appointed apostles, prophets, evangelists, pastors, and teachers ("doctors" of the church) for the work of ministering the Word.[85] Though God can do as he pleases, he chose to use human means to accomplish his purpose, partly in accommodation to our weakness, partly to test our obedience (and teach us humility).[86] Here is how Calvin describes the ministry of the Word in his *Genevan Catechism* (1537): "This power attributed to pastors in the Scriptures is entirely contained in and limited by the ministry of the Word; for Christ has not given this power to men as such, but to his word whose ministers men are."[87]

The Reformers were somewhat flexible as to the exact form that church government could take. However, they agreed, first, that some order was necessary; second, that Christ had instituted the basic office of overseer; and third, that whatever form of order was decided on, it must not be set against the royal priesthood. Rather, church order and church offices exist to serve the congregation. The authority of church leaders is ministerial.

What are local churches for? While it is apostolic truth that constitutes the church (faith in the word of the gospel), it takes more than a believing community to constitute a local church. It takes an office—that is, some kind

---

82. Ibid., 13:334.

83. Martin Luther, "Sermons on Psalm 82" (1530), in Luther, *Luther's Works*, 13:65.

84. Brown, *Spirit of Protestantism*, 103 (emphasis original). Cf. Gerrish, "Priesthood and Ministry," 419.

85. Calvin goes on to say that only the last two offices, pastors and teachers, are "intended to be perpetual"—that is, an ongoing part of the church's polity (Calvin, *Commentaries on the Epistles of Paul to the Galatians and Ephesians*, trans. William Pringle [Edinburgh: Calvin Translation Society, 1854], 280).

86. Calvin, *Institutes* IV.3.1.

87. Cited in J. S. Whale, *The Protestant Tradition: An Essay in Interpretation* (Cambridge: Cambridge University Press, 1962), 157.

of official means of publicly recognizing who is and who is not a passport-carrying citizen of the gospel. The local church, I said, is an embassy of Christ's kingdom. An embassy is "an institution that represents one nation inside another nation."[88] One function (there are many) of the local church is to admit new members through baptism, a public act that acknowledges one's citizenship of the gospel. Another function is to make the unity that believers have in Christ visible in a particular place.

The special office of the pastor-teacher is to help equip church members to play their authorized roles faithfully as members of the royal priesthood. As a seventeenth-century Reformed theology text put it, "The right of public interpretation of Scripture and of adjudging the truth of interpretation in public do not belong to all, but only to those who have been supplied with both the gifts and the calling to the task."[89] It is a crucial distinction: on the one hand, like the Berean Jews who examined the Scriptures daily (Acts 17:11), all believers have the right to read the Bible for their own and others' edification; but this should not be confused with authorized public interpretation, which is a ministerial office (and authority).[90]

The Keys of the Kingdom: Household Security

The question being pursued throughout the present work concerns the economy of interpretive authority. Whose say-so counts when it comes to biblical interpretation, and why? There is a royal priesthood charged with embodying as a living parable the kingdom of God on earth. Mere Protestant Christianity is not at the mercy of every individual interpretive whim. Why not?

I begin to answer this question with a negative example of how *not* to live out one's citizenship of the gospel. Paul, in Galatians 2, recounts an unfortunate run-in that he had with Peter (Cephas). Peter had been eating with the gentiles in Antioch, but when emissaries from James arrived, Peter withdrew from the gentiles, fearing the circumcision party. Whether the incident happened before or after the Jerusalem Council matters little; Peter should have known better. Paul opposes Peter "to his face" and calls him out as a hypocrite (Gal. 2:11–13). What lies behind this strong language is Paul's realization that Peter's conduct "was not in step with the truth of

---

88. Leeman, *Church Membership*, 27.
89. *Synopsis purioris theologiae*, cited in Muller, *Post-Reformation Reformed Dogmatics*, 2:469.
90. See Allen and Swain, *Reformed Catholicity*, 102–3.

the gospel" (Gal. 2:14). Peter had denied Christ; that is, his actions denied the gospel, the truth of *what is in Christ*, namely, the gracious inclusion of gentiles in the new covenant. It is an instructive example. Though Paul was not a church, he was exercising something like the authority vested in the keys of the kingdom when he declared Peter's actions to be conduct unbecoming an officer and a churchman.

In another well-known passage about Peter—in connection with the rock on which Christ will build his church—Jesus says, "I will give you the keys of the kingdom of heaven, and whatever you bind on earth shall be bound in heaven, and whatever you loose on earth shall be loosed in heaven" (Matt. 16:19). Peter, perhaps representing the other disciples or the whole royal priesthood, thereby becomes chief steward of the household of God (Matt. 16:18–19). There are three relevant questions: What are the keys? What do the keys do? Who holds the keys? Everyone agrees that the keys symbolize authority, and that this authority is exercised in the church. After that, opinions diverge.

The Keys according to Roman Catholicism

On the Roman Catholic view, the keys belong to the Petrine office (i.e., ordained priests, especially the bishop of Rome, the pope). Those who hold the keys receive them from Peter via apostolic succession—that is, from those previously ordained as priests. The keys' function is to grant or withhold admission to the institutional church, and thus to an abundant supply of saving grace. To "loose" is to exercise the power to restore a sinner to the church and its sacraments. Hence the power of the keys is effectively the right to include or exclude an individual from the company of the saved.

The Keys according to the Reformers

In sharp contrast, the Reformers view Peter as standing in for the apostles in general. Moreover, apostolicity refers not to an unbroken line of succession but to the apostles' message, the testimony and tradition preserved in Scripture. Jesus prays for "those who will believe [in him] through their [the apostles'] word" (John 17:20).

Luther understood the power of the keys to refer to absolution, itself a ministry of the Word: "To bind and loose clearly is nothing else than to proclaim and to apply the gospel. For what is it to loose, if not to announce the forgiveness of sins before God?"[91] Luther considered the keys not a conferring of power but a proclamation of the gospel, the communication of a promise. This is a privilege of the universal priesthood of all believers; in the only other passage where Jesus mentions binding and loosing (Matt. 18:18–19), he is addressing all the disciples.[92]

Calvin shared Luther's concern that the Roman hierarchy had appropriated to itself something that Christ gave to the royal priesthood of believers as a whole: "They [papists] know so well how to fit their keys to any locks and doors they please that one would say they had practiced the locksmith's art all their lives!"[93] Peter is the recipient of the keys in his capacity as spokesperson for everyone who confesses Christ. Like Luther, Calvin explains the keys as the proclamation of forgiveness of sins (i.e., the gospel), which makes the person who wields the keys an "ambassador of Christ."[94] The power of the keys "rests in the fact that, through those whom the Lord had ordained, the grace of the gospel is publicly and privately sealed in the hearts of the believers."[95] Calvin here relates the keys not to the forgiveness that accompanies conversion and regeneration but rather to the forgiveness that is to mark our ongoing life in the communion of saints.[96]

Calvin goes beyond Luther later in the *Institutes* when he returns to the power of the keys in the context of church discipline. The relevant text here is Matthew 18:15–18, where Jesus mentions binding and loosing in relation to disciplining an errant brother in order to restore him to fellowship. Calvin thinks that Matthew 16 is about the preaching of the gospel entrusted to ministers of the Word, whereas Matthew 18 is about "the discipline of excommunication which is entrusted to the whole church."[97] Here the keys are the basis of the church's power to make authoritative decisions and pronounce judgments: "For as no city or township can function without . . . polity, so the church of God . . . needs a spiritual polity."[98] Interestingly, Matthew 16 and 18 are the only two texts in the New Testament where Jesus explicitly refers to the church as *ekklēsia*.

91. Luther, *Luther's Works*, 40:27–28.
92. See further Eastwood, *Priesthood of All Believers*, 31–37.
93. Calvin, *Institutes* IV.11.2.
94. Calvin, *Institutes* III.4.14. In the same paragraph Calvin also describes the proclamation of absolution as an "embassy," a theme to which we return below.
95. Calvin, *Institutes* III.4.14.
96. Calvin, *Institutes* IV.1.22.
97. Calvin, *Institutes* IV.11.2.
98. Calvin, *Institutes* IV.11.1.

RETRIEVING THE KEYS: AN APOSTOLIC POLITY FOR AN EVANGELICAL *POLIS*

The Reformers did not have the advantage of modern biblical scholarship concerning Second Temple Judaism. They may have been unaware that the Jewish rabbis routinely spoke of "binding" and "loosing" the law in the context of determining whether or not a commandment applied to such and such a situation.[99] Nevertheless, what they did say about forgiving and disciplining anticipates in an impressive way more recent research. What I particularly want to retrieve from the Reformers is Calvin's point about the keys being the basis of church jurisdiction, and I want to relate this to judgments that the church makes about commanding or forbidding certain actions by interpreting not law (as the rabbis did) but gospel.[100] Binding and loosing becomes a constitutive aspect of the church's mission, namely, to become a people of the gospel, a holy nation that aims to discern what does or does not belong to good citizenship of the gospel.[101] To anticipate: the power of the keys is that of declaring what does or does not belong in the royal household of God.[102]

In Matthew's Gospel, "Jesus consistently exemplifies the right way to bind and loose the Scriptures while the scribes and Pharisees consistently exemplify the wrong way to do so."[103] For example, Jesus binds the law prohibiting murder so as to be applicable to anger (Matt. 5:21–23) and looses the law prohibiting work on the Sabbath with regard to plucking grain to satisfy one's hunger (Matt. 12:1–9). Note that loosing means not that a biblical text is no longer authoritative, but only that it is not *applicable* in such and such a situation: "The law was never wrong when it was rightly interpreted."[104]

99. "By 'binding' a decision a scribe declared something to be forbidden; by 'loosing' he declared something to be permitted" (Verlyn D. Verbrugge, "The Power to Bind and Loose," *Reformed Journal* 30, no. 7 [1980]: 16).

100. "It was the Law inscribed by Moses at the command of God which was to regulate life in Israel and settle any questions in dispute. Those holding the office of priest were simply commanded 'to judge according to the law of the Lord'" (Thompson, *Sure Ground*, 231).

101. Compare Leon Morris's summary of the power of the keys: "Jesus meant that the new community would exercise divinely given authority both in regulating its internal affairs and in deciding who would be admitted to and who excluded from its membership" (*The Gospel according to Matthew*, Pillar New Testament Commentary [Grand Rapids: Eerdmans, 1992], 427).

102. Cf. Isa. 22:22, which speaks of bestowing the "key of the house of David" upon a steward who has the authority to open and shut. The steward thus functions as a royal priest. See also Jacob Neusner, "The Kingdom of Heaven in Kindred Systems, Judaic and Christian," *Bulletin for Biblical Research* 15, no. 2 (2005): 279–305.

103. Mark Allan Powell, "Binding and Loosing: Asserting the Moral Authority of Scripture in Light of a Matthean Paradigm," *Ex Auditu* 19 (2003): 85.

104. Ibid., 83.

Jesus gives this interpretive authority—the right to make judgments about what is or is not evangelical (in the sense of "according to the gospel")—to the church. Jesus's words in Luke 11:52 make clear how contentious a move this is: "Woe to you lawyers! For you have taken away the key of knowledge. You did not enter yourselves, and you hindered those who were entering." The dominical authorization to define correct doctrine is the main thrust of Matthew 16:19 ("I will give you the keys of the kingdom of heaven"), and what immediately prompted it was the apostolic confession, the acclamation "You are the Christ, the Son of the living God" (Matt. 16:16). In Matthew 18's mention of binding and loosing, Jesus links the judgment of the church to his ongoing presence, though the context here is not articulating doctrine but disciplining a sinner: "For where two or three are gathered in my name, there am I among them" (Matt. 18:20). The implication is that when the community issues a judgment, "that decision is to be regarded as a declaration of the risen Christ who acts and speaks through the community."[105]

The keys thus represent the authority that accompanies apostolicity. They are given to the local church ("where two or three are gathered"), where they open or close the door of its earthly embassy. Believers do not need the institutional church in order to be united to Christ—the Spirit's gift of faith in the Word does that—yet "members of Christ's body politic still need to be publicly recognized and affirmed as a body politic. . . . Members need to be authorized in the work of the . . . kingdom."[106] Something more than faith is needed to make the church visible and to preserve its public integrity: "People need to be deputized and named as citizens of [Christ's] kingdom."[107] That, of course, is one of the chief purposes of baptism.

Jonathan Leeman has developed, over a number of books, an account of the church's authority to exercise the keys to preserve the integrity of both the gospel and the people who officially represent it as its "authorized version"—the royal priesthood, earthly citizens of Christ's heavenly kingdom.[108] There is not space here to do his work full justice, but here is Leeman's bottom line: "The keys of the kingdom authorize their holder to pronounce on

105. Ibid., 88. "Binding and loosing" thus has two different yet related meanings: first, the apostolic authority to define doctrine; second, the ecclesial authority to deal with unrepented sin. Both are necessary in order to maintain the integrity of the household of God.

106. Leeman, *Political Church*, 332.

107. Ibid., 333.

108. See esp. ibid., chap. 6.

heaven's behalf a judgment concerning the *who* and the *what* of the gospel: *what* is the right confession and practice of the gospel, and *who* is a right confessor."[109] Think of it as dominical authorization to rule on what is or is not evangelical, what does or does not correspond to the gospel: "The authority of the keys is the authority to assess a person's gospel words and deeds and to render a judgment."[110] *The keys thus represent the authority of the local church as an interpretive community.*

Polity ultimately matters, then, because it is a question not simply of the structure of church government but of its function and exercise. In giving the royal priesthood the keys of the kingdom, Jesus appoints the church to exercise his authority to (1) proclaim and preserve the integrity of the gospel; (2) admit those who profess faith in Christ into a local embassy; (3) expel those whose beliefs and actions fall short of the standard of citizenship of the gospel; and (4) determine whether or not a doctrine or practice is commensurate with good citizenship of the gospel: "The keys, in short, are the authority over a church's statements of faith and membership."[111]

Leeman calls our attention to the political nature of a local church, which he defines as "a group of Christians who regularly gather in Christ's name to officially affirm and oversee one another's membership in Jesus Christ and his kingdom through gospel preaching and gospel ordinances."[112] The local church is the practical outcome of Christ's Great Commission, in which, again in the context of his authority, he gives this charge to the disciples: "Go therefore and make disciples of all nations, baptizing them in the name of the Father and of the Son and of the Holy Spirit, teaching them to observe all that I have commanded you" (Matt. 28:19–20). There is something "institutional" about this task of making disciples. Baptism publicly identifies a believer as incorporated into the body of Christ: "The sacraments, baptism and the Lord's Supper, are what 'knit' the church together, giving it 'institutional form and order.' They make the church visible; they tell us where the church is."[113] God's people on earth need institutional procedures "to mark off who credibly speaks for [Jesus], to hold them together, to teach them, and

---

109. Jonathan Leeman, "A Congregational Approach to Unity, Holiness, and Apostolicity: Faith and Order," in Dever and Leeman, *Baptist Foundations*, 354.

110. Leeman, *Church Membership*, 59.

111. Leeman, "Congregational Approach to Unity," 355.

112. Leeman, *Church Membership*, 62–63.

113. Bobby Jamieson, *Going Public: Why Baptism Is Required for Church Membership* (Nashville: B&H Academic, 2015), 143.

to oversee their lives together."[114] It is in local gatherings that Jesus enacts his rule through the ministry of his word. The local church is that place where God's people gather together to make Christ's kingdom visible on earth as it is in heaven. Note well: the church is not just a group of Jesus people; rather, it is wherever two or more gather in Jesus's name to exercise his authority *as* a peculiar public: an evangelical *polis*, a place where people live under God's rule and enact their corporate citizenship of the gospel.

Solus Christus for Bible, Church, and Interpretive Authority

The church is a creature of the Word in which the word of Christ dwells richly, ministered by the Spirit and administered by those whom Christ has authorized to bind and loose interpretations, as well as interpreters. I conclude this chapter with four more summary theses, the last of which raises further problems that point to our fifth *sola* and final chapter.

13. Mere Protestant local churches have the authority to make binding interpretive judgments on matters pertaining to statements of faith and the life of church members insofar as they concern the integrity of the gospel.

The power of the keys is reflected in Paul's rebuke of Peter (Gal. 2) as well as in the decrees of the Jerusalem Council (Acts 15). In each case, at stake is what it means to be "in step with the truth of the gospel" (Gal. 2:14)—in this instance, the gracious inclusion of gentiles in the new covenant. If I belabor the point, it is because I am responding to the common misconception that the priesthood of all believers, one of the hallmarks of the Reformation, loosed interpretive anarchy upon the world. Far from being a charter for every individual interpreter to read in a way that is right in his or her own eyes, the royal priesthood is an ordered and disciplined community that exists largely to interpret Scripture, binding and loosing certain doctrines and those who hold them in order to preserve its integrity as a local embassy of the kingdom of God. Individual interpreters do not, therefore, have the run of God's house, and if they get too rambunctious, they may find themselves locked out, at least temporarily.

14. Christ authorizes both the congregation as a whole and its officers in particular to minister the same word in different ways.

114. Leeman, *Church and the Surprising Offense*, 183.

James Bannerman, a nineteenth-century Presbyterian, says something similar, though he relies on the distinction between possessing authority (whole church) and exercising it (church leaders).[115] All royal priests exercise the power of the keys (e.g., make formal judgments concerning the *what* and *who* of the gospel), but ordained ministers have authority to teach in public and to make recommendations to the congregation as to their use of the keys. The distinction, then, is between *possessing* and *leading in the use of* the keys—call it advisory authority.[116] It is one thing to teach doctrine, another to formally affirm the faith in a binding theological judgment.[117]

15. Christ authorizes the local church to be an authoritative interpretive community of the Word of God.

Mere Protestant Christians belong both to the church universal and to local churches. Reading Scripture ought to take place in the context of the local church; biblical interpretation is a communal exercise. Abraham Kuyper observes that the Christian reader "is no isolated worker, but . . . is in his way the organ of restored humanity."[118] The community of biblical interpreters is the vanguard of this restored humanity, a royal priesthood of readers.

I can now spell out the various elements in the pattern of authority in conjunction with the *solas*. *Sola gratia*: God has given the church as an external means of grace and officers of the church as ministers of the word of grace, namely, the gospel of Jesus Christ. *Sola fide*: the church is a creature of the Word, which it receives in faith as authoritative testimony to the truth of the gospel. *Sola scriptura*: Christ reigns over the church via his word, the commissioned testimony of the prophets and apostles. *Solus Christus*: all authority in heaven and on earth has been given to Jesus Christ. But this is not the end of the story. Christ distributes the power and authority to offer binding judgments concerning the meaning of the gospel (the keys) to the church and its officers. The church too, then, is part of the economy of the gospel and the pattern of theological authority. Indeed, the royal priesthood is arguably the

115. James Bannerman, *The Church of Christ: A Treatise on the Nature, Powers, Ordinances, Discipline and Government of the Christian Church*, vol. 1 (Edinburgh: T&T Clark, 1868; repr., Birmingham, AL: Solid Ground Christian Books, 2009).

116. Leeman, *Don't Fire Your Church Members*, chap. 3.

117. Leeman remarks, "In other words, exercising the keys is more like what a judge does than what a law professor does" (*Political Church*, 341).

118. Abraham Kuyper, *Principles of Sacred Theology*, trans. J. Hendrik De Vries (Grand Rapids: Eerdmans, 1968), 581.

whole point of the triune economy of the gospel, the recovery of the image of God in the body of Christ and fellowship of the Holy Spirit: "One could say that part of the saving activity of God is to make us a people: 'Once you were not a people, but now you are God's people' is the call of 1 Peter 2:10."[119] The centrality of the church in the pattern of interpretive authority emboldens us to suggest another *sola*: *sola ecclesia.* Each local church is "wholly the church, but not the whole church,"[120] and the local church alone is authorized to make binding interpretive judgments about the meaning of Scripture.[121]

> 16. Mere Protestant local churches have an obligation to read in communion
>   with other local churches.

I have not yet argued for this thesis, but a moment's reflection ought to indicate why it, or something like it, is necessary.

Matthew's Gospel never addresses the question "What if the (local) church is wrong?" Church history is, unfortunately, replete with examples of churches making decisions that "were later regarded (even by their own admission) as wrong decisions regarding ethical behavior."[122] One has only to think of the conflict between northern and southern churches at the time of the American Civil War.[123] What happens when the members of a local church are unable to agree? One of the reasons why there are over thirty thousand denominations is that doctrinal controversies are usually resolved not by a TKO but rather by split decisions that all too often result in the minority party deciding to split.

Recall the case of Anne Hutchinson. Her pastor, John Cotton, wrote *The Keyes of the Kingdom of Heaven* in 1644, in part because of the fallout from her trial. Cotton was a Congregationalist who believed that Christ gives each local church the power to rule its own affairs: each local congregation "is indowed with a Charter to be a body-politique to Christ."[124] Perhaps because

119. Greggs, "Priesthood of No Believer," 392.
120. Jean-Jacques von Allmen, "L'Église locale parmi les autres églises locales," *Irénikon* 43 (1970): 512.
121. William Whitaker summarizes the church's service to Scripture in four points. The church (1) witnesses to and guards Scripture; (2) distinguishes canonical Scripture from the noncanonical; (3) translates, publishes, and proclaims Scripture; and (4) expounds and interprets Scripture (*A Disputation on Holy Scripture: Against the Papists, Especially Bellarmine and Stapleton* [1588; repr., Morgan, PA: Soli Deo Gloria, 2000], 283–84).
122. Powell, "Binding and Loosing," 91.
123. See Mark A. Noll, *The Civil War as a Theological Crisis* (Chapel Hill: University of North Carolina Press, 2006).
124. John Cotton, *The Keyes of the Kingdom of Heaven* (1644; repr., Boston: Tappan & Dennet, 1843), 5.

of his own experience, he goes on to say that Christ directs local churches to give heed to a communion of churches: councils. The ruling of such a council is advisory only, however: "They are to leave the *formall act* of this censure to that authority which can only execute it, placed by Christ in those *Churches* themselves."[125] If a local church refuses to follow the advice of the council, then the churches may withdraw communion from it. What's a mere Protestant Christian to do?

The most important thing to do is remember this: the church does not have to work for church unity because, in an important sense, Christ has already established it ("There is neither Jew nor Greek . . . ," Gal. 3:28). What the church must do, however, is witness to the reality of Christ's finished work—to his having broken down the dividing wall of hostility (Eph. 2:14), reconciling us to God (and to one another) by creating a new humanity—and to do so on the ground. Bearing witness to the unity that we already have in Christ requires the church to make what is the case in Christ in the heavenlies visible (somehow) here on earth. There are different ways to do this. One way is through fraternal association. Another is through denominations. Still other Protestant churches attempt this through the office of the bishop who represents a local church or group of local churches. John Webster rightly observes that the bishop does not establish the unity of the church or even actualize it; rather, "the office of bishop *indicates* the unity of the church, testifying in a public manner to the oneness of the people of God as it is set out in the gospel."[126] But there are other ways to testify to our oneness in Christ. My final chapter tackles this ecclesial variation on the ancient problem of the "one and the many" under the improbable (but entirely appropriate) heading *soli Deo gloria*.

125. Ibid., 7.
126. Webster, *Word and Church*, 206.

5

For the Glory of God Alone

The Wealth of Holy Nations

The end of all priesthood is to draw near to God and to enable others to draw near. . . . At every service of Holy Communion the believer is vividly reminded of the End to which he has always aspired.[1]

Mere Protestant Christianity is a retrieval of the gospel—both its material principle (our share in Christ's death, resurrection, and ascension by grace through faith) and its formal principle (the supreme authority of the biblical testimony). More surprising (and controversial) is the claim that to retrieve the gospel we must also retrieve the church: first, as an implication of the gospel, the new humanity in which there is neither Jew nor Greek, free or slave, male or female; second, as the people and place where the written and proclaimed gospel is grasped, celebrated, understood, and enacted. The church is the domain where Christ's rule becomes flesh, embodied in the royal priesthood. Why, then, the need for another chapter? Is not *solus Christus* a fitting climax, not least because we finally answered the question of interpretive authority in the church? Or did we?

1. Eastwood, *Priesthood of All Believers*, 256.

179

This book began by considering the problematic legacy of the Reformation as a legitimation crisis: the seeming inability of Protestants to come up with criteria with which to resolve the conflict of ever-proliferating biblical interpretations. The previous chapter proposed a local solution to this problem by drawing on Jesus's teaching concerning who holds the house keys of the kingdom. However, there was a fly in this balm of Gilead, for it does not address these questions: What if the church is wrong? What happens when a church becomes infected with false teaching or practices incommensurable with the gospel? This is an important leftover problem, and one that I need to address if I am to avoid concluding the present book the way Rupert Davies concludes *The Problem of Authority in the Continental Reformers*. Davies had hoped to identify a clear criterion for discerning religious truth, but on the very last page he writes, "That hope has been disappointed, and the problem is still unsolved."[2]

"Hope" is the operative term. Mere Protestant Christianity aims not only to retrieve but also *to achieve* what the Reformers never could, namely, the teleological principle of the gospel: communion with God and all the saints. For, as the history books make painfully plain, Protestant churches have not always loved their Protestant neighbors. Discord on Evangel Way impedes the final purpose of the gospel, and the glory of God. To glorify God is to publish his greatness, which entails making it public; it is for the glory of God alone that the communion of the saints must somehow become *visible*. We glorify God when we show the world the goodness of his attributes and the goodness of his gospel, including our unity in Christ.

"By their fruits ye shall know them" (Matt. 7:20 ASV). How do mere Protestant churches glorify God? What kind of fruit do they bear? What kind of goods do they produce? Adam Smith's *The Wealth of Nations* (1776) was one of the first economic treatises to give an account of how a nation builds wealth in an industrial age.[3] If the church is a holy nation, what kind of wealth does it generate? Mere Protestant churches have nothing to do with the health-and-wealth gospel that has unfortunately become one of North American Christianity's major exports. The so-called prosperity gospel—that it is God's will that believers accumulate literal wealth, and that donations to Christian ministries will increase the odds of one's attaining this blessed state—is a false gospel that nullifies the cross. Interestingly for our purposes,

2. Davies, *Problem of Authority*, 154.
3. Adam Smith, *The Wealth of Nations*, book 3, chap. 4.

it is particularly nondenominational churches led by a single pastor that seem to be the most susceptible to this theological virus.[4]

Some critics might argue that the prosperity gospel is simply a mutation or new strain of something Reformational, that Max Weber was right that Protestantism (especially the Calvinist variety) encouraged sixteenth-century North Europeans to develop secular enterprises to accumulate wealth, and justified it with a distinct spirituality. Such was Weber's thesis in his *The Protestant Ethic and the "Spirit" of Capitalism* (1905), which opens by observing that business leaders and owners of capital in the early twentieth century "tend to be predominantly *Protestant*."[5] Protestants were successful, Weber argued, because their faith fostered a mentality conducive to professional advancement. In particular, they believed that work is a divinely ordained vocation, not a necessary evil to be avoided, and this belief led them to labor mightily to the glory of God.

A holy nation generates wealth of an entirely different order, and what generates this wealth are God's grace and Christian gratitude. Paul thanks God for the grace that God gave the Corinthians in Christ Jesus, for they were "*enriched* in him in all speech and knowledge" (1 Cor. 1:5). Elsewhere Paul speaks of the "riches" of God's glory (Rom. 9:23) and of his glorious inheritance in the saints (Eph. 1:18), but here in 1 Corinthians he focuses on speech (*logos*) and knowledge (*gnōsis*). Christ is the one "in whom are hidden all the treasures of wisdom and knowledge" (Col. 2:3). The wealth of holy nations is their accumulated insights into the mystery of Christ, the gospel of our salvation. When the first church came together, members shared their material goods (Acts 2:42–47; 4:32–37). How much more should God's people share their wealth of wisdom!

In an important sense, of course, Christ himself is the wealth of the church's wisdom, and it is he who bestows it on local churches, not local churches on one another. Yet we also know that not every church is as mature as another. If the gathering of a single church builds up congregations as different people exercise their gifts (1 Cor. 14:26), it is not unreasonable to expect one local congregation to be able to edify another. It is only in communion with one

---

4. For a description and critique of prosperity theology, see Gordon D. Fee, *The Disease of the Health and Wealth Gospels* (Vancouver: Regent College Publishing, 2006); David W. Jones and Russell S. Woodbridge, *Health, Wealth, and Happiness: Has the Prosperity Gospel Overshadowed the Gospel of Christ?* (Grand Rapids: Kregel, 2011).

5. Weber, *Protestant Ethic*, trans. Peter Baehr and Gordon Wells (London: Penguin, 2002), 1.

another—with other members and, perhaps, with other local bodies—that Christians fully appreciate the length and width of the train that adorns the wedding dress of the church, the bride of Christ.[6] What glorifies God is not the prosperity gospel but the *catholicity gospel*, namely, the coming together of mere Protestant churches from east and west, Anglican and Baptist, Pentecostal and Presbyterian, to "recline at table in the kingdom of God" (Luke 13:29), and there to feast on the unsearchable riches of Christ (Eph. 3:8). But we are not there yet.

Soli Deo Gloria: The Lord's Supper as a Test of Christian Unity

Soli Deo gloria, like the other *solas*, is partially intended to exclude an error. In this case, what is excluded is not human works but the end for which we work: human glorification. It was precisely this desire to make a name for themselves that led people to build the tower of Babel (Gen. 11:4). No one at the time of the Reformation was explicitly denying the rightness of glorifying God alone. However, the intent of the other four *solas* was to ensure that *all* the glory for salvation and true interpretation alike be given to God alone.[7] This is also the intent of mere Protestant Christianity, and the present work primarily aims to help Protestants clean their own houses, not to condemn the houses of others. In particular, the present work is a call to recover unitive (catholic) Protestantism, a lived ecclesiology that glorifies God by exemplifying the fellowship that the saints have in Christ through the Spirit, and this despite differences over biblical interpretation and (nonessential) doctrine.

One of the most characteristic practices that takes place in houses, in addition to table talk, is table fellowship—mealtime. "So, whether you eat or drink, or whatever you do, do all to the glory of God" (1 Cor. 10:31). This Pauline exhortation, like the earlier statement about being "enriched in [Christ]" (1 Cor. 1:5), precedes a more ominous word: "I hear that there are divisions among you" (1 Cor. 11:18; cf. 1:10). The Greek word for "divisions" sounds as scissors-like as its meaning: *schismata*. It occurs three times

6. Here it is interesting to note how Paul moves in 1 Cor. 12–14 from the gifts of the Spirit, to interdependence and love, to prophecy (biblical exposition?) as a means of building up the church. (I am grateful to Kessia Bennett for pointing this out.)

7. David VanDrunen refers to *soli Deo gloria* as the "lifeblood" or "glue that holds the other *solas* in place, or the center that draws the other *solas* into a grand, unified whole" (*God's Glory Alone: The Majestic Heart of Christian Faith and Life* [Grand Rapids: Zondervan, 2015], 15).

in John's Gospel, and in all three instances it refers to a division among the people over Jesus (John 7:43; 9:16; 10:19). It is to be expected that the gospel will divide those who accept it and those who reject it. Divisions in the church are an entirely different matter, however, especially when they occur, as they did at Corinth, in connection with the Lord's Supper, which is intended to be a place to celebrate togetherness: *communion.*

Alas, history repeated itself in sixteenth-century Protestant Europe, where there was again a falling-out over the Lord's Supper—except this time the division was doctrinal. With Calvin, I lament the "unhappy contests" that have divided Christians over the interpretation of Jesus's words "This is my body."[8] It is tragic that Protestants broke fellowship over the very doctrine and practice intended to symbolize it. The very place where Christians ought to have come together in communion became instead a place of consternation. We may not need to repent the Reformation as a whole, but certainly we should weep over this particular result, not least because celebrating Communion is one of the key evangelistic practices of the church: "For as often as you eat this bread and drink this cup, you proclaim the Lord's death until he comes" (1 Cor. 11:26).

Squabble at Marburg (1529)

"Protestants have taken protest and schism to be a model for handling differences when they arise."[9] Sadly, the stereotype of Protestants making only negative protests contains an element of truth. Fortunately, however, it is not the whole story, because for every centrifugal Protestant force there is a more powerful centripetal force: the oneness of the loaf. If mere Protestant Christianity had patron saints, Martin Bucer (1491–1551) surely would be a candidate. After Luther and Melanchthon, he was the most important Protestant leader in Germany, the reformer of the city of Strasbourg, and he influenced the English Reformation as a professor of theology at Cambridge University.[10] Bucer was involved in a number of initiatives to broker doctrinal

8. See Thomas J. Davis, *This Is My Body: The Presence of Christ in Reformation Thought* (Grand Rapids: Baker Academic, 2008), esp. chap. 9, "Discerning the Body: The Eucharist and the Christian Social Body in Sixteenth-Century Protestant Exegesis" (149–68).

9. Ronald P. Byars, *Finding Our Balance: Repositioning Mainstream Protestantism* (Eugene, OR: Wipf & Stock, 2015), 34.

10. In Bucer's most famous treatise, *De Regno Christi*, he suggests how Christ's kingdom might be realized in England. See David C. Steinmetz, *Reformers in the Wings: From Geiler von Kaysersberg to Theodore Beza*, 2nd ed. (Oxford: Oxford University Press, 2001), 85–92.

agreement between Protestants and Catholics (most notably, at Regensburg in 1541) but also between various Protestant factions. His biographer Martin Greschat entitled one of his chapters "A Champion of Protestant Unity."[11]

It was Bucer who brought Luther and Zwingli together at the Marburg Colloquy in 1529, which met to address the contentious issue of the nature of Christ's presence in the Lord's Supper. Bucer set forth a mediating position—"sacramental union"—agreeing with Zwingli that Christ's body is in heaven but agreeing with Luther that the bread and wine are objective means of nurturing grace. Luther was not impressed: "Your spirit and our spirit do not coincide."[12] Ouch. Luther felt that Calvin's doctrine of "real spiritual presence"—that communicants are united to the ascended Christ through the Holy Spirit—was too close to Zwingli's memorialist view. Later, after Luther's death, effigies of Calvin would be burned in Lutheran cities.

Concord at Wittenberg (1536)

Bucer exercised the perseverance of a saint as he worked tirelessly to achieve an accord between the Wittenberg Lutherans and the Reformed Protestants of southern Germany and Switzerland on the question of Christ's presence in the Lord's Supper. He eventually achieved a consensus with Luther and Melanchthon on the Lord's Supper in the Wittenberg Concord of 1536. It did not begin well: Luther said that meaningful talks could take place only if Bucer and the southern Germans "recanted their false understanding of the Lord's Supper and henceforth taught that unbelievers as well as believers actually received the body and the blood of Christ in their mouths."[13] The eventual solution involved a fine piece of prepositional theology that stipulated that the body and blood of Christ are truly and substantially present *with* (rather than *in*) the bread and wine. It also involved Luther's willingness to overlook Bucer's demurral on the question of whether unbelievers receive the body and blood of Jesus. Luther's final response is worth repeating: "We do not want to quarrel over this—. . . we are in agreement, we recognize and accept you as our dear brethren in the Lord."[14] Remember the bit about "we *recognize*."

11. Martin Greschat, *Martin Bucer: A Reformer and His Times*, trans. Stephen E. Buckwalter (Louisville: Westminster John Knox, 2004), chap. 5.
12. Cited in ibid., 93.
13. Ibid., 137.
14. Cited in ibid., 138.

The result of this meeting was "a concord in the true sense of the word— an agreement on fundamentals that still left enough leeway for differing emphases."[15] While dogmatics may entail polemics, it should also entail ire- nics: "In essentials unity, in nonessentials freedom, in all things charity."[16]

Harmony at Last? (1581)

Another early effort to articulate mere Protestant Christianity was the col- laborative work coordinated by the French minister Jean-François Salvard with help from Theodore Beza and others. *The Harmony of Confessions of Faith* (1581) demonstrates the substantial theological agreement on most doctrines that existed among not only the dozen Reformed confessions set forth in the harmony but also the Lutheran Augsburg Confession. The volume does exactly what its title promises, setting out in a series of comparative analytic tables the main lines of doctrinal agreement, both in what they affirm and in what they deny. For example, the fourteenth section treats the Lord's Supper and includes the relevant sections from twelve confessions from various Protestant regions (e.g., Helvetia, Bohemia, France, Scotland, Augsburg).

The preface makes a catholic gesture in its first line, which refers to a church father: "Ambrose in a certain place saith notably, 'There ought to be no strife, but conference, among the servants of Christ.'"[17] By "conference" is meant the cut and thrust of fraternal dialogue and debate, by which the church eventually comes "to very great light."[18] We will return to the idea of conference below.[19]

Church Unity: Other Views

"We believe in one holy catholic and apostolic Church." Interestingly, this line from the Nicene Creed substitutes the word "one" for the "the" in the Apostles'

15. Ibid.

16. Attributed to Peter Meiderlin, but published under the pen name Rupertus Meldenius, *A Reminder for Peace at the Church of the Augsburg Confession of Theologians* (1626). The original Latin quotation is: *In necessarilis unitatem, in non necessarilis libertatem, in utrisque caritem.*

17. Peter Hall, ed., *The Harmony of Protestant Confessions: Exhibiting the Faith of the Church of Christ*, rev. ed. (London: J. F. Shaw, 1842), xxix.

18. Ibid.

19. See further Scott M. Manetsch, *Calvin's Company of Pastors: Pastoral Care and the Emerging Reformed Church, 1536–1609* (Oxford: Oxford University Press, 2013), 228.

Creed: "the holy catholic Church." Would that unity were so easy! Jesus prayed that those who believe in him "may be one" (John 17:11), but what might a positive answer to his prayer look like? In what sense is the church "one"? We know the Roman Catholic answer: it means being institutionally united in a single magisterial structure (a tower whose interpretive authority reaches up to heaven). Peter Leithart asks the question to which this chapter attempts a response: "Can Protestants be Protestants, and yet also be committed to the unity of the Church?"[20] The present section sketches three broad Protestant approaches to the prospect of church unity, three alternatives to the position that I will identify with mere Protestant Christianity.

Ecumenism: The One

Ecumenism broadly conceived names the project of promoting unity among the Christian churches of the world despite differences of doctrine and polity. Mere Protestant Christians must exercise due vigilance at this point with regard to the *kind* of unity in view (and the kind of division).

In the computer strategy game *Europa Universalis III*, players control nations and make decisions about war, diplomacy, economy, and so on. The game starts in 1453 and ends in 1789, which means that players can decide what to do about the Reformation (one of the commands is "send missionary"). Players can also select "Ecumenism" as their National Idea, a choice that results in "heretical religions"—those that are not part of the state religion—within the player's domain being tolerated rather than suppressed. The twentieth-century ecumenical movement was no game, but a response to the devastation of World War I focused on uniting the various churches to provide help to those in physical and spiritual need. A worldwide organization sprung up for this purpose, and to display the visible unity of the church.

John Woodhouse offers some wise words concerning church unity.[21] Clearly, there is a kind of unity that honors God and is biblical: God is one, and the saints are one "in Christ." Yet there is also a unity that is ungodly:

20. Peter J. Leithart, foreword to *The Mercersburg Theology and the Quest for Reformed Catholicity*, by W. Bradford Littlejohn (Eugene, OR: Pickwick, 2009), xi.

21. See John Woodhouse, "When to Unite and When to Divide," *The Briefing* 279, December 1, 2001, http://matthiasmedia.com/briefing/2001/12/when-to-unite-and-when-to-divide/; Woodhouse, "The Unity of the Church," *The Briefing* 281, February 1, 2002, http://matthias media.com/briefing/2002/02/the-unity-of-the-church/; Woodhouse, "Christian Unity and Denominations," *The Briefing* 284, May 1, 2002, http://matthiasmedia.com/briefing/2002/05/christian-unity-and-denominations/.

the tower of Babel was a godless scheme to achieve a unity through human industry alone (i.e., the works of the flesh). That unity is not always unequivocally good is an important insight: people can be united in evil causes as well as good. Similarly, some divisions are godly (e.g., between light and dark, holy and unholy) and some ungodly (e.g., discrimination on the basis of race). Significantly, the kinds of divisions in the church that concerned Paul were divisions *within* particular congregations, not divisions *between* congregations.

True and godly church unity is a peculiar kind of unity, something that comes about only by God's grace, and the Spirit of God. To the extent that the ecumenical movement single-mindedly pursues unity as if it were always a good, and assumes that unity is a human creation, we must be wary. In sum, we need to distinguish between ecumenical unity—visible unity of an organizational kind—and evangelical unity, where the focus is on the gospel, which both unites (in Christ) and divides (cf. Luke 12:51).

Mere Protestant Christianity is not an ecumenism after the flesh.

Sectarianism: The Many

The Reformers were not sectarians, even if that is how Roman Catholics often described them. A sect is a breakaway group that thinks that it alone is the pure society of Jesus.[22] Sects typically refuse to recognize the legitimacy of other gatherings of two or three in Christ's name, which effectively means denying Christ's presence among those gatherings. Perhaps this is why Philip Schaff's Mercersburg colleague John Nevin, with a view to 1 John 4:1–3, describes the "spirit of sect and schism" as "AntiChrist." For Nevin, both forms of division, external (heresy) and internal (schism), are cut from the same spiritual cloth: "Heresy is theoretical schism; and schism is practical heresy. . . . All heresy is in principle schismatic; all schism is in its inmost constitution heretical."[23] Calvin mentions two sectarian groups, the Donatists and the Anabaptists. Augustine remarks about the former that they are too fond of their own contentions: "Puffed up in their pride, mad in their stubbornness, deceitful in their slanders, and turbulent in their seditions, they draw the shade of a rigid severity to hide their lack

22. Schaff defines sectarianism as a "one-sided practical religious subjectivism" (*Principle of Protestantism*, 227).

23. John W. Nevin, *AntiChrist; or, The Spirit of Sect and Schism* (New York: J. S. Taylor, 1848), 15.

of the light of truth."[24] "The dwarfs are for the dwarfs!" might be a good sectarian motto.

Of course, one person's sect is another's denomination. After visiting the United States, Max Weber wrote his celebrated essay on "'Churches' and 'Sects' in North America." Weber describes the church as institutional, hierarchically organized, and inclusive (because it ministers to all). By way of contrast, a sect is a voluntary society that lives apart from everyone else, claiming to represent the pure church and restricting its membership to those who meet its select criteria. Weber classifies Baptists and Methodists and other denominations with a Puritan background as "sects" rather than "churches."[25]

This is not the place to enter into debate with sociologists about the semantic range of "sect." What I mean by "sect" is any group that presents itself as a church that so sets itself apart—holier than thou and thou and thou—that it fails to acknowledge other groups as Christian or denies its connection with other local bodies of believers. Methinks they do protest too much!

Mere Protestant Christianity is not sectarian.

Denominationalism: The Fissiparously Many

Denominationalism is an interesting phenomenon, difficult to define, not least because we do not yet have a satisfying theological account of what a denomination is.[26] Minimally, however, we can say that denominations provide "a form in which Christians can live their affirmation that the church is more than their local congregation."[27] A denomination is "an association of some churches which does not include all churches."[28]

WEAK DENOMINATIONALISM

Many denominations are unable to provide a compelling account of their existence or raison d'être. This is a particularly acute problem when they downplay their theological commitments, as this leaves potential members with

24. Cited in Calvin, *Institutes* IV.12.12.
25. Weber, "'Churches' and 'Sects' in North America," in *Protestant Ethic*, 203–20.
26. Barry Ensign-George comments, "Systematic theology offers at present no meaningful help in understanding denomination theologically" ("Denomination as Ecclesiological Category: Sketching an Assessment," in *Denomination: Assessing an Ecclesiological Category*, ed. Paul M. Collins and Barry Ensign-George [London: T&T Clark, 2011], 1).
27. Ibid., 14.
28. Woodhouse, "Christian Unity." Woodhouse goes on to clarify that denominations are not churches but rather associations of churches.

no particular reason to join. This gets no farther than *weak* denominational-ism. At the limit, some denominations become so nondoctrinal that they lose the gospel altogether, at which time faithful congregations are faced with the decision to remain as salt and light or to associate with some other group.

RADICAL DENOMINATIONALISM

At the other extreme are *radical* denominationalists, who are fervently committed to preserving static structures, identity, and traditions. Denomi-nationalism is radical when it becomes too parochial and thus susceptible to the idolatry of the (denominational) tribe. This leads to serious problems. The first temptation of radical denominationalism is pride: a sinful desire to hoard the marks of the one true church for one's own congregations only. Radical denominationalists may be more inclined to exercise the nuclear op-tion (i.e., go to war) and push the proverbial button if doing so could make certain other denominations disappear. The second temptation of radical denominationalism is to substitute zeal for denominational processes and machinery for zeal for the gospel. Preoccupation with denominational affairs risks distracting the local church from its primary mission, which is to serve as an embassy of Christ's kingdom, not the denomination: "It is a mistake to think that the Christian unity for which Jesus prayed finds its expression in the uniting of denominations. Denominations are not churches, but are service structures to assist congregations which are real churches."[29]

STRONG DENOMINATIONALISM

Despite their flaws, denominations at their best are potentially one of God's good gifts to the church. The idea of a denomination "provides a form in which new insights into the faith, or new applications of old insights to changing contexts and circumstances, can be tested by being lived out."[30]

We usually can trace a denomination's origins to a specific theological or missiological crisis (e.g., Lutheranism). Viewed in this light, denomination-alism is part of the history of Christian mission, a contextualization of the gospel in and for a specific situation that nevertheless produces lasting insights of transcontextual significance. Churches with a strong denominational identity

29. D. Broughton Knox, *Selected Works*, vol. 2, *Church and Ministry* (Kingsford, Australia: Matthias Media, 2003), 36.
30. Ensign-George, "Denomination as Ecclesiological Category," 3.

are confident enough in their own skins to cooperate with other denominations. They have a healthy self-image, which includes an acknowledgment of their own partiality: "No denomination is ever the full embodiment of the church universal in this time."[31] Many denominations therefore allow leeway on questions and issues that have not been pivotal in their development. Denominations are *strong*, then, when they provide "a structure for a living disagreement in matters about which faithful Christians may disagree."[32]

Mere Protestant Christianity is not denominationalism, at least not first and foremost, though it does recognize the value of what I am here calling *strong* denominationalism.

Communion in the Church (and between Churches)

The unity of the church matters because Jesus cared enough to pray for it explicitly: "that they may be one" (John 17:11). Paul encourages the Romans to "be of one mind" but then adds "according to Christ Jesus" (Rom. 15:5). This was the Reformers' justification for their protest: they were not "leaving" the church but rather preserving the truth of the gospel, and the gospel must be the touchstone for unity. As John Jewel, bishop of Salisbury in the sixteenth century, pointedly observed, being "of the same mind" is not difficult: "For there was the greatest consent . . . amongst them that worshipped the golden calf and among them which with one voice jointly cried against our Saviour Jesus Christ, 'Crucify him!'"[33] Unity in Christ is something else. Moreover, because it is real, it raises the question of how churches now on earth should express it with believers beyond their own local congregations.

Our retrieval of this last *sola*—for the glory of God alone!—signals once again the Reformers' theology of the church as a vital element in the economy of the gospel, namely, as "one" and "catholic" as well as "holy" and "apostolic." My intent throughout the present work has been to rehabilitate the Reformers' retrieval (and reform) of the catholic church, not least for the sake of responding to the problem of pervasive interpretive pluralism. I have also been at pains to show how Protestant catholicity fits hand in glove with the Reformation *solas*. The *solas* preserve both the integrity of the gospel and

31. Ibid., 7.
32. Ibid., 6.
33. Cited in Philip E. Hughes, *Theology of the English Reformers*, new ed. (Grand Rapids: Baker, 1980), 254.

the unity of the church inasmuch as the latter is rooted in the former. For mere Protestant Christians, catholicity is not primarily geographical (e.g., Roman) but qualitative (biblical): "Where the gospel is, Christ is; where Christ is, there is the Church."[34]

Mere Protestant Unity: The One Church

That the church exists in space and time is, in the words of one recent writer on the subject, a "most inconvenient" fact, because however we define church, it is always possible to point to some group of people whose existence contradicts it.[35] To be sure, not every group of people is a church. Let us therefore define a church as two or more people, gathered in Jesus's name, that sets itself apart by its new-covenant ordinances (baptism and Lord's Supper), preaching of the gospel, and exercise of the power of the keys, in order to be a parable of the kingdom, an embassy of Christ's rule. In specifying the church as a "gathering," the implication is that churches are local bodies, and they are. However, we still have to deal with how to express visible unity on two distinct levels: local and catholic.[36] There is a communion *within* a church and a communion *between* churches. In chapter 3 we examined the principle of conciliarism in connection with the pattern of interpretive authority. Here, we return to the central conviction of conciliarism and its key ecclesiological presupposition: "the belief that responsibility for the well-being . . . of the Church rests with the whole Church."[37]

THE POLITICS OF RECOGNITION: "ONE SPIRIT"; "ONE LOAF"

Everything the church does should be done for the glory of God. Earlier we suggested that holy nations do this by sharing their interpretive capital: the wealth of the doctrinal riches that they have discovered by contemplating what is in Christ. Speaking of the wealth of nations, readers may be interested to learn of the Agreement on Mutual Recognition in Relation to Conformity

34. Avis, *Church in the Theology of the Reformers*, 221. On "qualitative" catholicity, see Gustav Aulén, *Reformation and Catholicity*, trans. Eric H. Wahlstrom (Edinburgh: Oliver & Boyd, 1960), 181.

35. John P. Bradbury, *Perpetually Reforming: A Theology of Church Reform and Renewal* (London: Bloomsbury, 2013), 1–2.

36. There is one church, with two aspects. The one church is both seated in the heavenlies with Christ and located in particular places on earth. Similarly, the local church is wholly the church, but it is not the whole church.

37. Avis, *Beyond the Reformation?*, 184.

Assessment. It is an international agreement between the European Union and other countries to recognize one another's technical standards and to comply with the necessary requirements, say, in academic qualifications or quality control in food processing. Food processing is the operative notion for us, as we reflect on what it means to recognize other people as those with whom we can share the Lord's Supper.

Much in contemporary politics turns on the need, or often the demand, for *recognition*. The need for recognition "is one of the driving forces behind nationalist movements in politics."[38] It is precisely because we are social beings that we are vulnerable to the ways in which we are perceived and character- ized by others. Israel and Palestine's mutual refusal to recognize each other's right to exist is more or less a tacit declaration of war.

Everyone has a deep desire to be recognized; nobody wants to be ignored. This was the burden of Ralph Ellison's *Invisible Man* and of other works that fall into the realm of identity politics. Failing to recognize a particular denomination as genuinely Christian is not what "invisible" church is supposed to mean! If space permitted, I would argue that mutual recognition—not just of the other's right to existence, but of the "other" as a sibling in Christ—is made possible by the doctrine of justification by faith, which gives every believer the same status in Christ.[39]

Mere Protestant Christianity needs both a theology and a practice of recog- nition. Whom, for example, should we recognize for admission to the Lord's Table, and what kind of recognition do we owe those with whom we share table fellowship? This question becomes especially pressing when we are dealing with professing Christians who do not belong to our local church or denomination.

The New Testament provides some powerful examples of recognition, of which the most notable is Peter's acknowledgment that Cornelius, a gentile, was not unclean and had received the Holy Spirit just as he had (Acts 10). That the Jerusalem Council recognizes gentiles as fully part of the society of Jesus, without them having to undergo circumcision, is one of the high points of the book of Acts, as it is of church history (Acts 15). Recognition means extending the right hand of fellowship, which is precisely what James

---

38. Charles Taylor, *Multiculturalism: Examining the Politics of Recognition* (Princeton: Princeton University Press, 1994), 25. See also Paul Ricoeur, *The Course of Recognition*, trans. David Pellauer (Cambridge, MA: Harvard University Press, 2004).

39. The other doctrinal help for recognizing another human as human is the *imago Dei*, but what we recognize here is the image of God in humanity, not union with Christ.

and the other pillars of the Jerusalem church offered Paul and Barnabas (Gal. 2:9), a tangible sign that they recognized the apostolicity of their mission to the gentiles.

The unity of the church is a complex notion. It can refer to the unity in a local church, the unity that a denomination provides, and the unity that exists between churches and denominations. There is also an "already but not yet" aspect to church unity. The oneness of the church is "already," thanks to our communion in Christ, but the historical situation on the ground has not yet caught up to this reality. The unity of the church is thus both indicative and imperative: the church's vocation, and challenge, is to become on earth what it is, in Christ, in heaven. It has to do with the importance of "discerning the body" (cf. 1 Cor. 11:29), which in context probably means not simply discerning the spiritual presence of Christ in the Lord's Supper but also (and more importantly for present purposes) the discerning of the body—the organic unity—of those assembled around the Lord's Table. Calvin eloquently expresses this very point: "Inasmuch as he [Christ] makes himself common to all, [he] also makes all of us one in himself."[40] We fail to discern the body when we fail to discern the truth of what is in Christ: the communion of saints. This failure in recognition leads to divisions in the church, flesh wounds in the body of Christ. Disunity is ultimately a failure to recognize the full measure of the one body of Christ.

Approaches to Unity: "A Communion of Communions"

Are there properly Protestant resources that help get churches past the former divisions over the theology of the Lord's Supper? How can Protestants embody catholicity while engaged in a conflict of biblical interpretations? May we hope for a "communion of communions"? A full inventory of approaches to the question of church unity is beyond the scope of the present chapter. What follows is only a brief sampling of various Protestant strategies for conceiving the unity and catholicity of the church, especially as this touches on the relationship of one church or association of churches to other churches where there is interpretive disagreement. The hope is to retrieve examples of best Protestant practice.

John Howard Yoder presents an interesting case: a Mennonite committed to the ecumenical task, "a congregationalist with Catholic sensibilities."[41]

---

40. Calvin, *Institutes* IV.17.38.

41. Stanley Hauerwas, *Approaching the End: Eschatological Reflections on Church, Politics, and Life* (Grand Rapids: Eerdmans, 2013), 100. In context, Hauerwas is using this phrase to describe his own position, but it fits Yoder too.

This is best seen in his collection of essays *The Royal Priesthood: Essays Ecclesiological and Ecumenical*. The final part of the book is entitled "Radical Catholicity," and that is where we find the essay that interests me for present purposes: "Binding and Loosing."[42] Yoder begins by citing Proverbs 27:5–6: "Better is open rebuke than hidden love. Faithful are the wounds of a friend." Binding and loosing—the practice of church discipline—is one of the key practices that make up what Yoder calls the "politics" of Jesus. In Yoder's Anabaptist tradition, discipleship means continuing the practices that characterized Jesus's life.

Binding and loosing—otherwise known as fraternal admonition or what the first Anabaptists called "the rule of Christ"—is a central church practice, derived from Jesus's teaching in Matthew 18:15–20 about how the church should deal with a recalcitrant sinner. One of the Anabaptist catechisms poses the question "What power do those in the church have over one another?" and answers, "The authority of fraternal admonition."[43] Yoder claims that binding and loosing constitutes a group of Christ followers as a church: "*The process of binding and loosing in the local community of faith* provides the practical and theological foundation for the centrality of the local congregation."[44] Where binding and loosing fails to take place, "'church' is not fully present."[45]

Yoder maintains that the unity of the churches is an imperative of the gospel because it renders credible witness to the unity of the Father and Son.[46] As Stanley Hauerwas notes, where there is no Christian unity, "quite simply the gospel is not true in that place."[47] Yoder further claims that the unity of the churches is an implication of the practice of fraternal admonition. He is not interested in denominationalism: local churches are not small companies to be gobbled up by large multinationals. Unity is decided not in executive jet planes at thirty-five thousand feet but rather in the trenches, in the costly practice of fraternal admonition and forgiveness, a practice that, like brush fire, jumps roads—and denominational divides.

---

42. Sadly, it appears that Yoder may not have practiced the politics of Jesus consistently. In 2014 the Anabaptist Mennonite Biblical Seminary issued a formal condemnation of Yoder's sexual victimization of women. See further Rachel Waltner Goosen's article "The Failure to Bind and Loose: Responses to Yoder's Sexual Abuse," *The Mennonite*, January 2, 2015, https://themennonite.org/feature/failure-bind-loose-responses-john-howard-yoders-sexual-abuse/.

43. Cited in Yoder, *Royal Priesthood*, 339.

44. Ibid., 352 (emphasis original).

45. Ibid., 337.

46. Ibid., 291.

47. Hauerwas, *Approaching the End*, 110.

There will be conflict in the church: Jesus, as recorded in Matthew's Gospel, is only being realistic when he speaks about the need for confronting and forgiving sinners. Yoder affirms this realpolitik: church unity is based not only on agreements but also on the awareness that disagreements need not lead to division but, rather, prove the existence of a reconciling community. Yoder acknowledges the mixed pedigree of his position: "It gives more authority to the church than does Rome, trusts more the Holy Spirit than does Pentecostalism, has more respect for the individual than humanism, [and] makes moral standards more binding than puritanism."[48]

According to Hauerwas, "catholicity" may be a better term than "unity" for expressing the church's oneness because it does not deny difference. Catholicity—in this context, fraternal admonition between churches—is "the commitment by the church . . . to be ready to challenge as well as be challenged by other Christian traditions."[49] The aim of the exchange is to determine whether a church is a faithful local expression of the universality of the gospel. Catholicity, on this view, becomes not merely a description of the church but an *ecclesial virtue*: a willingness to engage other church traditions. What counts is embodying this virtue (catholicity); of less importance is the institutional form that such embodiments take.[50]

Jonathan Leeman distinguishes the invisible unity that unites churches that confess the gospel from the visible unity that characterizes a local congregation. The New Testament never speaks of churches separating themselves from one another at a denominational level, only of divisions within particular local congregations.[51] As we have seen, the local congregation is independent because it possesses the keys of the kingdom: "They possess authority over their own members and statements of faith."[52] Though this is clearly a plea in favor of independent churches, it is not a charter for autonomous Christians. On the contrary, believers ought to become baptized members of local churches: "Christians do not have the authority to declare themselves Jesus's representatives."[53]

48. Yoder, *Royal Priesthood*, 325.

49. Hauerwas, *Approaching the End*, 116.

50. Hauerwas draws on Bruce Kaye's "Reality and Form in Catholicity" (*Journal of Anglican Studies* 10, no. 1 [2012]: 3–12), and he suggests that Yoder's form of Anabaptism has significant similarities to an Anglican approach to catholicity.

51. Jonathan Leeman, "A Congregational Approach to Catholicity: Independence and Interdependence," in Dever and Leeman, *Baptist Foundations*, 367.

52. Ibid., 368.

53. Ibid., 369.

One implication of this free-church view is that one local church is not bound by another's decision to "bind" or excommunicate an individual. The second church, if it is wise, should make inquiries into the circumstances, but in the final analysis, the second church "possesses its own authority in the keys to receive the individual into membership."[54] To what kind of catholicity does such a free-church approach give rise?

Though the New Testament knows nothing of denominational structures, it does have a lot to say about close family ties between local churches. "All the churches of Christ greet you" (Rom. 16:16); "The churches of Asia send you greetings" (1 Cor. 16:19). We also know that they supported one another financially (Rom. 15:25–26; 1 Cor. 16:1–3; 2 Cor. 9:12). There is a kind of "political" unity insofar as members of different embassies represent the same kingdom (and king), and there certainly is a degree of corporate responsibility: when one church presents a poor witness, the whole church in the area likely suffers.

Congregationalist catholicity involves, first, praying for other churches, especially in one's locale but also throughout the world. Second, churches can cooperate in certain gospel ministries even if they cannot work together to plant churches (if they do not share the same polity). While Leeman encourages local churches to learn from one another, including from churches in the past, he does not appear to have a place for the fraternal admonition of one church by another.

Curtis Freeman wrote his *Contesting Catholicity* in order to retell the Baptist story "as a community of contested convictions *within* the catholic church."[55] Freeman insists that early Baptist groups "conceived of their gathered communities as local and visible expressions of the church universal, not merely as independent congregations or voluntary associations."[56] Freeman traces the roots of a properly baptistic sense of catholicity to the sixteenth-century cleric and theologian William Perkins, who argued that the proper description of a Protestant is "Reformed Catholic."[57]

Earlier I said that Martin Bucer may well be the patron saint of mere Protestant Christianity. Fans of Thomas Cranmer may beg to differ. Cranmer was

---

54. Ibid., 372.
55. Curtis W. Freeman, *Contesting Catholicity: Theology for Other Baptists* (Waco: Baylor University Press, 2014), 10.
56. Ibid., 13.
57. Cited in ibid., 17.

deeply troubled by the prolonged dispute among the Continental Reformers about the Lord's Supper, and he made strenuous efforts toward achieving a biblically based unity on this issue. As early as 1537 he wrote to one Swiss Reformer, "It cannot be told how greatly this so bloody controversy has impeded the full course of the Gospel both throughout the whole Christian world and especially among ourselves."[58]

Cranmer invited a number of the Continental Reformers to England to deliberate the issue and formulate a form of the doctrine that would be both biblical and an expression of their common mind. Calvin was all in: "As far as I am concerned, if I can be of any service, I shall not shrink from crossing ten seas, if need be, for that object."[59] Cranmer also wrote to Melanchthon in 1552, citing the example of the Jerusalem Council and urging him to participate, for "it is truly grievous that the sacrament of unity is made by the malice of the devil for disagreement and (as it were) the apple of contention."[60] Unfortunately, Cranmer's Continental Congress of Protestant churches never took place.

Nevertheless, John Woodhouse rightly reminds us that the unity of the church, the fellowship seated in the heavenlies with Christ, is not under threat, for the Lord has built his church, and "the gates of hell shall not prevail against it" (Matt. 16:18). We must not think that the one body of Christ refers to a worldwide organization—an ecclesial-institutional complex—as if unity were something that could be politically engineered. The New Testament focuses on divisions *within* congregations, not between them. Sometimes, if a local church is too concerned with keeping the denominational peace, it risks being unfaithful to the gospel. The unity of the Spirit trumps the unity of human ingenuity.[61]

Woodhouse here follows the Knox-Robinson hypothesis—the proposition that when the New Testament speaks of *ekklēsia*, it refers to either a local or a heavenly gathering (with an emphasis on the activity or actuality of the gathering). According to D. Broughton Knox and Donald Robinson, there is no evidence of a "third place," an earthly ecclesial entity larger than a local congregation. The local congregation clearly gets the bulk of the New Testament authors' attention. The Bible does not prescribe denomination-like

---

58. Cited in Hughes, *Theology of the English Reformers*, 257.
59. Cited in ibid., 261.
60. Cited in ibid., 261–62.
61. See Woodhouse, "When to Unite."

entities, but neither does it prohibit them. Knox and Robinson place particular emphasis on the heavenly church. The ascended Christ is in heaven, and it is the heavenly church that is one in Christ. Still, we ought not to forget Jesus's promise to be with his followers "where two or three are gathered" on earth in his name (Matt. 18:20).

Where does authority reside according to this view? As we have seen, the church is ruled by the Word of God alone. Furthermore, there is no church beyond that which is identified in local gatherings. The local church is therefore autonomous, because it is directly accountable to God's Word alone: "There is no institutional authority over the local church as there is no earthly ecclesial reality beyond the local church."[62] Indeed, it might not be an exaggeration to describe the Knox-Robinson view in terms of *sola ecclesia*: the *local church alone* has the right to direct its own affairs, in contrast to situations in which local churches are but small cogs in larger denominational wheels.

There is much to admire in this view, especially when one remembers the pressures to conform to denominational policy or to fall in step with the ecumenical movement in pursuit of the ideal of visible universal unity. We may nevertheless wonder how Acts 9:31 fits into the biblical-theological picture: "So the church throughout all Judea and Galilee and Samaria had peace and was being built up." Some translations read "the churches" (plural), and this is what we find in the Textus Receptus ("received text"—the Greek text on which most Reformation-era translations were based) but, significantly, *only* in the Textus Receptus. Might there be biblical support after all for the notion of one, translocal, visible church?[63]

Mere Protestant Catholicity: The Many Churches

When confronted with theological diversity, the first reflex of the mere Protestant is to appeal to the supreme authority of Scripture, the formal principle

---

62. Chase Kuhn, "The Ecclesiology of Donald Robinson and David Broughton Knox: A Presentation, Analysis and Theological Evaluation of Their Thought on the Nature of the Church" (PhD thesis, University of Western Sydney, 2014), 209.

63. Donald Robinson thinks not. He admits that Acts 9:31 seems to refer to a regional as distinct from local church. However, "as the context beginning at 8:1 reveals, this is still the Jerusalem church, attenuated or dispersed through persecution. But the conception of a church which extends territorially while remaining the same church, however it may appeal to our modern frame of mind, has no further development in the NT" (*Donald Robinson: Selected Works*, vol. 1, *Assembling God's People*, ed. Peter Bolt and Mark Thompson [Camperdown, NSW: Australian Church Record; Newton, NSW: Moore College, 2008], 216–17). My thanks to Mark Thompson for calling my attention to this quotation.

of the Reformation. However, the second mere Protestant reflex is to consult tradition, the catholic substance of the Reformation. The catholic tradition contains a wealth of resources, the combined wealth of many holy nations. Think about it: today's biblical sermons, commentaries, and theologies will tomorrow join the ranks of church tradition.

I initially resisted but then reluctantly agreed with Richard Muller's observation that as soon as a theologian publishes a work of systematic theology, it becomes *historical* theology. In the unlikely event that future church historians will pore over what I have written, they will doubtless see how my thinking was shaped not only by the biblical text but also by the trends, controversies, and conversations that were happening as I was writing. It has always been so. This is not something to bemoan: God created us finite and declared it "very good." It is also good for biblical interpreters not to be alone, locked up in their own culture and epoch. We read the Bible best when we stand on the shoulders of giants—and also when we're open to what shorter people in cultural locations other than our own see in the text. Simply put: the best Protestants are catholic Protestants—people centered on the gospel but also alert to how the gospel has been faithfully received across cultures and centuries.

"Catholicity" (from Gk. *kata* + *holos*, "according to the whole") is the quality of being comprehensive in scope. As such, it catches an aspect of *mere*, though *mere* is equally apostolic, because centered on the gospel. To be Protestant is to focus on the gospel; to be catholic is to be mindful of the scope of the gospel's wide reception. A mere Protestant like Martin Bucer went far beyond the second mile in his attempts to unify the Reformers (his biographer has a section on "roads" and estimates that Bucer traveled thousands of miles just to keep negotiations from stalling).[64] We too must travel on, leaving Bucer in sixteenth-century Strasbourg as we travel to more recent Protestant burgs. For there is a remnant of mere Protestant Christians that remains.

Mercersburg: Protestant Catholicity

Philip Schaff left Europe in 1843 to become professor of church history at the German Reformed Theological Seminary in Mercersburg, Pennsylvania. His inaugural address, *The Principle of Protestantism*, has been called "one of the most significant events in the history of the American church."[65] Schaff

---

64. Greschat, *Martin Bucer*, 129–32.
65. Bart Thompson and George H. Bricker, preface to Schaff, *Principle of Protestantism*, 14.

arrived in the United States at a tumultuous moment in American church history, when familiar Protestant denominations existed beside a multitude of new churches, many of them independent, which had sprung up during decades of spiritual revival. Schaff spoke out against subjectivism and sectarianism, arguing that the Reformation—and this includes, by implication, the *solas*—was the unfolding of true catholicity.[66]

We best understand Schaff when we see that, for him, the Protestant principle means the "Reformed Catholic" principle.[67] To return to (and correct) Alister McGrath's metaphor: Protestantism is not the virus that divides and attacks the body; it is the antibodies that set to work attacking the body's infections (e.g., late medieval Roman Catholicism).[68] Schaff rejects the caricature of the Reformation as the event that freed individuals from church authority and promoted "private judgment to the papal throne."[69] On the contrary, the Reformation was the curative process that restored health and organic unity to the body of Christ, precisely by recovering the wealth of catholic tradition.

Schaff was a church historian. No doubt, a radical postmodern today, listening to Schaff through a hermeneutic of suspicion, might think, "*Of course* he gives pride of place to church history." The truth, of course, may be the reverse: perhaps he became a church historian *because* he thought that catholic tradition was tremendously important. In any case, he was convinced that a lack of respect for church history, and a preoccupation with the biblical interpretation of one's own community, amounts to a neglect of the Spirit's leading of the whole church into the truth over time.[70] Such a myopic attitude is less than epistemically conscientious. Neglecting the history of the Spirit's effects gets us only as far as abbreviated Protestantism, whereas the true Protestantism, the one represented by the Reformers themselves, is a catholic Protestantism. Recall that Schaff was responding to his historical situation: in his day, the problem was not that there was too much authority but that there was too little, which is why he and his colleague John Nevin sought to retrieve the doctrine of the church.[71]

66. Schaff, *Principle of Protestantism*, 73.

67. Ibid., 56.

68. Schaff himself suggests this imagery (ibid., 223).

69. Ibid., 224.

70. Ibid., 227.

71. See further W. Bradford Littlejohn, *The Mercersburg Theology and the Quest for Reformed Catholicity* (Eugene, OR: Pickwick, 2009).

Nevin wanted to recover Calvin's high regard for the church as an external means by which God nurtures us in the society of Christ: "Individualism without the church is as little to be trusted as ecclesiasticism without individual experience."[72] Nevin found in Calvin an alternative to the rampant religious subjectivity sweeping the United States in the mid-nineteenth century.[73]

LEUENBERG: PROTESTANT ECUMENICITY

Whatever happened to Protestantism in Europe? We know about the divisions, but in 1973 the Reformation churches in Europe reached a new concord in the Leuenberg Agreement, reaffirming the unique mediation of Christ at the heart of the Scriptures and that "the message of justification as the message of God's free grace is the measure of all the Church's preaching."[74] In assenting to the agreement, the churches articulated a common understanding of the gospel and declared their fellowship with one another. In the context of the agreement, church fellowship meant "that on the basis of the consensus they have reached in their understanding of the gospel, churches with different confessional positions accord each other fellowship in word and sacrament and strive for the fullest possible co-operation in witness and service to the world."[75] The hope was that unanimity concerning doctrine would serve not as the *precondition* of church fellowship but as its hopeful *consequence*.

As of today, over one hundred Protestant denominations have signed the Leuenberg Agreement and are now known as the Communion of Protestant Churches in Europe (CPCE). The agreement trades on a distinction between

---

72. John W. Nevin, introduction to Schaff, *Principle of Protestantism*, 37.

73. Darryl G. Hart, "The Use and Abuse of the Christian Past: Mercersburg, the Ancient Church, and American Evangelicalism," in *Evangelicals and the Early Church: Recovery, Reform, Renewal*, ed. George Kalantzis and Andrew Tooley (Eugene, OR: Cascade, 2012), 85–103. Douglas Sweeney's reply to Hart helpfully suggests asking whether there are further lessons to be learned from Mercersburg ("Mercersburg Doctrine as a Double-Edged Sword—A Response to Darryl G. Hart," in Kalantzis and Tooley, *Evangelicals and the Early Church*, 104–7). Sweeney asks,

> Were [Nevin and Schaff] onto something that might well instruct evangelicals and bolster evangelicalism? Or do they simply teach us that we have to make a choice between the latest forms of modern evangelical religion and the whole enchilada of traditional Catholicism (whether in Roman or Eastern flavors)? Can we have it both ways? Can we find a healthy balance of tradition, Protestant doctrine, and evangelical relevance? Can Nevin and Schaff help us to be "evangelical catholics"? (107)

74. "Agreement between Reformation Churches in Europe (The Leuenberg Agreement)," March 16, 1973, http://www.leuenberg.net/leuenberg-agreement.

75. Ibid.

the foundation of the church (faith) and its organizational shape (order). As to the foundation, it is the shared understanding (a "minimal consensus") of the gospel as "the justifying action of the triune God."[76] As to its shape, the agreement acknowledges that the church has taken various historical forms but concludes that these need not be an impediment to fellowship. All the churches agree that the ministry of the Word in proclamation, instruction, and pastoral care "always depends on the universal priesthood of the congregation and should serve it."[77] No one particular form of oversight (*episkopē*) is required: "Such differences in church structures do not impede a 'church fellowship.'"[78]

Churches can mutually *recognize* one another, and thus establish fellowship, "if there is agreement between them on the understanding of the gospel."[79] The particular shape and structure of ministry "belongs to the sphere of legitimate historically and locally conditioned diversity."[80] Differences over the Lord's Supper, while important, are no longer viewed as impediments to full fellowship. The Community of Protestant Churches in Europe practices "reconciled diversity." Hence, wherever a church displays the marks of the true church, it is to be recognized as part of the one, holy, catholic, and apostolic church, and, if necessary, "this has to be done unilaterally."[81]

Not all churches have signed up. For example, the Evangelical Lutheran Church of Finland rejected the agreement on theological grounds, namely, that the consensus about the gospel and the key concept of "church fellowship" are too vague and remain open to various (mis)interpretations.[82] Tellingly (and somewhat ironically), the most difficult single problem mentioned is the formulation of the doctrine of the Lord's Supper, which failed to satisfy the Finnish Lutherans.

76. Leuenberg Church Fellowship, "The Church of Jesus Christ: The Contribution of the Reformation towards Ecumenical Dialogue on Church Unity," May 9, 1994, http://www.reformiert-online.net/agora2/docs/309.pdf.

77. Ibid.

78. Ibid.

79. Ibid.

80. Ibid.

81. Ibid.

82. See Tomi Karttunen, "Useful and Possible? The Evangelical Lutheran Church of Finland and Membership in the Communion of the Protestant Churches in Europe," February 16, 2008, http://sakasti.evl.fi/sakasti.nsf/0/2EEE800EEBB8BA41C225773400279C85/$FILE/Leuenberg-CPCE%20and%20ELCF%20netti.pdf.

Ecclesial Unity and Diversity: Toward Which Catholicity?

Mercersburg and Leuenberg represent two Protestant takes on catholicity, the one a catholic Protestantism, the other a Protestant ecumenism. Here I need to declare myself: a catholicity that is not firmly anchored in apostolicity—the authoritative scriptural witness to the gospel of Jesus Christ—risks achieving only ecumenical or organizational unity, not evangelical or organic unity in Christ. The question remains: How ought churches to make their organic unity in Christ visible? If individual Christians are, as far as possible, to live peaceably with all others (Rom. 12:18), how much more ought local churches strive to do so with other churches? I agree with Oliver O'Donovan: Christians' "universal communion in the truth of the gospel will not come about by the denial of denominational traditions, but only by the critical appropriation and sharing of them."[83] I turn now to consider some strategies for doing this.

David Buschart's *Exploring Protestant Traditions: An Invitation to Theological Hospitality* follows the way of "humble recognition that all traditions of Christianity contain an admixture of truth and error, wisdom and weakness."[84] Both "humble" and "recognition" are the operative terms, and Buschart makes good on them in the epilogue, where he acknowledges his own tradition (Reformed) and then goes on to say how he has been challenged by listening to each of the other traditions (in addition to Reformed, he discusses Lutheran, Anabaptist, Anglican, Baptist, Wesleyan, Dispensational, and Pentecostal theology).

Buschart advocates neither a minimizing of differences nor an either/or approach, but rather an attitude of both/and: "Is it possible for someone to both stand within a tradition and stand with other Christians outside that tradition? Such a 'both/and' view of the church is not only possible, but is also, I propose, the proper and the most realistic and constructive view."[85] How is it possible? By understanding that not all differences need be divisive.[86] Recall Hauerwas's point that catholicity refers to what enables a gathered assembly to "refuse to let worldly divisions determine their relation to one another."[87] The

---

83. Oliver O'Donovan, *On the Thirty-Nine Articles: A Conversation with Tudor Christianity*, Latimer Monographs (Exeter, UK: Paternoster, 1986), 10.

84. Buschart, *Exploring Protestant Traditions*, 28.

85. Ibid., 258.

86. For example, there are several models of the atonement that differ largely in the emphasis that they give to a particular biblical metaphor and its related semantic field: penal substitution (law court); *Christus Victor* (battlefield); ransom (hostage situation).

87. Hauerwas, *Approaching the End*, 119.

church ought to exhibit both unity and diversity. Ontologically, the church *is* one, in Christ, even if organizationally it is not. Still, it is part of the church's mission to become more fully (and visibly) what it is in Christ: united, one. Again, it is the Word and the Spirit that make the church one in Christ; unity is achieved not by theological formulas or by politicking, though these can help to make the unity that we have in Christ more visible. The telltale sign of Christian unity is our love for Christ and for one another in Christ (see John 13:34–35), "not agreement with them in every matter of theology."[88]

We turn now to examine other ways of making good on the promise of the "both/and" approach to church traditions.

Mere Protestant Hospitality: The Prospects of Communion

In the introduction I compared mere Protestant Christianity to a block party and neighborhood watch. Those who have been raised in a particular confessional tradition live in one of the houses on Evangel Lane. Here, fences do not make good neighbors, especially when what is fenced off is the Lord's Table, and hence the possibility of table fellowship. The golden rule for confessional traditions is to practice hospitality, to visit one's neighbors and invite them to (the Lord's) Supper. Protestant traditions should be inviting homes, not mighty bulwarks (at least not toward one another). It is possible to fellowship with one's neighbors without betraying one's identity. What follows are further suggestions in aid of mere Protestant theological hospitality.

DOGMATIC RANK: THE KEY TO UNITY-IN-DIFFERENCE?

"Dogmatic rank" is the idea that not all doctrines are created equal. The basic premise of this way of thinking about theology is that not every doctrine is an essential of the faith. I submit that the framework of dogmatic rank may be helpful in negotiating interpretive disagreement between Protestant churches. I cannot call the roll of every doctrine here; it must suffice to provide a sketch of the framework and a few examples.[89]

Some doctrines are closer to the core events that make up the story of salvation, such that if we were to lose them, we could not tell the same story. Doctrines that are essential to the logic of the gospel story are thus of higher

---

88. Buschart, *Exploring Protestant Traditions*, 260.
89. For a related attempt to distinguish levels of doctrine, see Kevin DeYoung, "Where and How Do We Draw the Line?," *Tabletalk* 36, no. 7 (2012): 13–14.

rank than doctrines that are not. On these essential doctrines, there must be unity. We get some indication of what these essentials are from the Pastoral Epistles, where we have trustworthy sayings (1 Tim. 1:15; 3:1; 4:9–10; 2 Tim. 2:11–13; Titus 3:4–8), prototypical creedal formulas (1 Tim. 1:17; 2:5; 3:16; 6:15–16; Titus 2:11–15), warnings about false teaching (1 Tim. 1:8–11; 4:1–3; 2 Tim. 2:18; Titus 1:16), and exhortations to preserve sound doctrine (1 Tim. 1:8–10; 2:8; 2 Tim. 3:14–17). We find similar help in 1 John, where strong warnings about the antichrist ("he who denies the Father and the Son," 1 John 2:22) underline the centrality of the incarnation (i.e., confessing "that Jesus Christ has come in the flesh," 1 John 4:2). If God did not become human, the gospel is fatally short-circuited.

These first-level doctrines are "dogmas": formulations of revealed biblical truth that the whole church considers authoritative.[90] We have seen that tradition is not a second source of revelation but rather corporate testimony to the meaning and implications of the Bible. Dogmatic statements reflect the mind of the church as to the mind of the Scriptures. It is no accident that the doctrine of the Trinity was the first dogma on which the communion of saints formed a consensus, at the Council of Nicaea (325). When we attend closely to the Jesus of the Bible we will necessarily arrive at the Trinity, for the good news at the heart of Christianity concerns what the Father has done in the Son through the Spirit to incorporate people from every race, tribe, and class into his family as adopted children. That there is one God in three persons is a level-one teaching because it identifies the main persons of the gospel story. To differ at this first level is to disagree about the gospel itself. Level-one doctrines concern what the apostle Paul says is of "first importance" (1 Cor. 15:3), namely, doctrines such as the bodily resurrection of Jesus (1 Cor. 15:4), without which the gospel story loses its integrity. As to what and how many these level-one doctrines are, catholicity is a helpful criterion. Simply put: level-one doctrines are catholic doctrines—what every follower of Jesus, anywhere and at all times, must believe to preserve both the intelligibility of the gospel and the fellowship of the saints.

Disagreements about level-two doctrines do not disqualify a person from the fellowship of the saints, but they may lead to a parting of the ways. Paul and Barnabas went their separate ways to pursue different ministries,

90. On dogmas and dogmatic theology, see Bavinck, *Reformed Dogmatics*, 1:28–34.

though each continued to minister Christ. Paul and Barnabas foreshadow what happened during the Reformation, when Protestants from different regions—southern Germany, Switzerland, and so on—decided to go their separate ways over, for example, the theology of the Lord's Supper. Yes, there were doctrinal differences, but they tended to be differences about ambiguities and incidentals in the gospel story (e.g., the precise nature of Christ's presence in the bread and wine) rather than the story itself. Whereas level-one doctrines answer questions pertaining to the who and what of the gospel (e.g., Who is Jesus? What happened after he died?), level-two doctrines typically respond to questions of how (e.g., How does Jesus's death on the cross save sinners? How are the bread and the wine Jesus's body and blood?).

Finally, level-three doctrines, though important, are not regarded as necessary for everyone to affirm even in the same confessional tradition or denomination. There are areas on which there can be a legitimate diversity of opinions, even in a local church. Often these answer questions that the biblical text itself leaves somewhat open (e.g., When is Jesus coming back, and will his return precede or follow the tribulation of the church?). Such differences impede neither table fellowship nor collaboration in ministry. Put simply: level-three doctrines have a low degree of catholicity.

Table Talk: Theological Conference

Time is God's gift to the church—an opportunity for growth and mission. It took time for Jesus's disciples to realize who he was ("What I am doing you do not understand now, but afterward you will understand," John 13:7). Like the disciples on the way to Emmaus, who were "talking with each other about all these things that had happened [to Jesus at Jerusalem]" (Luke 24:14), Christians have been discussing among themselves for centuries, though not always as amicably. Talk can be threatening, especially if people feel that their most cherished views are at risk. Difference itself, whether great or small, can often be perceived as a threat.

Why do Christians who agree about *sola scriptura* differ as to what the Bible means? There are several factors, less reasons than rationalizations. To begin with, it is easier to disagree than to agree. Agreement requires patient listening, and time. It is more convenient simply to categorize others as "wrong" Christians. Such mental shortcuts enable us to make snap judgments, but labeling fails to do justice to others.[91] Nor should we overlook the possibility that Satan, the accuser, is on the lookout to exploit every difference of opinion by turning it into an excuse for church division. Mere Protestant Christians must remember, however, that not all differences need be divisive. Indeed, some differences may be divine, intended by God for the enrichment of the church.

I am struck by a parallel between Luke's account of the word of the gospel growing, Andrew Walls's account of the church's understanding of Christ growing through the process of cross-cultural mission and translation, and Mikhail Bakhtin's ideas about the importance of dialogue for textual understanding.[92] In a genuine dialogue, neither conversation partner is absorbed into the other (Bakhtin resists Gadamer's notion of a "fusion" of horizons for precisely this reason). Rather, each partner in a true dialogue remains "outside" the other. Bakhtin's basic insight is that interpreters gradually realize the "meaning potential" of a text by dialoguing with those who read differently. Dialogue does not add new meaning to the text, but, as a result of the different perspectives, each person in the dialogue discovers something in the text that he or she had not previously seen. Without "outsideness" (i.e., a *different* perspective), people see less, not more. To read by oneself is to imprison the text within one's own cultural moment or historical horizon—a prescription for interpretive tunnel vision. These points cast Protestant differences in an interesting new light.

Dialogue takes time. Interpreters must take care not to entrap or enclose the text either within its own epoch (in which case it cannot speak to us) or in ours (in which case we hear only ourselves). To entrap either the text or the reader in the past or the present is to fall prey to "small time." Luke-Acts presents a counterexample: as the word of God sets out on its communicative mission to Rome, it "increases" over time (Acts 6:7; 12:24; 19:20). The canon is closed, to be sure; not so the process of the church's increase in understanding. Understanding of God's word grows, not when people simply repeat what it says, but rather when they enter into a conversation about it with others, past and present. This kind of dialogue—the kind that explores the meaning

91. Christena Cleveland, *Disunity in Christ: Uncovering the Hidden Forces That Keep Us Apart* (Downers Grove, IL: InterVarsity, 2013), 47.

92. See Mikhail Bakhtin, *Problems of Dostoevsky's Poetics*, ed. and trans. Caryl Emerson (Minneapolis: University of Minnesota Press, 1984); Bakhtin, *Speech Genres and Other Late Essays*, trans. Vern W. McGee, ed. Caryl Emerson and Michael Holquist (Austin: University of Texas Press, 1986). See also Michael Holquist, *Dialogism: Bakhtin and His World*, 2nd ed. (London: Routledge, 2002).

potential of the text—takes time, "great time," as Bakhtin calls it. There is one gospel, but it takes many voices from various times and places, and perhaps even different confessional traditions, to actualize and comprehend fully its meaning.

Bakhtin's notion of realizing the meaning potential of a text through dialogue with "outsiders" who read the text differently corroborates not only Protestant conciliarism but also the weekly meetings of the Genevan *congrégations*, also called *conférences des Écritures* (Scripture conferences).[93] It also helps us see how denominational differences can work for the catholic good—the good of "great understanding." Engaging in dialogue has the benefit of resisting premature resolutions to difficult questions. Dialoguing can even be a means of sanctification and transformation to the extent that it affords individuals and churches the opportunity to grow in the conversational and interpretive virtues. But the basic point is that dialogue with other denominations affords a kind of catholic "outsideness"—that is, a view from beyond the perspective of our own confessional traditions or independent churches. Indeed, we can view a church's confession as a statement of what a denomination different from our own has seen in Scripture. Karl Barth had something like this in mind when he described a Reformed confession of faith as "the spontaneously and publicly formulated presentation to the Christian Church in general of a provisionally granted insight from the revelation of God in Jesus Christ attested in Holy Scripture alone by a geographically circumscribed Christian fellowship."[94]

Interestingly enough, Walls uses language almost identical to Bakhtin's to describe the process of coming to understand the gospel: "We need each other's vision to correct, enlarge, and focus our own; only together are we complete in Christ."[95] What begin as local insights (e.g., Nicaea's emphasis on *homoousios*) can blossom into catholic truths. The idea that we need others to correct us is but a variation on the theme of fraternal admonition. We are here a long way from the accusation that the Reformation gives rise to individual autonomy and anarchy. On the contrary, dialogue requires us to become the kind of people who can accept correction: humble and patient interlocutors.

---

93. See further de Boer, *Genevan School of the Prophets*.

94. Karl Barth, "Wünschbarkeit und Möglichkeit eines allgemeinen reformierten Glaubensbekenntnisses," in *Vorträge und kleinere Arbeiten, 1922–1925*, ed. Holger Finze (Zürich: Theologischer Verlag, 1990), 610 (cited in McCormack, "End of Reformed Theology?," 61).

95. Walls, *Cross-Cultural Process*, 79.

It takes "great time" for the church to achieve a "great understanding" of the greatest story ever told. Mere Protestant Christianity provides a way to think about ecclesiology that encourages various churches and denominations to continue talking, both in order to resolve differences that impede fellowship and to grow into a mature understanding of the wisdom that is in Christ.

THE GIFT OF PEACE: BEYOND CONTROVERSY

It is no accident in the Anglican liturgy of the sacrament that church members exchange the sign of peace just before the celebration of the Eucharist: "the peace of Christ." Nor is it insignificant that John Webster frames his discussion of theological controversy with a discussion about the peace of God's own life, a peace that unfolds over the course of the economy of redemption, and a peace that the church gathers to enact.[96]

Jesus preached peace (Eph. 2:17), made peace through the blood of his cross (Col. 1:20), and greeted his disciples after his resurrection saying, "Peace be with you" (John 20:19). Paul exhorts the Colossians, "And let the peace of Christ rule in your hearts, to which indeed you were called in one body" (Col. 3:15). As the church is an external means by which God holds us in the society of Christ (Calvin), so theology may serve as a creaturely aid to preserving peace to the extent that it rightly hears and heeds the gospel. Christians too are finite and do not know everything at once: "The scope of the gospel has to be learned over time and in a work of cooperative intellect."[97]

John Owen argues that gifts of insight into the gospel must be communicated, not hoarded. His *Discourse concerning Evangelical Love, Church Peace, and Unity* (1672) is a serious attempt to grapple with theological discord, as discord works against both the peace of the church and the glory of God. Webster agrees, urging theologians to engage in controversy not after the fashion of the world but with the aim of mutual edification, and he proposes some rules for doing so. Theological debate must (1) be within the communion of saints and have as its aim the furtherance of communion; (2) magnify the truth of the gospel; (3) have an eye to the catholicity of Christian confession; and (4) trust in the illumining power of the Spirit unifying the church through Scripture.[98]

---

96. Webster, *Domain of the Word*, 150–70. Webster also notes that conflict lacks ontological weight, because both Creator and the order of creation are intrinsically peaceful (156–57).
97. Ibid., 165.
98. Ibid., 169–70.

Soli Deo Gloria for Bible, Church, and Interpretive Authority

This examination of the authority of interpretive communities after Babel has nearly reached its end. We have seen the initial attraction of having a magisterium that adjudicates between rival interpretations, but this is not the path that I have pursued. I concluded that Roman Catholicity is not catholic enough, that the Roman Catholic view of tradition departs from church tradition, that the unity of the church is not a function of institutional organization, and that the priesthood is not restricted to a certain class of Christians but is the universal privilege and responsibility of every believer "in Christ."

On a more positive note, I have situated the question of the authority of interpretive communities within a biblical-theological and dogmatic framework (the triune economy), and I have insisted that unity and catholicity are a creation of Word and Spirit together ministering the gospel. Finally, I have suggested some ways for Protestant churches to negotiate their interpretive disagreements and, at the limit, benefit from them. We are therefore now in a better position to see why mere Protestant Christianity leads not to anarchy but rather to a peaceful, though often exciting, unity-in-diversity. To that end, I offer four last theses.

> 17. Mere Protestant Christianity, far from encouraging individual autonomy and interpretive anarchy, calls individual interpreters to join with other citizens of the gospel as members of a universal royal priesthood and local embassy of Christ's kingdom in order to represent God's rule publicly.

The center of mere Protestant Christianity is the gospel, but its circumference is catholicity. "Catholic" qualifies "Protestant": the Word of God in Scripture gathers the church, and "catholicity" designates the scope of the gospel's reception. To qualify Protestantism as catholic is to prohibit any one particular reception of the gospel from lording it over others and to urge all particular local receptions of the gospel to be open to enrichment and, if necessary, correction from other embassies of the gospel. Catholicity helps to address, even cure, the problem of pervasive interpretive pluralism by countering it with comprehensive interpretive unity—at least as concerns the economy of the gospel.

> 18. Mere Protestant Christianity is a confederacy of holy nations (local churches) united by a single constitution, and committed to reform and renewal through a continued rereading of Scripture.

Sola ecclesia may not have been one of the official Reformation *solas*, but together they imply a mere Protestant understanding of the church: by grace alone the church is an elect nation; through faith alone the church is a creature of the Word; according to Scripture alone the church governs its life and thought; in Christ alone the church is constituted a royal priesthood; for the glory of God alone the church as a holy nation accumulates its wealth—its worship, wisdom, and witness to the God of the gospel.

All the holy nations—every local church—are under the rule of God's Word. The church submits its judgment to correction by Scripture, comparing all the relevant passages on a given topic and interpreting them to avoid substantial contradictions: "Like every other rule, it may be misapplied, but . . . constitutional provision is made for correction by an objective standard. This is unique."[99] The Word of God gives direction as to how everyone everywhere at all times and places has a role to play in glorifying God (and loving one another to God's glory).

19. The genius of mere Protestant Christianity is its distinct converse (i.e., conversational "conference"), generated and governed by Scripture, and guided by a convictional conciliarism that unites diverse churches in a transdenominational communion.

I began by thinking about the Reformation and its impact on western Europe—what McGrath called "Christianity's dangerous idea." More recently, George Steiner has addressed the question of whether or not Europe is still a good idea. Steiner, a humanist, is primarily interested in Western culture, at the heart of which is the literary classic. To be a teacher, he has said, is "To invite others into meaning."[100] What is left of the glory that once was Europe after the demeaning of deconstruction? Steiner admits that the idea of Europe may have run its course (some are saying something similar about Protestantism). He is aware that the Continent has produced both great poets and terrible dictators, classic works of art and wars of ethnic cleansing. The "ideal of unison" is undeniable (Steiner was writing before Greece's recent debt crisis). Yet Steiner identifies the real genius of Europe with what William Blake terms "the holiness of the minute particular": "It is that of linguistic, cultural, social diversity, of a prodigal mosaic which

99. Blocher, "Analogy of Faith," 27.
100. George Steiner, *The Idea of Europe: An Essay* (London: Overlook Duckworth, 2015), 19.

often makes a trivial distance, twenty kilometers apart, a division between worlds."[101]

The genius of mere Protestant Christianity, similarly, is its great unity-in-diversity, a vision of churches from many traditions gathered around the Lord's Table to share insights into his person and work in mutually enriching conversation—table talk—that builds up the church into maturity, until our knowledge and wisdom attain to "the measure of the stature of the fullness of Christ" (Eph. 4:13).

> 20. The glory of mere Protestant Christianity is the conference and communion of holy nations, itself a gift that glorifies God in magnifying Jesus Christ.

In Revelation 21 the kings bring their "glory" to Christ, who reigns in the new Jerusalem (Rev. 21:24). There is an allusion here to the "wealth of nations" that Isaiah prophesied would be brought by kings as tribute (Isa. 60:5, 11), and even eaten (Isa. 61:6).[102] "Tribute," in addition to referring to periodic payment owed a ruler, can refer to a statement intended to show gratitude, respect, or worship. "Say to God, 'How awesome are your deeds!'" (Ps. 66:3). This is the essence of praise: *saying to God what God is*. Giving praise is sibling to doing theology, the project of saying who God is, and what the Triune God is doing in Jesus Christ.

The wealth of holy nations is the sum total of doxology and dogmatics alike. The church glorifies God when local churches share their biblical interpretations and doctrinal reflections with one another, especially when this is done in the overarching context of table fellowship. "Oh, the depth of the riches and wisdom and knowledge of God!" (Rom. 11:33). The church glorifies God when each household brings its wealth—its respective insights into the gospel and the measure of Christ—to the table. Table talk and table fellowship should be the norm on Evangel Way. While not every Protestant house may be in as good repair as another, everyone benefits by showing hospitality and neighborly concern.

The wealth of holy nations is the mystery of Jesus Christ celebrated in the Lord's Supper, on the Communion table: one body, broken for every believer; one body, of which every believer is a part. The Lord's Table must no longer

---

101. Ibid., 59.

102. See Charles E. Cruise, "The 'Wealth of Nations': A Study in the Intertextuality of Isaiah 60:5, 11," *Journal of the Evangelical Theological Society* 58, no. 2 (2015): 283–97. Cruise argues that the wealth depicted in Isaiah is booty taken from conquered gentile nations, whereas in Revelation the gentiles are not vanquished but are part of God's people (293–94).

be a place of division but instead be one of celebration—celebration of the unity and catholicity of the gospel. After all, faithful Protestant households eventually will find themselves seated round not a conference table, or even a Communion table, but the table on which is set the marriage supper of the Lamb (Rev. 19:9). The church begins and ends in corporate praise and table fellowship, union and communion, its members sharing the wealth of the knowledge of God with one another to God's eternal glory.

Conclusion

From Catholic Protestantism to Protestant Evangelicalism

The previous chapter ended with a picture of various churches—holy nations—bringing their wealth to the marriage supper of the Lamb. In conclusion, I wish to suggest that this "transnational" communion—the genius and glory of mere Protestant Christianity—is best realized in the transdenominational movement known as evangelicalism. The true catholicity of the church is a catholicity determined by the gospel.

"And in the Morning, It Was Leah!"

To suggest that Protestant evangelicalism is the present-day instantiation of catholic Protestantism will strike some readers as a non sequitur. In particular, as concerns the problem of the authority of interpretive communities, they will think that I am proposing to jump out of the frying pan into a roaring campfire. Some readers may even feel betrayed. This was not the bride for whom we have been working seven years—or rather, five chapters—is it? "And in the morning, behold, it was Leah!" (Gen. 29:25)—an unpleasant surprise. I therefore understand if some readers might want to demand, with some exasperation, "What is this you have done to me? Did I not serve with you for five laborious chapters? Why then have you deceived me?" (see Gen. 29:25).

"Deception" is the operative term. Some, like D. G. Hart, doubt whether evangelicalism even exists. For Hart, evangelicalism is nothing more than a hasty generalization, the mistake with which a person is left after forgetting not to reify abstractions. Put differently: Hart contends that evangelicalism is a social construction of religious historians, and therefore a movement that needs to be deconstructed. In particular, Hart argues that evangelicalism owes its amorphousness to the lack of an identifiable and unifying creed and church polity.[1]

"Leah's eyes were weak" (Gen. 29:17). Critics say something similar about the "mind's eye" of evangelicalism. Mark Noll famously opined in 1994: "The scandal of the evangelical mind is that there is not much of an evangelical mind."[2] The anti-intellectual evangelical Leah resembles nothing more than a loose woman in the (nonalcoholic) lounge bar of popular culture. David Wells laments her fall from *sola gratia* into *sola cultura*.[3] Others have discovered her in a variety of compromising social and theological positions.[4]

"Leah's eyes were weak." There is an interesting parallel between what Lesslie Newbigin calls the two cardinal weaknesses of Protestantism and what David Wells calls the two inherent weaknesses of evangelicalism, a parallel all the more striking in light of Wells writing fifty-five years after Newbigin, and apparently unaware of his similar diagnosis. The first problem that Newbigin mentions is "an overintellectualizing of the content of the word 'faith,'" which leads to an overemphasis on correct doctrine.[5] The first problem with evangelicalism, according to Wells, is also theological, but in the opposite direction: the "shrinking" of doctrine for the sake of minimizing disagreement and maximizing cooperation.[6] As to the second problem, though the causes are different, the result is virtually identical, with Newbigin speaking of the "disappearance" and Wells of the "vanishing" of the (visible) church.[7] In the case of Protestantism, the visible unity of the church shattered into visible disunity; in the case of evangelicalism, the church itself dissolved into parachurch organizations.

There is a third weakness in both Protestantism and evangelicalism. Newbigin explicitly names it, but it is implicit in Wells's account: the question of

1. Darryl G. Hart, *Deconstructing Evangelicalism: Conservative Protestantism in the Age of Billy Graham* (Grand Rapids: Baker Academic, 2004), 29, 196.
2. Mark A. Noll, *The Scandal of the Evangelical Mind* (Grand Rapids: Eerdmans, 1994), 3.
3. Wells, *Courage to Be Protestant*, 4.
4. See the essays in John H. Armstrong, ed., *The Compromised Church: The Present Evangelical Crisis* (Wheaton: Crossway, 1998).
5. Newbigin, *Household of God*, 51.
6. Wells, *Courage to Be Protestant*, 7–9.
7. Ibid., 10–12; Newbigin, *Household of God*, 53–58.

church authority and, in particular, interpretive authority. If the continuity of the church consists in the identity and integrity of the one gospel preached ever anew, who is authorized to give or withhold authority to minister this word? Or rather: Who can legitimately claim to belong to the unity and continuity of the one people of God in all times and all places?

It goes without saying that to lose the gospel is to lose the raison d'être of the church. Without the gospel, it's "Good night, Christianity." Similarly, it may be worth saying, and explicitly so, that to lose the visible church is to lose a precious element in the economy of the gospel, as well as of the economy of divine authority. The visible church has a visible (and audible) role to play in the economy of the gospel, not least as the dynamic domain of God's Word. But we can, and must, go further: the church is not simply the agent of the gospel but the culmination of God's saving purpose—a theme and result and, in an important sense, the goal of the gospel. The church is therefore no mere appendix to evangelical theology. On the contrary, the church is the domain of the gospel, and speak-acting according to the gospel is the raison d'être of the church. A people of the gospel must therefore be pro-ecclesial, precisely because they are pro-evangel. In particular, the church is that distinct interpretive community whose peculiar vocation is to minister the biblical word: to proclaim and practice the word in a fellowship of the Spirit that embodies and makes contextually concrete the lordship of Jesus Christ. After all, the special mandate of the church (the Great Commission), given by the risen Christ, is to "make disciples . . . , teaching them to observe all that I have commanded you" (Matt. 28:20). This involves articulating and defending doctrinal truth.

I here summarize the argument of this book, and my response to the three aforementioned weaknesses concerning the core doctrines, visible unity, and interpretive authority, respectively, of the evangelical church, by making good on my claim that the glory and genius of mere Protestant Christianity is "mere evangelicalism."[8]

Protestant Evangelicalism: A Marriage Made in Heaven?

Let me begin by acknowledging the counterintuitive nature of my proposal. If Protestantism is Christianity's dangerous idea (because it lacks an authoritative

---

8. See further Kevin J. Vanhoozer and Daniel J. Treier, *Theology and the Mirror of Scripture: A Mere Evangelical Account* (Downers Grove, IL: InterVarsity, 2015).

head and control on biblical interpretation), then evangelicalism is surely more dangerous because, if anything, it is even more fissiparous. A critic might even go so far as to say that evangelicalism is Christianity's dangerous idea gone viral. On a descriptive level, there is more than an element of truth to this judgment. My purpose is not to defend evangelical fissiparousness but rather to recall evangelicals to their identity as "greatly awakened" Protestants. Timothy George's definition is apt: "Evangelicalism . . . is a renewal movement within historic Christian orthodoxy with deep roots in the early Church, the Reformation of the sixteenth century, and the great awakenings of the eighteenth century."[9] Despite initial appearances, I believe that evangelicalism is an essentially centripetal force. Fissiparousness is no match for the gravitational pull of the gospel toward oneness in Christ.

Christian Smith, after studying recent iterations of American evangelicalism, declared the movement to be both "embattled and thriving."[10] It is thriving in a pluralistic context, surprisingly enough, because it is an effective subculture with its own identity. It is embattled because, precisely as a subculture, its interpretive authority extends only to those who identify with the movement, and thus it is unable to effect broader social change—unable to transform the world for Christ.[11] My own analysis moves in a different direction. I am more concerned with the dynamics of the household of faith itself.

While both evangelicalism and Protestantism have been described as "renewal movements within historic Christian orthodoxy"[12]—or what I have here called "retrievals"—with common concerns and overlapping histories, not all evangelicals think of themselves as "Protestant." Nor, for that matter, do all Protestants think of themselves as "evangelicals." Nevertheless, "evangelical" and "Protestant" belong together and need each other in order to thrive; left alone, each will only continue to be embattled. Consider: Protestants provide

9. Timothy George, "Evangelicals and Others," *First Things*, February 2006, http://www.firstthings.com/article/2006/02/evangelicals-and-others. See also the definition by Timothy Larsen, "Defining and Locating Evangelicalism," in *The Cambridge Companion to Evangelical Theology*, ed. Timothy Larsen and Daniel J. Treier (Cambridge: Cambridge University Press, 2007), 1.

10. Christian Smith, *American Evangelicalism: Embattled and Thriving* (Chicago: University of Chicago Press, 1998).

11. Ibid., 218–19.

12. See Timothy George, "The Unity of Faith: Evangelicalism and 'Mere Christianity,'" *Touchstone: A Journal of Mere Christianity* 16, no. 6 (July/August 2003), http://www.touchstonemag.com/archives/article.php?id=16-06-058-f.

(ecclesial) structure and (liturgical) order to the ministry of word and sacrament. Evangelicals bring new (spiritual) life and (devotional) energy to declining and weakened forms and structures. Evangelicalism is a booster shot in the arm to a tired and decrepit Protestantism, opening up the possibility of a unity of confession on first-order doctrines but not necessarily on second- and third-order doctrines. At the same time, the evangelical movement has become riddled with cultural cancers: thanks to a doctrinally deprived immune system, it has also caught a social disease, MTD (moralistic therapeutic deism). Protestantism can now return the favor by supplying confessional stem cells to the compromised evangelical body.

Evangelical churches and theology thrive insofar as they inhabit the catholic tradition as inflected by the Reformation *solas* and strive for the unity not of pragmatism but Protestantism; evangelical churches and theology are embattled insofar as they forget their proximate roots in the Reformation, and their ultimate roots in the gospel. Likewise, Protestantism thrives insofar as it is evangelical in its commitment to Christ and the Scriptures, and is embattled insofar as it seeks unity, integrity, or relevance anywhere else than in the gospel.

For evangelicals, to recover the Reformation means insisting on the utter sufficiency of God and protesting any absolutizing of the created order or purely human. Os Guinness posits an essential connection between this signature Protestant gesture and an evangelical approach to theology: "Protestant and evangelical are two faces of the same truth. Protestant is the critical stance of evangelicalism, just as evangelical is the positive content of Protestantism."[13] To steal a formula from the philosopher Immanuel Kant (and with only slight exaggeration): evangelicalism (devotional energy) without Protestantism (form) is blind; Protestantism (structure) without evangelicalism (substance) is empty.[14] To be sure, both movements are biblicist and crucicentric. Yet Protestantism brings a catholic sensibility and robust ecclesiology to the table that often is lacking in evangelicalism, while evangelicals bring a renewed fervor for biblical authority and union (i.e., personal relationship) with Christ that often is lacking in present-day Protestantism. Generalizations of complex

---

13. Os Guinness, introduction to *No God but God: Breaking with the Idols of Our Age*, ed. Os Guinness and John Seel (Chicago: Moody, 1992), 25.

14. Kant's own formulation stresses the importance for theories of knowledge to blend rationalism and empiricism: "Thoughts without content are empty, intuitions without concepts are blind" (*Critique of Pure Reason*, trans. Norman Kemp Smith [London: Macmillan, 1933], 93).

movements are risky, and I acknowledge that here I am painting in bold strokes with a broad brush on a big canvas. Still, the intuition-cum-concept that I wish to consider is that the marriage of Protestantism and evangelicalism is a win-win.

To restate the point in terms of our initial metaphor: evangelicals need to repossess the historic Protestant homes on Evangel Way. Too many evangelicals have been sleeping rough, in cardboard boxes—homeless. A good number live in tents left over from evangelistic rallies; others live in mobile homes. Meanwhile, the historic Protestant houses suffer from various states of disrepair, lessening the property value of the entire street. Protestants have historic homes but few inhabitants; evangelicals are numerous but nomadic. The way forward is for evangelicals to take possession of and inhabit Protestant houses, confessions and all, including ecclesiologies. For without the church as an external means of grace, evangelicalism fails to practice what it preaches: the supreme authority of Scripture, the lordship of Jesus Christ, and the catholicity of the gospel.[15]

Habitat for Humanity is a charitable organization that believes that everyone, everywhere, and at all times should have a home. The organization's mission is to build not simply homes but communities, and this includes a vision for neighborhood revitalization: "For families to succeed, sometimes the dynamics of their neighborhood have to change."[16] Indeed. How much more should churches strive to make a *habitat for the new humanity* that exists in Christ, his earthly body animated by his living Spirit. This, I submit, should be the godly ambition of Protestant evangelicalism: to form visible communities of Christ followers who seek first the kingdom of God and who seek second to live lives worthy of citizens of this kingdom. Protestant evangelicalism itself is a godly ambition, not an achievement. Churches that identify with the movement do not claim to instantiate the kingdom, much less to incarnate Christ. Rather, with hope and prayer they strive to work out their own salvation in faith, fear, and trembling (Phil. 2:12).[17]

15. John Woodhouse puts the point succinctly: "Wherever [the] gospel is preached and wherever it is believed, there is evangelicalism" ("When to Unite")—and, I would add, catholicity.

16. Habitat for Humanity, "Neighborhood Revitalization," http://www.habitat.org/neighborhood (accessed November 14, 2015).

17. John Stott personifies the Protestant evangelicalism described in this section. His book *Basic Christianity* (London: Inter-Varsity, 1958) makes him a strong candidate for the role of patron saint of mere evangelicalism. See further Alister Chapman, *Godly Ambition: John Stott and the Evangelical Movement* (Oxford: Oxford University Press, 2012), esp. 155–60.

After Babel, Pentecost: The Households of God and the Spirit of Mere Protestant Christianity

Why is there church rather than nothing? Calvin is clear that the church exists to serve as the external means "by which God invites us into the society of Christ and holds us therein."[18] The mission of the church is to build up disciples into a living temple, a holy dwelling place for God on earth. The New Testament regularly refers to the church as "the household of God" (Eph. 2:19; 1 Tim. 3:15; 1 Pet. 4:17). The church is neither afterthought nor appendix but rather a vital part of the economy of redemption. It is remarkable that, despite his historical context, Calvin insists on referring to the visible church as "mother" of believers.[19] The point is that God does not adopt children only to leave them homeless and unattended. On the contrary: the Triune God has provided both home and mother for his children. Why, then, are there so many churches rather than one? Will the real mother please stand up?

Location, Location, Location

Let us return a last time to Evangel Way. The seven-story mansion at the end of the street (it's actually at the intersection with Tiber Drive) is having another open house, with a twist: the head of the house is inviting everyone who lives on the street to "come home." And in the upstairs window, a votive candle is always lit. Not a few evangelicals have come in from the cold and accepted the offer, especially those who did not previously have a stable home. They feel the attractiveness of becoming part of such a large family with venerable family traditions. Other evangelicals, however, are put off by the family's tendency to invite them in, but never for dinner—unless, of course, they renounce their previous family allegiance and do as all Romans do. Still other evangelicals are suspicious of the family's sense of entitlement, which goes so far as seeking to exercise the right of eminent domain over the other houses on Evangel Way.

It may seem from the seven-story Roman high-rise that the block party that is mere Protestant Christianity, where every family keeps house in its own way, borders on the anarchic. It is indeed housekeeping—the structure of interpretive authority in the church—that continues to separate Protestant

18. Calvin, *Institutes* IV.1.
19. Calvin, *Institutes* IV.1.4.

evangelicals and Roman Catholics: "By the dogma of papal infallibility, Roman Catholicism has adopted a position incompatible with the notion that the church is *semper reformanda*, always to be reformed."[20] By way of contrast, it is the characteristic Protestant gesture to refuse any absolute claim made for a creaturely reality, including the church as a creature of the Word. The spirit of Protestantism is a reforming spirit, or rather, the Holy Spirit, who progressively reforms and transforms local churches to conform them progressively to the image of the Master of the house. The church is not a tower with its top in the heavens whose inhabitants all speak the same language (Latin). Does it follow that the authority of the Bible in Protestantism can never be more than a babbling book, or that having refused the magisterial tower of a single interpretive authority, Protestants are doomed to the eternal noxious punishment of mutual incomprehension?

Timothy George is an evangelical Protestant, a Baptist evangelical, and an evangelical Baptist. "So why am I a Baptist? I am a Baptist because it was through the witness of a small Baptist church that I first heard the gospel of Jesus Christ. Many of the things I still believe in I first learned in that modest Baptist community of faith."[21] The differences matter, but (1) they are second-order; (2) they distinguish but need not divide Baptists from other Protestant evangelicals; (3) they may be gifts to the catholic church; and (4) they may enhance rather than negate the unity of the church. I have touched on these themes in earlier chapters. Here I want to concentrate especially on the latter two points, especially in view of the critique that the Reformation begat schism.

The Holy Spirit leads the church into all truth over time. Different situations often lead to new insights. For example, it was thanks to the errors of Arianism that the early church came to have a firmer grip on the identity of God as Father, Son, and Spirit. Similarly, it was thanks to the excesses of certain late medieval practices that Martin Luther arrived at his deeper insight into the meaning of justification by faith. Just as various methods of exegesis focus on certain aspects of the text, so particular Christian traditions focus on the material insights that were most significant at the time of their origin. There is a sense in which these different insights, all generated by particular occasions, represent permanent gains in the church's grasp of the gospel

20. Brown, *Spirit of Protestantism*, 167.
21. Timothy George, "Why I Am an Evangelical and a Baptist," in *Why We Belong: Evangelical Unity and Denominational Diversity*, ed. Anthony Chute, Christopher W. Morgan, and Robert A. Peterson (Wheaton: Crossway, 2013), 108.

and its implications. What originated in specific contexts is now part of the catholic tradition.

Pentecostal Plurality and Plural Interpretive Unity

Protestant evangelicalism is not simply another name for "lowest common denominator" Christianity. The mere Protestant Christianity that I have advocated in these pages is neither "generic Protestantism"[22] nor "diluted catholicism."[23] What, then, is it? To state it succinctly: *mere (i.e., evangelical) Protestant Christianity is a kind of Pentecostal plurality*.[24] It is well known that Pentecost reverses Babel. The people who built the tower of Babel sought to make a name, and a unity, for themselves. At Pentecost, God builds his temple, uniting people in Christ. Unity—interpretive agreement and mutual understanding—is, it would appear, something that only God can accomplish. And accomplish it he does, but not in the way we might have expected. Although onlookers thought that the believers who received the Spirit at Pentecost were babbling (Acts 2:13), in fact they were speaking intelligibly in several languages (Acts 2:8–11). Note well: they were all saying the same thing (testifying about Jesus) in different languages. It takes a thousand tongues to say and sing our great Redeemer's praise.

Protestant evangelicalism evidences a Pentecostal plurality: the various Protestant streams testify to Jesus in their own vocabularies, and it takes many languages (i.e., interpretive traditions) to minister the meaning of God's Word and the fullness of Christ. As the body is made up of many members, so many interpretations may be needed to do justice to the body of the biblical text.[25] Why else are there four Gospels, but that the one story of Jesus was too rich to be told from one perspective only? Could it be that the various Protestant traditions function similarly as witnesses who testify to the same Jesus from different situations and perspectives? Perhaps we can put it like this:

22. Ronald Byars criticizes "mid-American generic Protestantism"—that is, the way mainstream Protestant churches have adopted the civil religion and moral prejudices of the surrounding culture (*Finding Our Balance*, 28).

23. See Brown, *Spirit of Protestantism*, 5.

24. Many rivulets and tributaries feed into and proceed from the river of Protestant evangelicalism, including Puritanism, Pietism, and, most recently, Pentecostalism. For present purposes, however, my use of the term "Pentecostal" refers primarily to the Spirit's work in forming communities able to communicate, and *denominate*, the gospel in many languages and church traditions.

25. I first used the idea of Pentecostal plurality in connection with biblical interpretation in Vanhoozer, *Is There a Meaning in This Text?*, 418–21.

each Protestant church seeks to be faithful to the gospel, but no one form of Protestantism exhausts the gospel's meaning. Rather, it takes the discussion ("conference") between the many Protestant churches to appreciate fully the richness of the one gospel. The particularity of each Protestant tradition is thus not a source of conflict but a servant of unity—the unity of the truth of the gospel. We ought not to call this "lowest common denominator/denominational" Christianity. It is rather a matter of "highest catholic denominator" biblical Christianity. Stated differently: evangelicalism offers a transdenominational denominator that makes of Protestantism not a pervasive interpretive pluralism but a unitive interpretive plurality—a mere Protestant Christianity.

Protestant evangelicals think it important to belong to Christ, to one another in Christ, and to denominations (houses) that seek to help local churches be salt and light for Christ. As we saw above, Timothy George works this out with a "hierarchy of ecclesial identity": it is possible for one and the same person to be, for example, a Protestant, Baptist, and evangelical, though the disciple's deepest identity is one who is "in Christ" by the grace of the Triune God. Yet individuals are "in Christ" in specific times, places, and associations. It is important to emphasize *both* Pentecostal plurality *and* the unity of the Spirit. The white light of mere Protestant Christianity is made up precisely of the diverse denominational colors. The differences, and the dialogue that they generate, really matter.

We may here recall that historic Protestantism itself possessed "an inward unitive principle."[26] Yet evangelicalism provides a unique transdenominational place for unitive Protestant plurality to flourish in the Spirit. Strictly speaking, "Protestant" plurality is the qualifier and "evangelical" the substantive. There is one gospel, but several interpretive traditions. What must not be missed, however, is the extent to which even in Protestantism there is a drive toward unity. That is largely because the economy of the gospel is oriented to unity—union and communion—too. As Christopher Morgan rightly argues, church unity showcases God's mission to bring about cosmic unity.[27] In the words of the apostle Paul: "Through the church the wisdom of God in its rich variety might now be known to the rulers and authorities in the heavenly

---

26. McNeill identifies it by the Reformers' emphasis on "the communion of believers, their claim of catholicity against the sectarianism of Rome, and their conciliar idea of church government" (*Unitive Protestantism*, 17).

27. Christopher W. Morgan, "Toward a Theology of the Unity of the Church," in Chute, Morgan, and Peterson, *Why We Belong*, 19–36.

places" (Eph. 3:10 NRSV). Morgan's gloss is apt: "The beings in the heavenly realms are put on notice: God is going to do cosmically . . . what he has done corporately with the Jews and Gentiles."[28] The unity of the church is itself part of God's cosmic housekeeping—that is, the economy of redemption, whose purpose is a new reconciled creation. In short, the unity of the church is both an indicative reality (we are one in Christ) and an imperative perennial pursuit (we must visibly display our unity in Christ).

Mere Protestant Christianity represents this same project: displaying the plural unity of the church as it exists now in Christ. To be sure, church unity is ultimately eschatological, a matter of hope, not sight. The church nevertheless ought to seek to render visible this unity "in and by the actual development of a community which embodies—if only in foretaste—the restored harmony of which it speaks."[29] Denominational differences need not impede the unity of the church; rather, they can enhance it. They do so not by diluting their denominational characteristics, including distinctive doctrines, but by offering them as prophetic gifts to the whole church. Indeed, it is by inviting others into our own homes and enjoying table fellowship that we come to maturity in Christ. We should check for pests in our own houses before pointing out the termites in those of our neighbors. Even better would be a situation where each house looked out and worked for the betterment of its neighbors. Each house is situated such that it can see only part of the whole street. An effective neighborhood watch observes from many houses' windows.

The Holy Spirit is not a spirit of confusion (cf. Isa. 19:14; 1 Cor. 14:33) but a spirit of peaceful yet plural unity (Eph. 4:3). Yes, there will be not only differences but also interpretive disagreements. Yet, for those who subscribe to biblical authority, even disagreements can be opportunities to explore and resolve important tensions within the context of evangelical communion. Epistemically conscientious mere Protestant Christians will want to engage in conversation with others who, under the supreme authority of Scripture, pray for the Spirit's illumination. Oliver O'Donovan describes how such a conversation might go:

> The only thing I concede in committing myself to such a process is that if I could discuss the matter through with an opponent sincerely committed to the church's authorities, Scripture chief among them, the Holy Spirit would

28. Ibid., 24.
29. Newbigin, *Household of God*, 161.

open up perspectives that are not immediately apparent, and that patient and
scrupulous pursuit of these could lead at least to giving the problem a different
shape. . . . The only thing I have to think . . . is that there are things still to be
learned by one who is determined to be taught by Scripture how to read the
age in which we live.[30]

Evangelicalism is a place (neighborhood) for converse and conference between the residents of many houses. The fruits of the Spirit include conversational virtues such as humility, gentleness, and patience (Eph. 4:1–3). These
conversational virtues are in fact virtues of the unitive interpretive plurality that
has been the consistent aim of our retrieval. Protestant evangelicals bear with
one another in love, "eager to maintain the unity of the Spirit in the bond of
peace" (Eph. 4:3). They speak the truth in love and so "grow up in every way
into him who is the head, into Christ" (Eph. 4:15). Paul might have Evangel
Way in mind when he exhorts the Ephesians, "Let each one of you speak the
truth with his neighbor, for we are members of one another" (Eph. 4:25).

"By their fruits ye shall know them." The fruit of the Protestant Reformation is ultimately not anarchy (pervasive interpretive pluralism) but abundance
(unitive interpretive plurality)—a rich diversity that makes for lively conversation around the table (table talk) without breaking table fellowship. Jesus is
both host and meal. But where does he live? When two of John the Baptist's
disciples began to follow Jesus, he asked them, "What are you seeking?" And
instead of saying, "You," they replied, "Where are you staying?" (John 1:38).
It was an interesting sectarian slip. They wrongly thought that Jesus lives in
one place or another rather than in the fellowship of those who are united to
him. No one Protestant house contains the fullness of Jesus.

The Spirit is a down payment of the church's unity. A local church or group
of churches is true to its own essential nature only when it sees as part of its
mission the demonstration of its existence as a cell in a catholic body. The
main tension that the church faces is between the conviction that its mission
is to preserve and propagate the truth of the gospel and the conviction that its
mission is to advance and display the unity of the gospel. The key, of course,
is to see that both missions are aspects of one another. Both missions are, of
course, daughters of time, and therefore eschatological hope: the church is
already and not yet "one." It is precisely because no church or denomination

---

30. Oliver O'Donovan, *A Conversation Waiting to Begin: The Churches and the Gay Controversy* (London: SCM, 2009), 32.

has arrived that we need the "communion of communions," a system of prophetic checks and priestly balances, until such time as they are presented to
Christ without spot or wrinkle (Eph. 5:27). Until such time of consummated
catholicity, however, when God will be all in all (1 Cor. 15:28), the church
must make do with Pentecostal (i.e., plural) unity.

The Gospel Alone: The *Solas* in the Pattern of Protestant Evangelical Interpretive Authority

Every residential street sometimes has to deal with noisy or unruly neighbors.
A news item from 2014 in the *Minneapolis-St. Paul Star Tribune* is all too
typical: a dispute over feeding deer erupted in gunfire and bloodshed. Here
is how the article begins: "Barking dogs. Untrimmed trees. Loud back-yard
barbecues. Poor parking etiquette. On the surface, such nuisances sound
minor. But they can trigger unrest in even the most idyllic neighborhoods,
especially when people haven't gotten to know each other."[31] Something
similar could be said about church history. How, then, are we to navigate
interpretive disagreement between interpretive communities, each of which
affirms the authority of the Bible? This question affords me a final opportunity
to explain how interpretive authority works in mere Protestant Christianity.
How should the church respond to pervasive interpretive pluralism, the pain
of acute interpretive disagreement? Which way should Christians go when
two (or more) authorities diverge in a Christian wood?

The Authority of Interpretive Communities (Reprise)

The path and pattern of Roman Catholic interpretive authority is well
known. Its principles are clear-cut, and its practice has clean lines. The structure of interpretive authority in the Roman Catholic house is hierarchical and
centralized (i.e., "monarchical"). This is only one form of catholicity, and a
narrow one at that, presupposing as it does that the one church is a single
visible social institution: "We should acknowledge the fact that the papacy
as we know it today, an essentially monarchical power possessed of sovereign
authority over the entire Roman Catholic Church worldwide, is very much

31. Shannon Prather, "Feuds between Neighbors Common, Hard to Solve, but Rarely Deadly,"
Minneapolis-St. Paul Star Tribune, July 22, 2014, http://www.startribune.com/may-10-feuds
-between-neighbors-rarely-deadly/258779441/.

the product of the second thousand years of Christian history."[32] Vatican I's dogmas of papal infallibility and papal primacy of jurisdiction mean that the Petrine office claims teaching authority over every local church or council, which, along with the teaching about the indefectibility of the church, effectively forecloses the possibility of reforming the church's teaching. According to Paul Avis, "These claims were not retracted by Vatican II (1962–65) which continued to assert the supreme, full, ordinary and immediate jurisdiction of the pope over all local churches and all Christians."[33] At this point, it is hard to avoid Robert McAfee Brown's conclusion: "Roman Catholicism has become master of the gospel rather than servant."[34] In particular, the Roman magisterium (teaching authority) functions as a de facto tower reaching up to heaven. Evangel Way is not zoned for such high-rise apartment complexes.[35]

"Neighborhoods . . . exist wherever human beings congregate, in permanent family dwellings; and many of the functions of the city tend to be distributed naturally . . . into neighborhoods."[36] A neighborhood association is a group of residents who advocate for or organize activities within a neighborhood. Such associations are voluntary in nature and elect their leaders. They are not to be confused with homeowners associations for which membership is mandatory and that have the legal authority to enforce rules that, for example, restrict the kind of buildings and decorations that are allowed. Roman Catholicism is a homeowners association. By way of contrast, neighborhood associations "work together for changes and improvements such as neighborhood safety, beautification and social activities."[37] The authority of a neighborhood association is strictly advisory in nature, not legal.

And we're back where we started (again!), with every ecclesial house (interpretive community) reading and using Scripture in ways that are right in its own eyes. Or are we? Some certainly think so. Simply exchanging labels, from

32. Francis Oakley, *The Conciliarist Tradition: Constitutionalism in the Catholic Church, 1300–1870* (Oxford: Oxford University Press, 2003), 3.

33. Avis, *Beyond the Reformation?*, 18.

34. Brown, *Spirit of Protestantism*, 167.

35. Not all Roman Catholic theologians accept the monarchical reading of the papacy. For a more collegial approach, see Gaillardetz, *By What Authority?*, esp. chaps. 4–5.

36. Lewis Mumford, "The Neighborhood and the Neighborhood Unit," *Town Planning Review* 24 (1954): 258. On the decline of community in neighborhoods, see Peter Lovenheim, *In the Neighborhood: The Search for Community on an American Street, One Sleepover at a Time* (New York: Perigee, 2010).

37. "Neighborhood Association," *Wikipedia*, https://en.wikipedia.org/wiki/Neighborhood _association (accessed November 15, 2015).

"Protestant" to "evangelical," solves nothing, according to Molly Worthen, whose *Apostles of Reason* exposes, as its subtitle states, "the crisis of authority in American evangelicalism."[38] The crisis is the movement's lack of a magisterium, a single authority that can navigate the winds and waves of interpretive disagreement.[39] According to Worthen, evangelicals assume the posture of open-minded intellectuals and academics but in reality close ranks (and minds) when anyone strays too far off the farm. In spite of claims that the Bible is their supreme authority, evangelicals are deeply conflicted by disagreements over what the Bible means, and they have adopted other authorities that support "the true interpretation of the Bible" (often labeled "the Christian worldview") in ad hoc fashion, only to then shut the door to any challenges to that interpretation, however faithful and reasonable they may be.[40] Evangelicals turn out to be *false* apostles of reason: fundamentalist wolves hiding behind sheepskins (academic diplomas).

No doubt there is more than an element of truth to Worthen's account, as there is to Brad Gregory's and Christian Smith's. It is all too easy to smuggle one's personal agenda into the church under the guise of biblical authority and interpretation. It is even easier to neglect other people's interpretation of Scripture when it conflicts with or challenges one's own. Make no mistake: perfect fear—that one's cherished biblical interpretations are vulnerable to critique—casts out love, and good listening. Let me conclude by sketching the more excellent way toward which the present work has been gesturing, a way that subjects Scripture not to secular reason but rather to scriptural and Spirited reasoning.

After Babel, and the loss of towering Roman uniformity, all believers are the Word's ministers—and martyrs. Every Protestant evangelical has a mandate to minister the good news of the gospel by communicating it to others. Every Protestant evangelical is a martyr to the Word in the double sense of (1) witnessing to what God says rather than one's own interpretations, and (2) suffering the conflict of interpretations with other Bible-believing Christians. This is the case with regard to individual Christians, local churches, and denominations alike: none is in a position to lord it over the others. Indeed,

---

38. Molly Worthen, *Apostles of Reason: The Crisis of Authority in American Evangelicalism* (Oxford: Oxford University Press, 2014).

39. See Noll, *Civil War as a Theological Crisis*, and note his ironic conclusion that it was left to Generals Grant and Sherman to decide, on the battlefield, what the Bible meant as concerns slavery.

40. Worthen, *Apostles of Reason*, 261.

as Anthony Thiselton observes, "If the only viable criterion of meaning is that which coheres with what their reading community regards as conducive to 'progress,' all interpretation becomes corporate self-affirmation."[41] Wretched interpreter that I am! Who will deliver me from this corporate will to interpretive power?

Catholic Council and Canonical Conference: The Magisterial Authority of God's Gospel

The strength of Protestant evangelicalism is its unitive interpretive plurality. It is precisely its diversity—the conspicuous presence of alternative interpretive communities and interpretations—that, in principle, keeps Protestant evangelicals honest, humble, and real. The more excellent way—a third way beyond monarchical (the authority of one) and anarchic (the authority of all)—is the way of catholic council and canonical conference (the ministerial authority of plural unity).

As we have seen, Protestants are, for lack of a better term, *convictional conciliarists*.[42] Convictional conciliarists affirm catholicity but insist that the church means the whole church (not just the clergy), and that interpretive authority is distributed throughout the whole church and is not concentrated in a single human head (monarch = pope). The authority distributed to the whole church best comes to expression in councils that represent the whole church on various levels: local, provincial, or general.[43] Councils are corporate expressions of Protestant ecclesial conscientiousness, namely, the awareness that the Spirit is at work illumining others who profess biblical authority and not only oneself (or one's own interpretive community). Catholic councils provide formal structures for the second condition of unitive interpretive plurality: canonical conference.

Protestant evangelicals meet to discuss and deliberate the meaning of Scripture. Put differently, Protestant evangelicals take counsel in council. Scripture alone is supremely authoritative. Discussion is not an aim in itself; consensus is ("It has seemed good to the Holy Spirit and to us," Acts 15:28). Canonical

41. Anthony Thiselton, *Can the Bible Mean Whatever We Want It to Mean?* (Chester, UK: Chester Academic Press, 2005), 18.

42. Paul Avis suggests that the Reformers can in some sense be called "conciliarists by conviction" (*Beyond the Reformation?*, xii). Avis's study is also valuable for tracing the history of pre-Reformation conciliarism.

43. Ibid., 22–23, 102.

conference is a way of describing gatherings that meet to form consensus about what a biblical passage means, or about what it means to be biblical in a particular area of doctrine or ethics. The *congrégations* of sixteenth-century Geneva and the *Prophezei* in Zurich remain helpful models. Canonical conference deserves to be recognized as a vital element in the triune economy of interpretive authority. Canonical conference—gathering together to reach a common understanding on the meaning of Scripture—is both unifying and edifying to the church. It is the informal counterpart to formal councils, and a concrete way of practicing canonical catholicity and catholic canonicity.

Let me be clear: Protestant evangelicals recognize a *magisterium* of the *evangelium*. Only the God of the gospel and the gospel of God carry ultimate authority. The Lord Jesus Christ is ultimately the Master of the house. Mere Protestant evangelicals keep house in different ways, but all of them are committed to deepening discipleship through canonical conference and keeping peace in the neighborhood through catholic council. "Protestant" qualifies "evangelical": the latter takes precedence because it is the substantive content of the councils and conferences, but the councils and conferences provide the structure and order that prevent interpretive anarchy when it comes to saying what the gospel is.

The spirit of mere Protestant Christianity involves not only the *magisterium* of the *evangelium* and the *ministerium* (ministerial authority) of the priesthood of all believers, but also, and primarily, the Holy Spirit. The Spirit is the unitive power that propels unitive Protestant interpretive plurality. The Spirit is the one who guides catholic councils deeper into understanding and truth. The Spirit is the one who enables the humility and peace without which canonical conferences fall apart. Again, the purpose of canonical conferences is to preserve both doctrinal truth and ecclesial unity. The Spirit who authored the Scriptures is also the Spirit who superintends catholic councils, communal conscientiousness, and canonical conferences.

Singing Sola: *Attuning Protestant Evangelicals to the Economy of the Gospel*

The ultimate purpose for interpreting the Scriptures is to hear the Word of God sounding through human words. These words direct us to the living Word, Jesus Christ, and to the possibility of union and communion in him. Communion in Christ is the ontological condition for Protestant evangelical catholicity, conciliarism, and conference alike. Christ now rules his church through the scepter of his Word (the Bible). The distinction between Christ's magisterial authority and the ministerial authority of the church is meaningful only if we preserve the distinction between the biblical text and its ecclesial interpretation. Scripture is the canon, the rule by which all speech in the Lord's name must be measured: "The authority of the church, in other words, finds expression . . . in the faithful interpretation of Holy Scripture."[44]

This book is not a handbook on hermeneutics. I have not pretended to offer detailed exegetical method or procedures for resolving interpretive difference. My primary aim has been to refute the charge that the Reformation loosed interpretive anarchy upon the world, and that the Reformation is responsible for the pervasive interpretive pluralism that bedevils society, the academy, and the church. I have sought to retrieve certain insights from the Reformation that move in a different direction: unitive interpretive Protestant plurality. In particular, I have argued for a retrieval of the doctrine of the church, the particular interpretive community in question. Contrary to the common accusation, Protestant ecclesiology is not about the right of private judgment. It is a caricature of Protestant ecclesiology to reduce it to "every man for himself," though too often evangelical ecclesiology amounts to no more than this counsel of desperation.

The *solas* are neither a confession of faith nor a substitute for the ancient Rule of Faith. Rather, as evangelicalism is a renewal movement in the heart of Protestantism, so the *solas* are a renewal of catholic Christianity, providing deeper insights into the triune logic of the gospel. Each *sola* contributes something to the pattern of interpretive authority, and, interestingly enough, each *sola* corresponds to one of the five distinguishing marks of evangelicalism.[45]

Sola gratia: evangelicalism is "crucicentric," and the Reformers understood better than any other group of Christians how the cross spells the end of the project of making oneself righteous through one's works. As to the pattern of interpretive authority, "grace alone" reminds us that the triune economy precedes any housekeeping that humans can do. The church is the household of God, created by the Word in the power of the Spirit. The church is God's

44. McCormack, "End of Reformed Theology?," 57.

45. David W. Bebbington lists four characteristics—crucicentrism, biblicism, conversionism, and activism—to which I am adding transdenominationalism as a fifth. See Bebbington, *Evangelicalism in Modern Britain: A History from the 1730s to the 1980s* (London: Unwin Hyman, 1989), 2–17.

house that, out of free love, he has opened up to undeserving sinners: "In my Father's house are many mansions" (John 14:2 KJV).

Sola fide: evangelicalism is "conversionist," and the Reformers emphasized the priority of the hearing of the Word for eliciting saving faith. As to the question of interpretive authority, I argued for the rationality of trust in testimony, and for the need for the kind of epistemic conscientiousness that inclines one to attend to the interpretations of others.

Sola scriptura: evangelicalism is "biblicist," but as we learned from the Reformers, this does not mean that the Bible is the sole source of theology; rather, the Bible is evangelicalism's supreme authority. As to the question of interpretive authority, we saw that attending to the ministerial authority of tradition affords precious insights into the way that the Spirit has illumined local churches that were serving not just themselves but the whole church. The genius of mere Protestant Christianity is its never-ending conference ("always reforming") about the meaning of the Bible under the magisterial authority of Scripture and the ministerial authority of catholicity.

Solus Christus: evangelicalism is transdenominational, as is Protestantism itself, recognizing that Christ is the head of every local church and not simply of those in our household. As to interpretive authority, I argued that Christ, as head of the church, has authorized local households to preserve the integrity of the gospel and has given each church its own set of house keys.

Soli Deo gloria: evangelicalism is "activist," but the example of the Reformation encourages us to work not only for social justice and the common good but also, in particular, for the unity of the church. The one church is a confederacy of local holy nations, united by a single constitution (Scripture), head (Jesus Christ), and ethos (Holy Spirit). As to interpretive authority, the glory of mere Protestant Christianity is its dedication to understanding Scripture in local and translocal conference, its desire to enter into a mutually correcting conversation, and its willingness to hold one another mutually accountable, in the fellowship of the Spirit, to the written word that creates, sustains, and guides it to the word of life.

The Reformation *solas* do a better job of preserving genuine (i.e., conciliar) catholicity than do the Roman anathemas against them pronounced by the Council of Trent.[46] Protestant evangelicals believe that one's *"fidelity to the church must be measured by the degree of the church's fidelity to the gospel."*[47]

---

46. Avis, *Church in the Theology of the Reformers*, 217.
47. Brown, *Spirit of Protestantism*, 15 (emphasis original).

The Protestant *solas* help evangelicals inch closer to the unitive interpretive plurality that is the (unrealized) hope of convictional conciliarists everywhere, including the Reformers. *Sola scriptura* need not lead to interpretive anarchy, and certainly does not lead there when taken together with the other *solas*: "These affirmations do not stand simply as solitary, disconnected sentinels, but they are the key points in an integrated, whole understanding of biblical truth."[48] It is this integrated, organic understanding of biblical truth, worked out in and through the triune economy of the gospel, that best represents the spirit of mere Protestant Christianity and the hope of holy nations.

48. Wells, *Courage to Be Protestant*, 21.

Bibliography

Agnew, F. H. "The Origin of the NT Apostle-Concept: A Review of Research." *Journal of Biblical Literature* 105 (1986): 75–96.

"Agreement between Reformation Churches in Europe (The Leuenberg Agreement)." March 16, 1973. http://www.leuenberg.net/leuenberg-agreement.

Alexander, T. Desmond, and Brian S. Rosner, eds. *New Dictionary of Biblical Theology.* Downers Grove, IL: InterVarsity, 2000.

Allen, Michael, and Scott R. Swain. *Reformed Catholicity: The Promise of Retrieval for Theology and Biblical Interpretation.* Grand Rapids: Baker Academic, 2015.

Allison, Gregg R. *Roman Catholic Theology and Practice: An Evangelical Assessment.* Wheaton: Crossway, 2014.

Allmen, Jean-Jacques von. "L'Église locale parmi les autres églises locales." *Irénikon* 43 (1970): 512–37.

Alsted, Johann Heinrich. *Theologia scholastica didacta.* Hanover, 1618.

Alston, Wallace M., Jr., and Michael Welker, eds. *Reformed Theology: Identity and Ecumenicity.* Grand Rapids: Eerdmans, 2003.

Anizor, Uche. *Kings and Priests: Scripture's Theological Account of Its Readers.* Eugene, OR: Pickwick, 2014.

Aquinas, Thomas. *Summa theologica.* Translated by Fathers of the English Dominican Province. 5 vols. Westminster, MD: Christian Classics, 1981.

Armstrong, John H., ed. *The Compromised Church: The Present Evangelical Crisis.* Wheaton: Crossway, 1998.

Atkinson, Bruce. "The Seven Solas: Toward Reconciling Evangelical and Anglo-Catholic Perspectives." *Virtue Online.* December 31, 2009. http://www.virtueonline.org/seven-solas-toward-reconciling-evangelical-and-anglo-catholic-perspectives.

Augustine. *Tractates on the Gospel of John 28–54*. Translated by John W. Retig. Fathers of the Church. Washington, DC: Catholic University of America Press, 1993.

———. *A Treatise on the Grace of Christ and on Original Sin*. Translated by Dr. Holmes. London: Aeterna, 2014.

Aulén, Gustav. *Reformation and Catholicity*. Translated by Eric H. Wahlstrom. Edinburgh: Oliver & Boyd, 1960.

Austin, Victor Lee. *Up with Authority: Why We Need Authority to Flourish as Human Beings*. London: T&T Clark, 2010.

Avis, Paul D. L. *Beyond the Reformation? Authority, Primacy and Unity in the Conciliar Tradition*. London: T&T Clark, 2006.

———. *The Church in the Theology of the Reformers*. Atlanta: John Knox, 1981.

Bainton, Roland. *Here I Stand: A Life of Martin Luther*. New York: Mentor, 1950.

Baker, William R., ed. *Evangelicalism and the Stone-Campbell Movement*. Downers Grove, IL: InterVarsity, 2002.

Bakhtin, Mikhail. *Problems of Dostoevsky's Poetics*. Edited and translated by Caryl Emerson. Minneapolis: University of Minnesota Press, 1984.

———. *Speech Genres and Other Late Essays*. Translated by Vern W. McGee. Edited by Caryl Emerson and Michael Holquist. Austin: University of Texas Press, 1986.

Bannerman, James. *The Church of Christ: A Treatise on the Nature, Powers, Ordinances, Discipline and Government of the Christian Church*. Vol. 1. Edinburgh: T&T Clark, 1868. Reprint, Birmingham, AL: Solid Ground Christian Books, 2009.

Barclay, John M. G. *Paul and the Gift*. Grand Rapids: Eerdmans, 2015.

Barr, James. *Fundamentalism*. London: SCM, 1981.

Barrett, Matthew. *God's Word Alone: The Authority of Scripture; What the Reformers Taught . . . and Why It Still Matters*. Grand Rapids: Zondervan Academic, 2016.

Barth, Karl. *Church Dogmatics*. Edited by G. W. Bromiley and T. F. Torrance. Translated by G. W. Bromiley et al. 4 vols. in 13 parts. Edinburgh: T&T Clark, 1936–77.

———. "Wünschbarkeit und Möglichkeit eines allgemeinen reformierten Glaubensbekenntnisses." In *Vorträge und kleinere Arbeiten, 1922–1925*, edited by Holger Finze, 604–43. Zürich: Theologischer Verlag, 1990.

Bavinck, Herman. "De Hervorming en ons nationale leven." In *Ter herdenking der Hervorming, 1517–1917: Twee redevoeringen, uitgesproken in de openbare zitting van den senaat der Vrije Universiteit op 31 October 1917*, edited by H. Bavinck and H. H. Kuyper, 7–36. Kampen: Kok, 1917.

———. *Reformed Dogmatics*. Edited by John Bolt. Translated by John Vriend. 4 vols. Grand Rapids: Baker Academic, 2003–8.

Baxter, Richard. *Church History of the Government of Bishops and Their Councils*. London: John Kidgell, 1680.

Bayer, Oswald. "Luther as an Interpreter of Holy Scripture." In *The Cambridge Companion to Martin Luther*, edited by Donald K. McKim, 73–85. Cambridge: Cambridge University Press, 2003.

———. *Martin Luther's Theology: A Contemporary Interpretation*. Translated by Thomas H. Trapp. Grand Rapids: Eerdmans, 2008.

———. *Theology the Lutheran Way*. Edited and translated by Jeffrey G. Silcock and Mark C. Mattes. Grand Rapids: Eerdmans, 2007.

Beale, G. K. *The Temple and the Church's Mission: A Biblical Theology of the Dwelling Place of God*. Downers Grove, IL: IVP Academic, 2004.

Bebbington, David W. *Evangelicalism in Modern Britain: A History from the 1730s to the 1980s*. London: Unwin Hyman, 1989.

Beeton, Isabella. *Mrs. Beeton's Book of Household Management*. Abridged ed. Oxford: Oxford University Press, 2000.

Belt, Henk van den. *The Authority of Scripture in Reformed Theology: Truth and Trust*. Leiden: Brill, 2008.

———. "The Problematic Character of *Sola Scriptura*." In *Sola Scriptura: Biblical and Theological Perspectives on Scripture, Authority, and Hermeneutics*, edited by Eric Peels, Arnold Huijgen, and Hans Burger. Leiden: Brill, forthcoming.

Berger, Peter L. *The Heretical Imperative: Contemporary Possibilities of Religious Affirmation*. Garden City, NY: Anchor, 1979.

Berger, Peter L., and Thomas Luckmann. *The Social Construction of Reality: A Treatise in the Sociology of Knowledge*. Garden City, NY: Doubleday, 1966.

Blocher, Henri. "The 'Analogy of Faith' in the Study of Scripture." *Scottish Bulletin of Evangelical Theology* 5 (1987): 17–38.

Block, Daniel I. *The Gospel according to Moses: Theological and Ethical Reflections on the Book of Deuteronomy*. Eugene, OR: Cascade, 2012.

Bock, Darrell. *Acts*. Baker Exegetical Commentary on the New Testament. Grand Rapids: Baker Academic, 2007.

Boer, Erik Alexander de. *The Genevan School of the Prophets: The Congrégations of the Company of Pastors and Their Influence in 16th Century Europe*. Geneva: Librairie Droz, 2012.

Boersma, Hans. *Heavenly Participation: The Weaving of a Sacramental Tapestry*. Grand Rapids: Eerdmans, 2011.

———. Nouvelle Théologie *and Sacramental Ontology: A Return to Mystery*. Oxford: Oxford University Press, 2009.

Bonhoeffer, Dietrich. *Life Together; Prayerbook of the Bible*. Edited by Geffrey B. Kelly. Translated by Daniel W. Bloesch and James H. Burtness. Dietrich Bonhoeffer Works 5. Minneapolis: Fortress, 1996.

―――――. *Sanctorum Communio: A Theological Study of the Sociology of the Church.* Edited by Clifford J. Green. Translated by Reinhard Krauss and Nancy Lukens. Dietrich Bonhoeffer Works 1. Minneapolis: Fortress, 1998.

Bonino, Serge-Thomas, ed. *Surnaturel: A Controversy at the Heart of Twentieth-Century Thomistic Thought.* Washington, DC: Catholic University of America Press, 2007.

Boone, Kathleen C. *The Bible Tells Them So: The Discourse of Protestant Fundamentalism.* Albany: State University of New York Press, 1989.

Bowald, Mark Alan. *Rendering the Word in Theological Hermeneutics: Mapping Divine and Human Agency.* Aldershot, UK: Ashgate, 2007.

Braaten, Carl E. "The Problem of Authority in the Church." In *The Catholicity of the Reformation*, edited by Carl E. Braaten and Robert W. Jenson, 53–66. Grand Rapids: Eerdmans, 1996.

Bradbury, John P. *Perpetually Reforming: A Theology of Church Reform and Renewal.* London: Bloomsbury, 2013.

Brown, Robert McAfee. *The Spirit of Protestantism.* Oxford: Oxford University Press, 1965.

Bruce, F. F. *The Acts of the Apostles: The Greek Text with Introduction and Commentary.* Grand Rapids: Eerdmans, 1951.

―――――. *The Book of the Acts.* Rev. ed. New International Commentary on the New Testament. Grand Rapids: Eerdmans, 1988.

―――――. *The Epistles to the Colossians, to Philemon, and to the Ephesians.* New International Commentary on the New Testament. Grand Rapids: Eerdmans, 1984.

Bultmann, Rudolf. *Jesus Christ and Mythology.* New York: Scribner, 1958.

Buschart, W. David. *Exploring Protestant Traditions: An Invitation to Theological Hospitality.* Downers Grove, IL: IVP Academic, 2006.

―――――. "The Nones and the Nons: Surprising Similarities?" *Patheos*, July 22, 2015. http://www.patheos.com/Topics/Future-of-Faith-in-America/Evangelicalism/The-Nones-and-the-Nons-David-Buschart-07-22-2015.html.

Buschart, W. David, and Kent D. Eilers. *Theology as Retrieval: Receiving the Past, Renewing the Church.* Downers Grove, IL: IVP Academic, 2015.

Byars, Ronald P. *Finding Our Balance: Repositioning Mainstream Protestantism.* Eugene, OR: Wipf & Stock, 2015.

Calvin, John. *Calvin: Theological Treatises.* Translated by J. K. S. Reid. Library of Christian Classics 22. Philadelphia: Westminster, 1954.

―――――. *Commentaries on Philippians, Colossians, and Thessalonians.* Edinburgh: Calvin Translation Society, 1851.

―――――. *Commentaries on the Catholic Epistles.* Edinburgh: Calvin Translation Society, 1855.

————. *Commentaries on the Epistles of Paul to the Galatians and Ephesians*. Translated by William Pringle. Edinburgh: Calvin Translation Society, 1854.

————. *Institutes of the Christian Religion*. Edited by John McNeill. Translated by Ford Lewis Battles. 2 vols. Library of Christian Classics 20–21. Philadelphia: Westminster, 1960.

————. *The Second Epistle of Paul the Apostle to the Corinthians and the Epistles to Timothy, Titus, and Philemon*. Translated by T. A. Small. Grand Rapids: Eerdmans, 1996.

————. *Selected Works of John Calvin: Tracts and Letters*. Vol. 3, *Tracts, Part 3*. Grand Rapids: Baker, 1983.

Caragounis, Chrys. *The Ephesian* Mysterion: *Meaning and Content*. Lund: Gleerup, 1977.

Carson, D. A. "Systematic Theology and Biblical Theology." In Alexander and Rosner, *New Dictionary of Biblical Theology*, 89–104.

Cary, Philip. "On Behalf of Classical Trinitarianism: A Critique of Rahner on the Trinity." *Thomist* 56 (1992): 365–406.

Chadwick, Henry. *East and West: The Making of a Rift in the Church; From Apostolic Times until the Council of Florence*. Oxford History of the Christian Church. Oxford: Oxford University Press, 2003.

Chadwick, Owen. *A History of the Popes, 1830–1914*. Oxford History of the Christian Church. Oxford: Oxford University Press, 1998.

Chapman, Alister. *Godly Ambition: John Stott and the Evangelical Movement*. Oxford: Oxford University Press, 2012.

Chemnitz, Martin. *Examination of the Council of Trent*. Translated by Fred Kramer. St. Louis: Concordia, 1971.

Chesterton, G. K. *What's Wrong with the World*. New York: Dodd, Mead, 1912.

Chillingworth, William. *The Works of William Chillingworth*. 10th ed. London, 1742.

Chung-Kim, Esther. *Inventing Authority: The Use of the Church Fathers in Reformation Debates over the Eucharist*. Waco: Baylor University Press, 2011.

Chute, Anthony, Christopher W. Morgan, and Robert A. Peterson, eds. *Why We Belong: Evangelical Unity and Denominational Diversity*. Wheaton: Crossway, 2013.

Clapp, Rodney. *A Peculiar People: The Church as Culture in a Post-Christian Society*. Downers Grove, IL: InterVarsity, 1996.

Cleveland, Christena. *Disunity in Christ: Uncovering the Hidden Forces That Keep Us Apart*. Downers Grove, IL: InterVarsity, 2013.

Coady, C. A. J. *Testimony: A Philosophical Study*. Oxford: Clarendon, 1992.

Colson, Charles, and Richard John Neuhaus, eds. *Your Word Is Truth: A Project of Evangelicals and Catholics Together*. Grand Rapids: Eerdmans, 2002.

Congar, Yves. *Tradition and Traditions: An Historical and a Theological Essay*. New York: Macmillan, 1967.

Cotton, John. *The Keyes of the Kingdom of Heaven*. 1644. Reprint, Boston: Tappan & Dennet, 1843.

Crews, Frederick C. *The Pooh Perplex*. London: Robin Clark, 1979.

Cruise, Charles E. "The 'Wealth of Nations': A Study in the Intertextuality of Isaiah 60:5, 11." *Journal of the Evangelical Theological Society* 58, no. 2 (2015): 283–97.

Davies, Rupert E. *The Problem of Authority in the Continental Reformers: A Study in Luther, Zwingli, and Calvin*. London: Epworth, 1946.

Davis, Thomas J. *This Is My Body: The Presence of Christ in Reformation Thought*. Grand Rapids: Baker Academic, 2008.

Dawkins, Richard. *The Selfish Gene*. Oxford: Oxford University Press, 1976.

De Chirico, Leonardo. *Evangelical Theological Perspectives on Post-Vatican II Roman Catholicism*. Bern: Peter Lang, 2003.

Delio, Ilia. *Making All Things New: Catholicity, Cosmology, Consciousness*. Maryknoll, NY: Orbis, 2015.

Dennett, Daniel C. *Darwin's Dangerous Idea: Evolution and the Meanings of Life*. New York: Simon & Schuster, 1995.

Derrida, Jacques. "Plato's Pharmacy." In *Dissemination*, translated by Barbara Johnson, 61–172. London: Athlone, 1981.

Dever, Mark, and Jonathan Leeman, eds. *Baptist Foundations: Church Government for an Anti-Institutional Age*. Nashville: B&H Academic, 2015.

DeYoung, Kevin. "Where and How Do We Draw the Line?" *Tabletalk* 36, no. 7 (2012): 13–14.

Diller, Kevin. *Theology's Epistemic Dilemma: How Karl Barth and Alvin Plantinga Provide a Unified Response*. Downers Grove, IL: IVP Academic, 2014.

Dryden, John. *Selected Poems*. London: Penguin, 2001.

Eastwood, Cyril. *The Priesthood of All Believers: An Examination of the Doctrine from the Reformation to the Present Day*. London: Epworth, 1960.

Ebeling, Gerhard. *The Word of God and Tradition: Historical Studies Interpreting the Divisions of Christianity*. Translated by S. H. Hooke. Philadelphia: Fortress, 1968.

Edwards, Jonathan. *The Sermons of Jonathan Edwards: A Reader*. Edited by Wilson H. Kimnach, Kenneth P. Minkema, and Douglas A. Sweeney. New Haven: Yale University Press, 1999.

———. *The Works of Jonathan Edwards*. Vol. 13, *The "Miscellanies."* Edited by Thomas A. Schafer. New Haven: Yale University Press, 1994.

Eire, Carlos M. N. *War against the Idols: The Reformation of Worship from Erasmus to Calvin*. Cambridge: Cambridge University Press, 1986.

Eliot, T. S. *Notes towards the Definition of Culture*. London: Faber & Faber, 1949.

Engelder, Theodore. "The Three Principles of the Reformation: Sola Scriptura, Sola Gratia, Sola Fides." In *Four Hundred Years: Commemorative Essays on the Reformation*, edited by W. H. T. Dua, 97–109. St. Louis: Concordia, 1916.

Ensign-George, Barry. "Denomination as Ecclesiological Category: Sketching an Assessment." In *Denomination: Assessing an Ecclesiological Category*, edited by Paul M. Collins and Barry Ensign-George, 1–21. London: T&T Clark, 2011.

Fee, Gordon D. *The Disease of the Health and Wealth Gospels*. Vancouver: Regent College Publishing, 2006.

Feingold, Lawrence. *The Natural Desire to See God according to St. Thomas and His Interpreters*. 2nd ed. Washington, DC: Catholic University of America Press, 2004.

Feuerbach, Ludwig. *The Essence of Christianity*. Translated by George Eliot. Buffalo: Prometheus, 1989.

Fish, Stanley. *Is There a Text in This Class? The Authority of Interpretive Communities*. Cambridge, MA: Harvard University Press, 1980.

Florovsky, Georges. *Bible, Church, Tradition: An Eastern Orthodox View*. Belmont, MA: Nordland, 1972.

Foley, Richard. *Intellectual Trust in Oneself and Others*. Cambridge: Cambridge University Press, 2001.

Forde, Gerhard O. *A More Radical Gospel: Essays on Eschatology, Authority, Atonement, and Ecumenism*. Edited by Mark C. Mattes and Steven D. Paulson. Grand Rapids: Eerdmans, 2004.

Forsyth, P. T. *The Church and the Sacraments*. 1917. Reprint, Eugene, OR: Wipf & Stock, 1996.

———. "The Cross as the Final Seat of Authority." In *The Gospel and Authority: A P. T. Forsyth Reader*, edited by Marvin W. Anderson, 148–78. Minneapolis: Augsburg, 1971.

Frame, John M. *The Doctrine of God*. Phillipsburg, NJ: P&R, 2002.

———. *The Doctrine of the Knowledge of God*. Phillipsburg, NJ: P&R, 1987.

Franzmann, Martin H. "Seven Theses on Reformation Hermeneutics." *Concordia Journal* 36, no. 2 (2010): 120–32.

Freeman, Curtis W. *Contesting Catholicity: Theology for Other Baptists*. Waco: Baylor University Press, 2014.

Frei, Hans W. *The Eclipse of Biblical Narrative: A Study in Eighteenth and Nineteenth Century Hermeneutics*. New Haven: Yale University Press, 1974.

Freud, Sigmund. *The Future of an Illusion*. Translated and edited by James Strachey. New York: W. W. Norton, 1989.

Gaffin, Richard B. "The Vitality of the Reformed Tradition." In *The Vitality of Reformed Theology: Proceedings of the International Theological Congress, June 20–24th 1994, Noordwijkerhout, the Netherlands*, edited by J. M. Batteau, J. W. Maris, and K. Veling, 16–50. Kampen: Kok, 1994.

Gaillardetz, Richard R. *By What Authority? A Primer on Scripture, the Magisterium, and the Sense of the Faithful*. Collegeville, MN: Liturgical Press, 2003.

———. *Teaching with Authority: A Theology of the Magisterium in the Church.* Collegeville, MN: Liturgical Press, 1997.

George, Timothy. "Evangelicals and Others." *First Things.* February 2006. http://www.firstthings.com/article/2006/02/evangelicals-and-others.

———. "The Priesthood of All Believers and the Quest for Theological Integrity." *Criswell Theological Review* 3 (1989): 283–94.

———. *Reading Scripture with the Reformers.* Downers Grove, IL: IVP Academic, 2011.

———. "A Thicker Kind of Mere." *First Things.* May 2015. http://www.firstthings.com/web-exclusives/2015/05/a-thicker-kind-of-mere.

———. "The Unity of Faith: Evangelicalism and 'Mere Christianity.'" *Touchstone: A Journal of Mere Christianity* 16, no. 6 (July/August 2003). http://www.touchstonemag.com/archives/article.php?id=16-06-058-f.

———. "Why I Am an Evangelical and a Baptist." In Chute, Morgan, and Peterson, *Why We Belong*, 93–110.

Gerrish, Brian A. *Grace and Gratitude: The Eucharistic Theology of John Calvin.* Minneapolis: Fortress, 1993.

———. "Priesthood and Ministry in the Theology of Luther." *Church History* 34, no. 4 (1965): 404–22.

Glodo, Michael J. "*Sola ecclesia*: The Lost Reformation Doctrine?" *Reformation and Revival* 9, no. 4 (2000): 91–97.

Goldsworthy, Graeme. *Gospel and Kingdom: A Christian Interpretation of the Old Testament.* Exeter, UK: Paternoster, 1981.

———. *Gospel-Centered Hermeneutics: Foundations and Principles of Evangelical Biblical Interpretation.* Downers Grove, IL: IVP Academic, 2006.

Goosen, Rachel Waltner. "The Failure to Bind and Loose: Responses to Yoder's Sexual Abuse." *The Mennonite*, January 2, 2015. https://themennonite.org/feature/failure-bind-loose-responses-john-howard-yoders-sexual-abuse/.

Gordis, Lisa M. *Opening Scripture: Bible Reading and Interpretive Authority in Puritan New England.* Chicago: University of Chicago Press, 2003.

Greggs, Tom. "The Priesthood of No Believer: On the Priesthood of Christ and His Church." *International Journal of Systematic Theology* 17, no. 4 (2015): 374–98.

Gregory, Brad S. *The Unintended Reformation: How a Religious Revolution Secularized Society.* Cambridge, MA: Belknap Press of Harvard University Press, 2012.

Greschat, Martin. *Martin Bucer: A Reformer and His Times.* Translated by Stephen E. Buckwalter. Louisville: Westminster John Knox, 2004.

Groves, Peter. *Grace: The Cruciform Love of God.* London: Canterbury, 2012.

Guinness, Os, and John Seel, eds. *No God but God: Breaking with the Idols of Our Age.* Chicago: Moody, 1992.

Habitat for Humanity. "Neighborhood Revitalization." http://www.habitat.org/neighborhood.

Hall, David D., ed. *The Antinomian Controversy, 1636–1638: A Documentary History*. 2nd ed. Durham, NC: Duke University Press, 1990.

Hall, Peter, ed. *The Harmony of Protestant Confessions: Exhibiting the Faith of the Church of Christ*. Rev. ed. London: J. F. Shaw, 1842.

Harris, Harriet A. *Fundamentalism and Evangelicals*. Oxford: Clarendon, 1998.

Hart, Darryl G. *Deconstructing Evangelicalism: Conservative Protestantism in the Age of Billy Graham*. Grand Rapids: Baker Academic, 2004.

———. "The Use and Abuse of the Christian Past: Mercersburg, the Ancient Church, and American Evangelicalism." In Kalantzis and Tooley, *Evangelicals and the Early Church*, 85–103.

Hauerwas, Stanley. *Approaching the End: Eschatological Reflections on Church, Politics, and Life*. Grand Rapids: Eerdmans, 2013.

———. *Unleashing the Scripture: Freeing the Bible from Captivity to America*. Nashville: Abingdon, 1993.

Hays, Christopher M., and Christopher B. Ansberry, eds. *Evangelical Faith and the Challenge of Historical Criticism*. Grand Rapids: Baker Academic, 2013.

Hegel, G. W. F. *The Philosophy of History*. Translated by J. Sibree. Mineola, NY: Dover, 1956.

Henry, Matthew. *A Brief Enquiry into the True Nature of Schism: Or a Persuasive to Christian Love and Charity*. London, 1690.

Hoffmeier, James K., and Dennis R. Magary, eds. *Do Historical Matters Matter to Faith? A Critical Appraisal of Modern and Postmodern Approaches to Scripture*. Wheaton: Crossway, 2012.

Holquist, Michael. *Dialogism: Bakhtin and His World*. 2nd ed. London: Routledge, 2002.

Hort, Fenton J. A. *The Christian Ecclesia: A Course of Lectures on the Early History and Early Conceptions of the Ecclesia*. London: Macmillan, 1914.

Horton, Michael. *People and Place: A Covenant Ecclesiology*. Louisville: Westminster John Knox, 2008.

———. "The *Sola*'s of the Reformation." In *Here We Stand! A Call from Confessing Evangelicals for a Modern Reformation*, edited by James Montgomery Boice and Benjamin E. Sasse, 99–130. Phillipsburg, NJ: P&R, 1996.

Howard, Thomas Albert, and Mark A. Noll. "The Reformation at Five Hundred: An Outline of the Changing Ways We Remember the Reformation." *First Things* 247 (November 2014): 43–48.

Howell, Clifford. *Of Sacraments and Sacrifice*. Collegeville, MN: Liturgical Press, 1953.

Hughes, Philip E. *Theology of the English Reformers*. New ed. Grand Rapids: Baker, 1980.

Huijgen, Arnold. "Alone Together: *Sola Scriptura* and the Other *Solas* of the Reformation." In *Sola Scriptura: Biblical and Theological Perspectives on Scripture, Authority, and Hermeneutics*, edited by Eric Peels, Arnold Huijgen, and Hans Burger. Leiden: Brill, forthcoming.

Husbands, Mark, and Daniel J. Treier, eds. *The Community of the Word: Toward an Evangelical Ecclesiology*. Downers Grove, IL: InterVarsity, 2005.

Jamieson, Bobby. *Going Public: Why Baptism Is Required for Church Membership*. Nashville: B&H Academic, 2015.

Jenkins, Allan K., and Patrick Preston. *Biblical Scholarship and the Church: A Sixteenth-Century Crisis of Authority*. Aldershot, UK: Ashgate, 2007.

Jenson, Robert W. *Lutheran Slogans: Use and Abuse*. Delhi, NY: American Lutheran Publicity Bureau, 2011.

Johnson, Terry L. *The Case for Traditional Protestantism: The Solas of the Reformation*. Edinburgh: Banner of Truth Trust, 2004.

Johnson, Todd M., and Kenneth R. Ross, eds. *Atlas of Global Christianity*. Edinburgh: Edinburgh University Press, 2009.

Johnson, William Stacy. "Theology and the Church's Mission: Catholic, Orthodox, Evangelical, and Reformed." In Alston and Welker, *Reformed Theology*, 65–84.

Jones, David W., and Russell S. Woodbridge. *Health, Wealth, and Happiness: Has the Prosperity Gospel Overshadowed the Gospel of Christ?* Grand Rapids: Kregel, 2011.

Jowett, Benjamin. "On the Interpretation of Scripture." In *The Interpretation of Scripture and Other Essays*, 1–76. London: George Routledge & Sons, 1907.

Kalantzis, George, and Andrew Tooley, eds. *Evangelicals and the Early Church: Recovery, Reform, Renewal*. Eugene, OR: Cascade, 2012.

Kaminsky, Howard. "The Great Schism." In *The New Cambridge Medieval History*. Vol. 6, *c. 1300–c. 1415*, edited by Michael Jones, 674–98. Cambridge: Cambridge University Press, 2000.

Kant, Immanuel. *Critique of Pure Reason*. Translated by Norman Kemp Smith. London: Macmillan, 1933.

Karttunen, Tomi. "Useful and Possible? The Evangelical Lutheran Church of Finland and Membership in the Communion of the Protestant Churches in Europe." February 16, 2008. http://sakasti.evl.fi/sakasti.nsf/0/2EEE800EEBB8BA41C2257734002 79C85/$FILE/Leuenberg-CPCE%20and%20ELCF%20netti.pdf.

Kasper, Walter. *Mercy: The Essence of the Gospel and the Key to Christian Life*. New York: Paulist Press, 2013.

Kaye, Bruce. "Reality and Form in Catholicity." *Journal of Anglican Studies* 10, no. 1 (2012): 3–12.

Kelly, J. N. D. *Early Christian Doctrines*. Rev. ed. San Francisco: HarperCollins, 1978.

Kerr, Fergus. *Twentieth-Century Catholic Theologians*. Oxford: Blackwell, 2007.

Kierkegaard, Søren. *The Present Age; and, Two Minor Ethico-Religious Treatises.* Translated by Alexander Dru and Walter Lowrie. Oxford: Oxford University Press, 1940.

Knox, D. Broughton. *Selected Works.* Vol. 2, *Church and Ministry.* Kingsford, Australia: Matthias Media, 2003.

Kolb, Robert. "Melanchthon's Doctrinal Last Will and Testament: The *Responsiones ad articulos Bavaricae inquisitionis* as His Final Confession of Faith." In *Philip Melanchthon: Theologian in Classroom, Confession, and Controversy,* edited by Irene Dingel et al., 141–60. Göttingen: Vandenhoeck & Ruprecht, 2012.

Kolb, Robert, and Charles P. Arand. *The Genius of Luther's Theology: A Wittenberg Way of Thinking for the Contemporary Church.* Grand Rapids: Baker Academic, 2008.

Koyzis, David T. *We Answer to Another: Authority, Office, and the Image of God.* Eugene, OR: Pickwick, 2014.

Kuhn, Chase. "The Ecclesiology of Donald Robinson and David Broughton Knox: A Presentation, Analysis and Theological Evaluation of Their Thought on the Nature of the Church." PhD thesis, University of Western Sydney, 2014.

Kuyper, Abraham. *Principles of Sacred Theology.* Translated by J. Hendrik De Vries. Grand Rapids: Eerdmans, 1968.

Lane, Anthony N. S. *John Calvin: Student of the Church Fathers.* Edinburgh: T&T Clark, 1999.

———. "Scripture, Tradition, and Church: An Historical Survey." *Vox Evangelica* 9 (1975): 37–55.

———. "*Sola Scriptura*? Making Sense of a Post-Reformation Slogan." In *A Pathway into the Holy Scripture,* edited by Philip E. Satterthwaite and David F. Wright, 297–327. Grand Rapids: Eerdmans, 1994.

Larsen, Timothy. "Defining and Locating Evangelicalism." In *The Cambridge Companion to Evangelical Theology,* edited by Timothy Larsen and Daniel J. Treier, 1–14. Cambridge: Cambridge University Press, 2007.

Lecerf, Auguste. *An Introduction to Reformed Dogmatics.* London: Lutterworth, 1949.

Leeman, Jonathan. *The Church and the Surprising Offense of God's Love: Reintroducing the Doctrines of Church Membership and Discipline.* Wheaton: Crossway, 2010.

———. *Church Membership: How the World Knows Who Represents Jesus.* Wheaton: Crossway, 2012.

———. "A Congregational Approach to Catholicity: Independence and Interdependence." In Dever and Leeman, *Baptist Foundations,* 367–80.

———. "A Congregational Approach to Unity, Holiness, and Apostolicity: Faith and Order." In Dever and Leeman, *Baptist Foundations,* 333–66.

———. *Don't Fire Your Church Members: The Case for Congregationalism.* Nashville: B&H Academic, 2016.

———. *Political Church: The Local Assembly as Embassy of Christ's Rule*. Downers Grove, IL: IVP Academic, 2016.

Legaspi, Michael C. *The Death of Scripture and the Rise of Biblical Studies*. Oxford: Oxford University Press, 2010.

Leithart, Peter J. *Athanasius*. Grand Rapids: Baker Academic, 2011.

———. *The End of Protestantism: Pursuing Unity in a Fragmented Church*. Grand Rapids: Brazos, 2016.

———. "Epistemological Crisis." *First Things*, August 9, 2013. http://www.firstthings .com/blogs/leithart/2013/08/epistemological-crisis.

———. "The Future of Protestantism: The Churches Must Die to Be Raised Anew." *First Things* 245 (August/September 2014): 23–27.

———. "Residual Extrinsicism." *First Things*, May 28, 2014. http://www.firstthings .com/blogs/leithart/2014/05/residual-extrinicism.

———. "Sola Scriptura, Una Ecclesia." *First Things*, May 1, 2014. http://www.first things.com/blogs/leithart/2014/05/sola-scriptura-una-ecclesia.

Letham, Robert. *The Work of Christ*. Downers Grove, IL: InterVarsity, 1993.

Leuenberg Church Fellowship. "The Church of Jesus Christ: The Contribution of the Reformation towards Ecumenical Dialogue on Church Unity." May 9, 1994. http:// www.reformiert-online.net/agora2/docs/309.pdf.

Lewis, C. S. *The Collected Letters of C. S. Lewis*. Vol. 2, *Books, Broadcasts, and the War, 1931–1949*. Edited by Walter Hooper. New York: HarperSanFrancisco, 2004.

———. *Mere Christianity*. New York: Touchstone, 1996.

Lightfoot, J. B. *The Epistle of St. Paul to the Galatians*. 10th ed. London: Macmillan, 1986.

Lindbeck, George. *The Nature of Doctrine: Religion and Theology in a Postliberal Age*. Philadelphia: Westminster, 1984.

Littlejohn, W. Bradford. *The Mercersburg Theology and the Quest for Reformed Catholicity*. Eugene, OR: Pickwick, 2009.

Loisy, Alfred. *L'Évangile et l'Église*. 2nd ed. Bellevue, 1903.

Long, D. Stephen. *Saving Karl Barth: Hans Urs von Balthasar's Preoccupation*. Minneapolis: Fortress, 2014.

Long, Steven A. *Natura Pura: On the Recovery of Nature in the Doctrine of Grace*. New York: Fordham University Press, 2010.

Lovenheim, Peter. *In the Neighborhood: The Search for Community on an American Street, One Sleepover at a Time*. New York: Perigee, 2010.

Lubac, Henri de. *Surnaturel: Études historiques*. Paris: Aubier, 1946.

Luther, Martin. "The Distinction between the Law and the Gospel: A Sermon Preached on January 1, 1532." Translated by Willard L. Burce. *Concordia Journal* 18, no. 2 (1992): 153–63.

———. *D. Martin Luthers Werke: Kritische Gesamtausgabe*. Weimar: H. Böhlau, 1883–2009.

———. *Luther's Works*. Edited by Jaroslav Pelikan et al. 55 vols. St. Louis: Concordia; Philadelphia: Fortress, 1958–86.

———. *Martin Luther's Basic Theological Writings*. Edited by Timothy F. Lull. Minneapolis: Fortress, 1989.

———. *On the Bondage of the Will*. In *Luther and Erasmus: Free Will and Salvation*, edited by E. Gordon Rupp and Philip S. Watson. Library of Christian Classics. Philadelphia: Westminster, 1969.

Manetsch, Scott M. *Calvin's Company of Pastors: Pastoral Care and the Emerging Reformed Church, 1536–1609*. Oxford: Oxford University Press, 2013.

Maritain, Jacques. *Three Reformers: Luther, Descartes, Rousseau*. London: Sheed & Ward, 1944.

Mathison, Keith A. *The Shape of Sola Scriptura*. Moscow, ID: Canon Press, 2001.

McCormack, Bruce. "The End of Reformed Theology?" In Alston and Welker, *Reformed Theology*, 46–64.

McCracken, George E., and Allen Cabaniss, eds. *Early Medieval Theology*. London: SCM, 1957.

McDowell, John. *Meaning, Knowledge, and Reality*. Cambridge, MA: Harvard University Press, 1998.

McGrath, Alister. *Christianity's Dangerous Idea: The Protestant Revolution—A History from the Sixteenth Century to the Twenty-First*. New York: HarperOne, 2007.

———. *Reformation Thought: An Introduction*. 2nd ed. Oxford: Blackwell, 1993.

McKnight, Scot. *A Fellowship of Differents: Showing the World God's Design for Life Together*. Grand Rapids: Zondervan, 2014.

McMyler, Benjamin. *Testimony, Trust, and Authority*. New York: Oxford University Press, 2011.

McNeill, John T. *Unitive Protestantism: The Ecumenical Spirit and Its Persistent Expression*. Richmond: John Knox, 1964.

Millar, J. G. "People of God." In Alexander and Rosner, *New Dictionary of Biblical Theology*, 684–87.

Morgan, Christopher W. "Toward a Theology of the Unity of the Church." In Chute, Morgan, and Peterson, *Why We Belong*, 19–36.

Morris, Leon. *The Gospel according to Matthew*. Pillar New Testament Commentary. Grand Rapids: Eerdmans, 1992.

Muller, Richard A. *Post-Reformation Reformed Dogmatics: The Rise and Development of Reformed Orthodoxy, ca. 1520 to ca. 1725*. 2nd ed. 4 vols. Grand Rapids: Baker Academic, 2003.

Mumford, Lewis. "The Neighborhood and the Neighborhood Unit." *Town Planning Review* 24 (1954): 256–70.

Nebeker, Gary L. "The Holy Spirit, Hermeneutics, and Transformation: From Present to Future Glory." *Evangelical Review of Theology* 27, no. 1 (2003): 47–54.

"Neighborhood Association." *Wikipedia.* https://en.wikipedia.org/wiki/Neighborhood_association.

Neusner, Jacob. "The Kingdom of Heaven in Kindred Systems, Judaic and Christian." *Bulletin for Biblical Research* 15, no. 2 (2005): 279–305.

Nevin, John W. *AntiChrist; or, The Spirit of Sect and Schism.* New York: J. S. Taylor, 1848.

Newbigin, Lesslie. *The Household of God: Lectures on the Nature of the Church.* New York: Friendship Press, 1953.

———. *Proper Confidence: Faith, Doubt, and Certainty in Christian Discipleship.* Grand Rapids: Eerdmans, 1995.

Niebuhr, H. Richard. *The Kingdom of God in America.* 1937. Reprint, Middletown, CT: Wesleyan University Press, 1988.

Noll, Mark A. *Between Faith and Criticism: Evangelicals, Scholarship, and the Bible in America.* 2nd ed. Vancouver: Regent College Publishing, 2004.

———. *The Civil War as a Theological Crisis.* Chapel Hill: University of North Carolina Press, 2006.

———. *Protestantism: A Very Short Introduction.* Oxford: Oxford University Press, 2011.

———. *The Scandal of the Evangelical Mind.* Grand Rapids: Eerdmans, 1994.

Oakley, Francis. *The Conciliarist Tradition: Constitutionalism in the Catholic Church, 1300–1870.* Oxford: Oxford University Press, 2003.

Oberman, Heiko A. *The Dawn of the Reformation: Essays in Late Medieval and Early Modern Thought.* Grand Rapids: Eerdmans, 1992.

———. *Forerunners of the Reformation: The Shape of Late Medieval Thought.* Translated by Paul L. Nyhus. London: Lutterworth, 1967.

O'Brien, Peter T. *The Letter to the Ephesians.* Pillar New Testament Commentary. Grand Rapids: Eerdmans, 2009.

O'Donovan, Oliver. *A Conversation Waiting to Begin: The Churches and the Gay Controversy.* London: SCM, 2009.

———. *The Desire of the Nations: Rediscovering the Roots of Political Theology.* Cambridge: Cambridge University Press, 1996.

———. *Ethics as Theology.* Vol. 2, *Finding and Seeking.* Grand Rapids: Eerdmans, 2014.

———. *On the Thirty-Nine Articles: A Conversation with Tudor Christianity.* Latimer Monographs. Exeter, UK: Paternoster, 1986.

———. *Resurrection and Moral Order: An Outline for Evangelical Ethics.* Grand Rapids: Eerdmans, 1986.

O'Malley, John W. *Trent: What Happened at the Council*. Cambridge, MA: Belknap Press of Harvard University Press, 2013.

Outler, Albert. *The Christian Tradition and the Unity We Seek*. Oxford: Oxford University Press, 1957.

Owen, John. *Causes, Ways, and Means of Understanding the Mind of God*. Edited by Thomas Russell. Works of John Owen 3. London: Richard Baynes, 1826.

Packer, J. I. *Taking God Seriously: Vital Things We Need to Know*. Wheaton, IL: Crossway, 2013.

Pannenberg, Wolfhart, ed. *Revelation as History*. London: Macmillan, 1968.

Pelikan, Jaroslav. *Acts*. Brazos Theological Commentary on the Bible. Grand Rapids: Brazos, 2005.

———. *Obedient Rebels: Catholic Substance and Protestant Principle in Luther's Reformation*. London: SCM, 1964.

Peterson, David G. *The Acts of the Apostles*. Pillar New Testament Commentary. Grand Rapids: Eerdmans, 2009.

Piper, John. "Feed the Flame of God's Gift: Unashamed Courage in the Gospel (2 Timothy 1:1–12)." In *Entrusted with the Gospel: Pastoral Expositions of 2 Timothy*, edited by D. A. Carson, 11–24. Wheaton: Crossway, 2010.

Plantinga, Alvin. *Knowledge and Christian Belief*. Grand Rapids: Eerdmans, 2015.

———. "Reason and Belief in God." In *Faith and Rationality: Reason and Belief in God*, edited by Alvin Plantinga and Nicholas Wolterstorff, 16–93. Notre Dame, IN: University of Notre Dame Press, 1983.

———. *Warranted Christian Belief*. Oxford: Oxford University Press, 2000.

Polanyi, Michael. *Personal Knowledge: Towards a Post-Critical Philosophy*. Corrected ed. Chicago: University of Chicago Press, 1962.

Popkin, Richard H. *The History of Scepticism: From Savonarola to Bayle*. Rev. and expanded ed. Oxford: Oxford University Press, 2003.

Powell, Mark Allan. "Binding and Loosing: Asserting the Moral Authority of Scripture in Light of a Matthean Paradigm." *Ex Auditu* 19 (2003): 81–96.

Prather, Shannon. "Feuds between Neighbors Common, Hard to Solve, but Rarely Deadly." *Minneapolis-St. Paul Star Tribune*, July 22, 2014. http://www.startribune.com/may-10-feuds-between-neighbors-rarely-deadly/258779441/.

Preus, Herman A. "Luther on the Universal Priesthood and the Office of the Ministry." *Concordia Journal* 5, no. 2 (1979): 55–62.

Radner, Ephraim. *The End of the Church: A Pneumatology of Christian Division in the West*. Grand Rapids: Eerdmans, 1998.

Rae, Murray. "On Reading Scripture Theologically." *Princeton Theological Review* 14, no. 1 (2008): 13–26.

Ramm, Bernard. *The Pattern of Religious Authority*. Grand Rapids: Eerdmans, 1957.

———. *Protestant Biblical Interpretation*. 3rd rev. ed. Grand Rapids: Baker, 1970.

————. *The Witness of the Spirit: An Essay on the Contemporary Relevance of the Internal Witness of the Holy Spirit*. Grand Rapids: Eerdmans, 1959.

Reid, Thomas. *Essays on the Intellectual Powers of Man*. Edited by Derek R. Brookes. University Park: Pennsylvania State University Press, 2002.

Richardson, Cyril C., trans. *Early Christian Fathers*. New York: Macmillan, 1970.

Ricoeur, Paul. *The Course of Recognition*. Translated by David Pellauer. Cambridge, MA: Harvard University Press, 2004.

Robinson, Donald. *Donald Robinson: Selected Works*. Vol. 1, *Assembling God's People*. Edited by Peter Bolt and Mark Thompson. Camperdown, NSW: Australian Church Record; Newton, NSW: Moore College, 2008.

Rose, Devin. *The Protestant's Dilemma: How the Reformation's Shocking Consequences Point to the Truth of Catholicism*. San Diego: Catholic Answers Press, 2014.

Sanders, Fred. *The Deep Things of God: How the Trinity Changes Everything*. Wheaton: Crossway, 2010.

Sarisky, Darren, ed. *Theology, History, and Biblical Interpretation: Modern Readings*. London: Bloomsbury T&T Clark, 2015.

Schaff, Philip. *Creeds of Christendom, with a History and Critical Notes*. Vol. 1, *The History of Creeds*. New York: Harper, 1877.

————. *The Principle of Protestantism*. Translated by John W. Nevin. Chambersburg, PA: Publication Office of the German Reformed Church, 1845. Reprint, edited by Bard Thompson and George H. Bricker. Lancaster Series on the Mercersburg Theology 1. Eugene, OR: Wipf & Stock, 2004.

Schleiermacher, Friedrich. *The Christian Faith*. Edited by H. R. Mackintosh and J. S. Stewart. Edinburgh: T&T Clark, 1999.

Schreiner, Susan E. *Are You Alone Wise? The Search for Certainty in the Early Modern Era*. Oxford: Oxford University Press, 2011.

Schroeder, H. J., trans. *The Canons and Decrees of the Council of Trent*. Rockford, IL: Tan Books, 1978.

Schütz, John Howard. *Paul and the Anatomy of Apostolic Authority*. Cambridge: Cambridge University Press, 1975.

Simon, Yves R. *A General Theory of Authority*. Notre Dame, IN: University of Notre Dame Press, 1980.

Smith, Christian. *American Evangelicalism: Embattled and Thriving*. Chicago: University of Chicago Press, 1998.

————. *The Bible Made Impossible: Why Biblicism Is Not a Truly Evangelical Reading of Scripture*. Grand Rapids: Brazos, 2011.

Smith, James K. A. *How (Not) to Be Secular: Reading Charles Taylor*. Grand Rapids: Eerdmans, 2014.

————. *Who's Afraid of Relativism? Community, Contingency, and Creaturehood*. Grand Rapids: Baker Academic, 2014.

Spellman, Chad. *Toward a Canon-Conscious Reading of the Bible: Exploring the History and Hermeneutics of the Canon*. Sheffield: Sheffield Phoenix Press, 2014.

Spinoza, Benedict de. *Theological-Political Treatise*. Edited by Jonathan Israel. Translated by Michael Silverthorne and Jonathan Israel. Cambridge: Cambridge University Press, 2007.

Stackhouse, John G., Jr. "Generic Evangelicalism." In *Four Views on the Spectrum of Evangelicalism*, edited by Andrew David Naselli and Collin Hansen, 116–42. Grand Rapids: Zondervan, 2011.

Stafford, Andrew Dean. *Nature and Grace: A New Approach to Thomistic Ressourcement*. Eugene, OR: Pickwick, 2014.

Starling, David. *Hermeneutics as Apprenticeship: How the Bible Shapes Our Interpretive Habits and Practices*. Grand Rapids: Baker Academic, 2016.

Steiner, George. *The Idea of Europe: An Essay*. London: Overlook Duckworth, 2015.

Steinmetz, David C. *Reformers in the Wings: From Geiler von Kaysersberg to Theodore Beza*. 2nd ed. Oxford: Oxford University Press, 2001.

Stendahl, Krister. "Biblical Theology, Contemporary." In *Interpreter's Dictionary of the Bible*, edited by G. A. Buttrick, 1:418–32. Nashville: Abingdon, 1962.

Stott, John R. W. *Basic Christianity*. London: Inter-Varsity, 1958.

———. *Christ the Controversialist: A Study in Some Essentials of Evangelical Religion*. Downers Grove, IL: InterVarsity, 1970.

Sullivan, Francis A. *Magisterium: Teaching Authority in the Catholic Church*. New York: Paulist Press, 1983.

Sungenis, Robert A. *Not by Scripture Alone: A Catholic Critique of the Protestant Doctrine of* Sola Scriptura. Santa Barbara, CA: Queenship Publishing, 1997.

Swain, Scott R. *Trinity, Revelation, and Reading: A Theological Introduction to the Bible and Its Interpretation*. London: T&T Clark, 2011.

Sweeney, Douglas A. "Mercersburg Doctrine as a Double-Edged Sword—A Response to Darryl G. Hart." In Kalantzis and Tooley, *Evangelicals and the Early Church*, 104–7.

Tanner, Kathryn. *Christ the Key*. Cambridge: Cambridge University Press, 2010.

Taylor, Charles. *Multiculturalism: Examining the Politics of Recognition*. Princeton: Princeton University Press, 1994.

———. *A Secular Age*. Cambridge, MA: Belknap Press of Harvard University Press, 2007.

Thiselton, Anthony. *Can the Bible Mean Whatever We Want It to Mean?* Chester, UK: Chester Academic Press, 2005.

Thompson, Mark D. *A Clear and Present Word: The Clarity of Scripture*. Downers Grove, IL: InterVarsity, 2006.

———. *A Sure Ground on Which to Stand: The Relation of Authority and Interpretive Method in Luther's Approach to Scripture*. Eugene, OR: Wipf & Stock, 2007.

Tillich, Paul. *A History of Christian Thought*. New York: Touchstone, 1967.

———. *The Protestant Era*. Chicago: University of Chicago Press, 1948.

Torrance, Thomas F. *The Mediation of Christ*. 2nd ed. Colorado Springs: Helmers & Howard, 1992.

Treat, Jeremy R. *The Crucified King: Atonement and Kingdom in Biblical and Systematic Theology*. Grand Rapids: Zondervan, 2014.

Troeltsch, Ernst. *Protestantism and Progress: The Significance of Protestantism for the Rise of the Modern World*. Philadelphia: Fortress, 1986.

Trueman, Carl R. *Reformation: Yesterday, Today and Tomorrow*. Ross-shire, Scotland: Christian Focus Publications, 2011.

Turretin, Francis. *Institutes of Elenctic Theology*. Vol. 1, *First through Tenth Topics*. Translated by George Musgrave Giger. Edited by James T. Dennison Jr. Phillipsburg, NJ: P&R, 1992.

VanDrunen, David. *God's Glory Alone: The Majestic Heart of Christian Faith and Life*. Grand Rapids: Zondervan, 2015.

Vanhoozer, Kevin J. "The Apostolic Discourse and Its Developments." In *Scripture's Doctrine and Theology's Bible: How the New Testament Shapes Christian Dogmatics*, edited by Markus Bockmuehl and Alan J. Torrance, 191–207. Grand Rapids: Baker Academic, 2008.

———. "Ascending the Mountain, Singing the Rock: Biblical Interpretation Earthed, Typed, and Transfigured." *Modern Theology* 28, no. 4 (2012): 781–803.

———. "At Play in the Theodrama of the Lord: The Triune God of the Gospel." In *Theatrical Theology: Explorations in Performing the Faith*, edited by Trevor Hart and Wesley Vander Lugt, 1–29. Eugene, OR: Cascade, 2014.

———. *The Drama of Doctrine: A Canonical-Linguistic Approach to Christian Theology*. Louisville: Westminster John Knox, 2005.

———. *Faith Speaking Understanding: Performing the Drama of Doctrine*. Louisville: Westminster John Knox, 2014.

———. *First Theology: God, Scripture, and Hermeneutics*. Downers Grove, IL: IVP Academic, 2001.

———. "Improvising Theology according to the Scriptures: An Evangelical Account of the Development of Doctrine." In *Building on the Foundations of Evangelical Theology: Essays in Honor of John S. Feinberg*, edited by Gregg R. Allison and Stephen J. Wellum, 15–50. Wheaton: Crossway, 2015.

———. "Interpreting Scripture between the Rock of Biblical Studies and the Hard Place of Systematic Theology: The State of the Evangelical (dis)Union." In *Renewing the Evangelical Mission*, edited by Richard Lints, 201–25. Grand Rapids: Eerdmans, 2013.

———. *Is There a Meaning in This Text? The Bible, the Reader, and the Morality of Literary Knowledge*. Grand Rapids: Zondervan, 1998.

———. "Is the Theology of the New Testament One or Many? Between (the Rock of) Systematic Theology and (the Hard Place of) Historical Occasionalism." In *Reconsidering the Relationship between Biblical and Systematic Theology in the New Testament: Essays by Theologians and New Testament Scholars*, edited by Benjamin Reynolds, Brian Lugioyo, and Kevin Vanhoozer, 17–38. Wissenschaftliche Untersuchungen zum Neuen Testament 2.369. Tübingen: Mohr Siebeck, 2014.

———. *Remythologizing Theology: Divine Action, Passion, and Authorship*. Cambridge: Cambridge University Press, 2010.

———. "The Spirit of Light after the Age of Enlightenment: Renewing/Reforming Pneumatic Hermeneutics via the Economy of Illumination." In *Spirit of God: Christian Renewal in the Community of Faith*, edited by Jeffrey Barbeau and Beth Felker Jones, 149–67. Downers Grove, IL: InterVarsity, 2015.

———. "Three (or More) Ways of Triangulating Theology: On the Very Idea of a Trinitarian System." In *Revisioning, Renewing, and Rediscovering the Triune Center: Essays in Honor of Stanley J. Grenz*, edited by Derek Tidball, Brian Harris, and Jason Sexton, 31–58. Eugene, OR: Cascade, 2015.

———. "Wrighting the Wrongs of the Reformation? The State of the Union with Christ in St. Paul and Protestant Soteriology." In *Jesus, Paul, and the People of God: A Theological Dialogue with N. T. Wright*, edited by Nicholas Perrin and Richard B. Hays, 235–58. Downers Grove, IL: IVP Academic, 2011.

Vanhoozer, Kevin J., and Daniel J. Treier. *Theology and the Mirror of Scripture: A Mere Evangelical Account*. Downers Grove, IL: InterVarsity, 2015.

Verbrugge, Verlyn D. "The Power to Bind and Loose." *Reformed Journal* 30, no. 7 (1980): 15–17.

Volf, Miroslav. *After Our Likeness: The Church as the Image of the Trinity*. Grand Rapids: Eerdmans, 1997.

Wahlberg, Mats. *Revelation as Testimony: A Philosophical-Theological Study*. Grand Rapids: Eerdmans, 2014.

Walls, Andrew F. *The Cross-Cultural Process in Christian History: Studies in the Transmission and Appropriation of Faith*. Maryknoll, NY: Orbis; Edinburgh: T&T Clark, 2002.

———. *The Missionary Movement in Christian History: Studies in the Transmission of Faith*. Maryknoll, NY: Orbis; Edinburgh: T&T Clark, 1996.

Walsh, Marcus. "Profession and Authority: The Interpretation of the Bible in the Seventeenth and Eighteenth Centuries." *Literature and Theology* 9 (1995): 383–98.

Ward, Timothy. *Word and Supplement: Speech Acts, Biblical Texts, and the Sufficiency of Scripture*. Oxford: Oxford University Press, 2002.

———. *Words of Life: Scripture as the Living and Active Word of God*. Downers Grove, IL: IVP Academic, 2009.

Weber, Max. *The Protestant Ethic and the "Spirit" of Capitalism and Other Writings*. Translated and edited by Peter Baehr and Gordon C. Wells. London: Penguin, 2002.

Webster, John. "The Church and the Perfection of God." In Husbands and Treier, *Community of the Word*, 75–95.

———. *The Domain of the Word: Scripture and Theological Reason*. London: Bloomsbury T&T Clark, 2012.

———. "God's Perfect Life." In *God's Life in Trinity*, edited by Miroslav Volf and Michael Welker, 143–52. Minneapolis: Fortress, 2006.

———. "'In the Society of God': Some Principles of Ecclesiology." In *God without Measure: Working Papers in Christian Theology*. Vol. 1, *God and the Works of God*, 177–94. London: Bloomsbury T&T Clark, 2016.

———. "*Ressourcement* Theology and Protestantism." In *Ressourcement: A Movement for Renewal in Twentieth-Century Theology*, edited by Gabriel Flynn and Paul D. Murray, 482–95. Oxford: Oxford University Press, 2014.

———. "Theologies of Retrieval." In *The Oxford Handbook of Systematic Theology*, edited by John Webster, Kathryn Tanner, and Iain Torrance, 583–99. Oxford: Oxford University Press, 2007.

———. "The Visible Attests the Invisible." In Husbands and Treier, *Community of the Word*, 96–113.

———. *Word and Church: Essays in Christian Dogmatics*. Edinburgh: T&T Clark, 2001.

Wells, David. *The Courage to Be Protestant: Truth-Lovers, Marketers, and Emergents in the Postmodern World*. Grand Rapids: Eerdmans, 2008.

Westphal, Merold. *Hegel, Freedom, and Modernity*. Albany: State University of New York Press, 1992.

———. *Whose Community? Which Interpretation? Philosophical Hermeneutics for the Church*. The Church and Postmodern Culture. Grand Rapids: Baker Academic, 2009.

Whale, J. S. *The Protestant Tradition: An Essay in Interpretation*. Cambridge: Cambridge University Press, 1962.

Whitaker, William. *A Disputation on Holy Scripture: Against the Papists, Especially Bellarmine and Stapleton*. 1588. Reprint, Morgan, PA: Soli Deo Gloria, 2000.

Winship, Michael. *Making Heretics: Militant Protestantism and Free Grace in Massachusetts, 1636–1641*. Princeton: Princeton University Press, 2002.

———. *The Times and Trials of Anne Hutchinson: Puritans Divided*. Lawrence: University Press of Kansas, 2005.

Wolterstorff, Nicholas. *The Mighty and the Almighty: An Essay in Political Theology*. Cambridge: Cambridge University Press, 2012.

———. *Thomas Reid and the Story of Epistemology*. Cambridge: Cambridge University Press, 2001.

Woodhouse, John. "Christian Unity and Denominations." *The Briefing* 284. May 1, 2002. http://matthiasmedia.com/briefing/2002/05/christian-unity-and-denominations/.

———. "The Unity of the Church." *The Briefing* 281. February 1, 2002. http://matthias media.com/briefing/2002/02/the-unity-of-the-church/.

———. "When to Unite and When to Divide." *The Briefing* 279. December 1, 2001. http://matthiasmedia.com/briefing/2001/12/when-to-unite-and-when-to-divide/.

Worthen, Molly. *Apostles of Reason: The Crisis of Authority in American Evangelicalism.* Oxford: Oxford University Press, 2014.

Wright, N. T. *Simply Good News: Why the Gospel Is News and What Makes It Good.* New York: HarperOne, 2015.

Yarnell, Malcolm B., III. *Royal Priesthood in the English Reformation.* Oxford: Oxford University Press, 2013.

Yeago, David S. "The Bible." In *Knowing the Triune God: The Work of the Spirit in the Practices of the Church*, edited by James J. Buckley and David S. Yeago, 49–94. Grand Rapids: Eerdmans, 2001.

———. "The New Testament and the Nicene Dogma: A Contribution to the Recovery of Theological Exegesis." In *The Theological Interpretation of Scripture: Classic and Contemporary Readings*, edited by Stephen Fowl, 87–100. Oxford: Blackwell, 1997.

Yoder, John Howard. *The Royal Priesthood: Essays Ecclesiological and Ecumenical.* Edited by Michael G. Cartwright. Scottdale, PA: Herald, 1994.

Zagzebski, Linda Trinkhaus. *Epistemic Authority: A Theory of Trust, Authority, and Autonomy in Belief.* Oxford: Oxford University Press, 2012.

Scripture Index

Subject Index